D1104823

INTERNATIONAL STUDIES AND
ACADEMIC ENTERPRISE

ᔰ ROBERT A. McCAUGHEY

INTERNATIONAL STUDIES AND ACADEMIC ENTERPRISE

A CHAPTER IN THE ENCLOSURE OF AMERICAN LEARNING

COLUMBIA UNIVERSITY PRESS
NEW YORK   1984

Library of Congress Cataloging in Publication Data

McCaughey, Robert A.
  International studies and academic enterprise.

  Bibliography: p.
  Includes index.
  1. Area studies—United States—History—19th century.
  2. Area studies—United States—History—19th century.
  3. United States—Intellectual life. 4. Intellectuals—
  United States. I. Title.
  D16.25.M38 1984   907'.2073   83-21038
  ISBN 0-231-05054-2 (alk. paper)

Columbia University Press
New York Guildford, Surrey
Copyright © 1984 Columbia University Press
All rights reserved

Printed in the United States of America

Clothbound editions of Columbia University Press Books are Smyth-
sewn and printed on permanent and durable acid-free paper

Designed by Ken Venezio

જ IN MEMORY OF
WILLIAM JOHN MCCAUGHEY, 1927–1981
REQUIESCAT IN PACE

CONTENTS

PREFACE

This book describes a heretofore unexamined but important chapter in the history of American learning. It is about a specific collectivity of intellectual pursuits, those through which Americans have sought greater knowledge and wider understanding of the world beyond their national borders and those of culturally akin Western Europe. These pursuits have a long history but only recently have they acquired a common name, "international studies."

This is not a book in but rather about international studies. It does not aspire to advance American understanding of distant areas or the "foreign" peoples who live there, except insofar as it seeks to advance understanding of those who have so aspired. Its purposes, accordingly, differ fundamentally from such books as Benjamin Keen's *The Aztec Image in Western Thought,* James A. Field's *America and the Mediterranean World,* or the recent collaborative effort of James C. Thomson, Peter W. Stanley, and John Curtis Perry, *Sentimental Imperialists: The American Experience in East Asia.* The focus of all these books has been on *what* Americans thought, taught, and wrote about cultures perceived to be different from their own; the focus here is on *why,* and, more pointedly, *how* they went about doing so.[1]

To be sure, our concerns overlap, as in the shared interest in personal motivations and policy implications. Yet the distinction between the history of the idea of a particular culture and the history of a particular intellectual enterprise is crucial to this undertaking and bears emphasizing at the outset. What follows is a form of intellectual history in which the analysis of intellectual content is subordinated to the scrutiny of social context. It is in many ways closer in approach to the work of such sociologists as Edward Shils and Joseph Ben-David than to that of such intellectual historians as Perry Miller and Richard Hofstadter. To the extent, however, that any single book has served as a model for this one, it is *The Rise and Fall of the Man of Letters,* by the English literary critic and bookman, John Gross.[2]

Several American intellectual historians have urged recently that efforts to develop a social history of American intellectuals or of the institutions they inhabit justify themselves only in so far as they contribute directly to the larger understanding of the ideas intellectuals have generated. This view, that the tasks of the social historian of American intellectual life and of the historian of ideas are not only different but that the success of the former ultimately depends upon the use made of his work by the latter, is one which I share. I do not believe, however, that these tasks must be undertaken simultaneously. On the contrary, I would argue that several recent attempts at combining them have in fact resulted in two quite separate books, albeit bound as one.[3]

There is, nonetheless, much here of interest to those primarily concerned with the ideas that Americans engaged in international studies have propounded and disseminated. Two examples may suffice. Surely the occupational marginality if not cultural alienation of many nineteenth-century Americans who took up non-Western studies affected their view of societies that had been spared the dissemination of the Protestant or capitalistic work ethic, as well as their view of societies in which both were making substantial headway. Similarly, the choice of areas and topics that international studies academics chose to investigate in the 1950s and 1960s would seem to have been influenced at least as much by professional and funding considerations as by national interest, student demand, or public ignorance. To have gone beyond such inferences and to attempt to analyze at every possible point the impact of changes in the social and institutional context of those engaged in international studies upon how they viewed their subject would have been to write a different book.

The one that has been written falls into two parts. The first, "In the Land of the Blind, 1810–1940," consists of four chapters on the following: the organizational beginnings of American international studies in the early nineteenth century; the peripheral place international studies acquired in the American university as it emerged in the late nineteenth century; the persistence of nonacademic and even antioccupational motives among Americans taking up international studies into the 1930s; and the effective founding and principal founders of academic international studies between 1900 and 1940. Part I concludes with an assessment of the state of American academic international studies on the eve of World War Two.

Part II, "The Years That Were Fat, 1941–1966," consists of four chapters which take up the following: the impact of World War Two and the onset of the Cold War on the academic international studies community, particularly on its self-perception as an important and promotable national asset; the reorganization of the Ford Foundation and its early interest in international studies; an internal history of the foundation's International Training and Research Program (ITR) from its launching in 1953 to its termination in 1966; and an assessment of the impact of ITR upon the American international studies community, American higher education, and American society generally. The book concludes with a consideration of the state of academic international studies in the years since ITR and with some general reflections on the contemporary "crisis" in and the future prospects of American international studies in light of the foregoing interpretation of its past.

Rather than anticipate further the actual contents of the book, it may be more useful here to define three terms contained in its title and crucial to its argument. By "international studies," I mean the serious inquiry by Americans into those parts of the world Americans have traditionally regarded as having histories, cultures, and social arrangements distinctly different from their own. For convenience and in keeping with current usage, this alien world has been divided into the following components: Eastern Europe and Russia; East Asia; South Asia; the Middle East (including North Africa); Africa; Latin America; and "Other" (e.g., Canada, Oceania). Such inquiry into one of these areas may seek to acquire knowledge about it as an end in itself (i.e., "area studies") or to serve a comparative, multi-area, or functional purpose (e.g., international relations, demographic studies).

The specific methodological approaches encompassed by this definition include those currently classified as falling within the social sciences—history, political science, economics, sociology, anthropology—and the humanities—language and literature, philosophy, religion, fine arts, musicology. Also included are inquiries that predate this classification system and went under such subsequently discarded labels as philology, sinology, and orientalism.

Both the geographical and methodological terms of definition present boundary problems, which, though unavoidable, should be acknowledged. For example, in view of the exclusion of Western Europe, on the grounds of familiarity and consanguinity, the inclusion of Canada among the "Other" areas may seem inconsistent. The reasons for doing so are historical and organizational. Work on Canada figured prominently in the once substantial academic specialization of "imperial studies," which at several institutions in the 1920s and 1930s constituted a major part of their international studies activities. At a few universities, Duke and the University of Rochester among them, this is still the case. Greece presents a somewhat different problem. It has been resolved here by excluding studies of classical Greece, on the ground that it is about the beginnings of the West and its cultural legacy, but including studies of modern Greece, on the ground that it is part of the Balkans region and is therefore properly included among the countries making up Eastern Europe.

The omission of the sciences from the list of disciplines involved in international studies would seem to overlook the fact that, for example, the subjects of some dissertations in psychology and geography fall within the terms of the above definition as readily as do those in the social sciences and humanities. Yet because proportionally so little work in psychology is "international" in the sense intended here, and because geography is a recognized doctoral field at only some of the universities considered here, their inclusion would have distorted any findings based on PhD counts more than has their exclusion. International relations, here considered part of political science, and such functional topics as those found in demographic studies present still another kind of problem. All such studies have been counted as being part of international studies whenever their geographical concerns extend beyond the United States and Western Europe and have been classified by area under the catch-all "Other."

The definitional imprecision of international studies, the book's subject, accounts for the use of the term "enterprise" in its title. By "enterprise," I mean any organized undertaking of sufficient magnitude and duration to permit its participants to derive a measure of identity from it. Intellectual enterprises concern us here, which for present purposes approximate one of two ideal types: those in which the learning that is their end is pursued outside the university by other than academics; and those in which it is pursued within the university by academics.

Prior to the emergence of the university, which in the United States occurred in the last third of the nineteenth century, American intellectual enterprises were necessarily of the first type. With its emergence, however, many such enterprises promptly moved many if not most of their activities into the university. The physical sciences are instances of already established intellectual enterprises that became partly "academicized" during the late nineteenth century and have remained so since. Philosophy is an intellectual enterprise that became almost wholly an academic enterprise, whereas sociology is one that began as an academic enterprise and has subsequently acquired extra-university standing. Still others, perhaps most notably contemporary literary criticism and political commentary, are intellectual enterprises that have to some extent resisted academicization and continue to be pursued at least as much and at as high a level outside the university as within.

It is through this rough but recognizable distinction between an intellectual enterprise as a general category and an academic enterprise as one of its subcategories that we arrive at the central argument of the book and the third term in its title in need of defining. The argument is this: The history of American international studies is best understood—and critically evaluated—as a specific and belated instance of the more general process by which the primary responsibility for the pursuit of learning in America has been transferred from the American intellectual community at large to the universities. That the transfer in the case of international studies occurred a half-century after it had been effected in many other sectors of American learning clearly distinguishes international studies from those intellectual enterprises and requires an explanation. Otherwise, its belatedness enhances its comparative utility as an instance of the larger process.

After considerable deliberation, I have chosen to describe this process as that of "enclosure," which the *Oxford English Dictionary* defines as "the action of surrounding or marking off (land) with a fence or boundary; the action of converting pieces of common land into private property." I have done so aware of the risks in putting an old term with its own specific connotations (i.e., in English agricultural history) to new purposes. I am also aware that other terms are available to me. One I have already used, "academicization," or, after Max Weber, "academic bureaucratization," might have served. Still closer to my purposes is Edward Shils' "institutionalization," which, in terms of an intellectual activity, he defines as "the relatively dense interaction of persons who conduct that activity within a social arrangement which has boundaries, endurance, and a name." Indeed, Shils' delineation of the institutionalization of sociology informs my understanding of what happened to international studies at several points, not least when the pattern for sociology, which has some claims to being an intellectual discipline as well as an academic enterprise, and

that for international studies, which has few such claims, di-
verge.[4]

Moreover, Shils' discussion of institutionalization, unlike
much of the sociological and historical literature on professionalization, does not assume that the process is necessarily
good. "All I contend," he writes, "is that its presence and form
make a difference," and further on, "to be well institutionalized is in a certain sense to be a success, but this is not the same
as intellectual success."[5] Yet for all its obvious virtues, "institutionalization," to my mind, implies a more balanced and
nonjudgmental position with respect to the process it deline-
ates than I am prepared to maintain with respect to that which
I seek to delineate. "Enclosure," especially as Adam Smith used
it—"The advantage of enclosure is greater for pasture than for
corn"—more nearly captures the profound ambivalence which
informs virtually every page of this book.

My ambivalence results from two opposite reactions to what
I take to be the consequences of the academic enclosure of
American international studies. The first is one of awe in the
face of the striking accomplishments that followed on enclosure, in terms not only of the amount, variety, and quality of
work published, or of the students trained, but also of the success international studies has enjoyed penetrating to the centers
of those American universities which presently constitute the
center of American intellectual life. Indeed, my willingness to
acknowledge these accomplishments exceeds that of the leading promoters of academic international studies, as well as their
principal outside underwriters, who in print at least remain
more concerned with present gaps than past achievements.

On the other hand, for all the good intentions and honest
zeal that went into the enclosure of international studies in the
decades after World War Two, I am not persuaded that the
success of the postwar academic international studies community is to be viewed as success all round. One can argue, of
course, that the academic enclosure of international studies was
inevitable and that the only question that ought to concern us
is why it took so long. To take this deterministic view, how-

ever, precludes asking just those "what if" questions that have
been both the making of most and the undoing of many historians. Yet such questions need to be asked, not only by historians to help understand what in fact did happen, but also
by those concerned with the consequences of what happened.

Among the questions this study obliged me to consider continuously without ever providing definitive answers were these:
Could the achievements that characterized international studies
as an academic enterprise have come except at the relative if
not actual expense of international studies as an intellectual enterprise? Might not the talent and energies that academic enclosure concentrated within the university have had a more
beneficial impact on American society had they been more
widely dispersed? Did enclosure advance or hinder the formulation of an enlightened American foreign policy and the
education of an internationally informed electorate? Need the
flourishing of international studies within the university in the
1950s and 1960s have been attended by the withering of non-
university components of the enterprise that seemed so vital as
late as the 1930s? Finally, might not somewhat less success on
the academic side in the 1950s and 1960s have left the entire
international studies enterprise in a stronger position to survive the era of the "steady state" university and declining
funding for intellectual activities generally that came in their
wake?

A legitimate inference from what follows is that, if pressed,
I would answer each of these hypothetical questions in a manner certain to displease members of the academic international
studies community who have committed much of their careers
to advancing its cause. Yet this book ought not to be read as
one academic's indictment of the enterprise of other academics. "Use every man after his desert, and who shall 'scape
whipping?" The acceptance or rejection of any particular conclusion advanced here as to the causes and consequences of the
academic enclosure of American international studies is less to
my ultimate purposes than that subsequent discussions of this

or any other instance of academic enclosure acknowledge not only its palpable benefits to academics but its possible costs to others, of whom—need we be reminded?—there are many more and upon whose sufferance all our careers depend.

Financial support for this book has been provided by the Faculty Research Fund of Barnard College; the Dunning Fund of the Department of History, Columbia University; and the John Simon Guggenheim Foundation. I thank all these organizations for their generosity, and the last for its patience.

My most immediate intellectual debts are owed to members of the international studies community in the Columbia University faculty who willingly served as "native informants." Particularly generous in sharing their knowledge of their enterprise were Wm. Theodore de Bary, Richard W. Bulliet, Ainslie Embree, William T. R. Fox, Graham W. Irwin, Herbert S. Klein, John Meskill, and Marc Raeff. Among colleagues not connected with international studies, Bernard Barber, Lawrence A. Cremin, John A. Garraty, Stephen E. Koss, and Eric L. McKitrick all made significant contributions to this project, as to my scholarly life generally.

International studies academics beyond Morningside Heights who proved helpful far beyond the requirements of professional protocol include Robert Byrnes, Richard D. Lambert, Ernest R. May, Robert D. Schulzinger, Milton Singer, and Robert Ward. As they have before, Donald Fleming, David Riesman, and Edward Shils provided critical guidance and personal encouragement.

I should also like to thank several individuals associated with the Ford Foundation—past and present. Elinor Barber, Melvin J. Fox, Ruebin Frodin, John Howard, Don K. Price, and Francis X. Sutton all were unstinting with their help, while scrupulously honoring the integrity of a project that impinged upon their own professional lives.

Finally, I wish to acknowledge the support provided by my wife Ann and our two children, Hannah and John. This book was to have been dedicated to them. But as with so much else in our lives together, I trust they understand.

ROBERT A. MCCAUGHEY

Barnard College, Columbia University
New York City

IN THE LAND OF THE BLIND, 1810–1940

The gift and graces of Christians lay in common,
till base envy made the first enclosure.

THOMAS FULLER, 1642

GENTLEMEN AND SCHOLARS

[Mine] are not the elaborate productions of one who has had the leisure and other advantages of a professor, but they are the efforts of a mere amateur in literature.

JOHN PICKERING, 1821 [1]

To assert the need for a critical history of American international studies is not to claim that the subject has been neglected. Neglect, Bernard Bailyn concluded after examining the historiography of American education, was only one affliction that could beset a subject. It might also suffer "from the opposite, from an excess of writing along certain lines and an almost undue clarity of direction." [2] Such has been the fate of American international studies.

Accounts depicting—without so labeling it—international studies as a distinct area of American learning with its own history first appeared in the late 1920s and 1930s. They were written by academics engaged in international studies and sponsored by academic organizations such as the American Council of Learned Societies and the Social Science Research Council. Since then sponsors have included the major foundations, various government agencies, and the several area associations organized in the late 1940s and the 1950s. The chronicling function, however, has for the most part remained the responsibility of academics professionally identified with the enterprise.[3]

The most persistent theme of these accounts has been American indifference to and ignorance of the rest of the world. The tone with which this indictment has been rendered has varied with the times. In the 1930s, when expectations of outside financial support were modest and those pursuing international studies within the university were few and scattered, it was plaintive. After World War Two, with the onset of the Cold War and the surge in higher education, it turned more assertive. In the early 1960s, when funding for academic international studies from foundations and the federal government reached levels undreamed of earlier (and unseen since), it became strained, even at times embarrassed. More recently, in the midst of the self-declared "crisis" in international studies, it has again turned plaintive, if not despondent.[4]

The utility of the indifference theme has not been lost on international studies' chronicler–promoters. Latin Americanists and East Asianists first invoked it in the 1930s, although those depicting the "primitive state" of Slavic studies and the "appalling condition" of South Asian studies after World War Two demonstrated a fuller appreciation of its possibilities. In the 1950s promoters of African studies regularly decried America's scholarly neglect of "their" part of the world, as did Southeast Asianists in the 1960s and those promoting Middle Eastern studies in the 1970s. Perhaps the most telling testimony to the promotional effectiveness of the indifference theme was its adoption in the early 1960s by academics who previously had not thought to characterize their work as "Western European Studies." Years of well-funded attention to more exotic areas, their spokesmen argued, had resulted in the comparative neglect of Western Europe by American scholars, which in turn helped account for its neglect by Americans generally. By a neat twist, scholarly inattention, viewed in the 1930s as a consequence of national inattention, had in the 1960s become its cause.[5]

For all its promotional utility, the indifference theme presents serious problems for the historian of American international studies. Like "neglect," "indifference" is a relative term and requires an historical or comparative context to have meaning. Yet this is precisely what existing accounts lack. Two reasons help explain this situation. First, those recruited to write the histories of the various components that make up international studies come from inside the enterprise and therefore have not been specialists in American intellectual history; they have lacked the wherewithal to provide that context in any significant detail. Second, and perhaps more crucially, the promotional purposes of these accounts, which require that the emphasis be placed on the present and future needs of academic international studies, are not served by a sympathetic rendering of pre-academic arrangements and accomplishments.

To be sure, some mention of nineteenth- and even eighteenth-century Americans, typically identified as "gentlemen amateurs" pursuing the study of distant parts, is made in most of these accounts. Usually, however, the main purpose in doing so is to provide the subject with a respectably long lineage. Later references to the efforts of "old hands," "ex-diplomats," and "wealthy expatriates" are also common, though made in such a way as to reinforce the point that the *real* history of American international studies dates from its entry into the university and its subsequent growth therein. Because these accounts do not take seriously the tradition of nonacademic cultivation of international studies they can only view its subsequent academic enclosure as a progressive and wholly desirable development. The result is a version of the history of American international studies foreshortened, predetermined, and in need of recasting.[6]

❧ I

Even granting the need for a running head start, the early nineteenth century seems an inauspicious point at which to seek the beginnings of American international studies, or, for that

matter, of any American intellectual enterprise. "American society," Alexis de Tocqueville noted two weeks into his 1831
visit to the United States, "suffers from taking too little account of intellectual questions." Eight months of additional
observation only confirmed his initial impression. "Few of the
civilized nations of our time," he concluded in *Democracy in
America,* "have made less progress than the United States in
higher sciences or had so few artists, distinguished poets, or
celebrated writers."[7]

Most contemporary reviewers of *Democracy in America* accepted this derisory assessment of American intellectual life, as
have most historians since. "We are a business-doing people,"
the Boston physician James Jackson, Sr., asserted in 1834. "We
are new. We have, as it were just landed on these uncultivated
shores; there is a vast deal to be done; and he who will not be
doing, must be set down as a drone." Only in the last two
decades have historians seriously questioned Tocqueville's view,
to which Richard Shryock gave classic form in 1948, that early
nineteenth-century American science was indifferent to theoretical considerations. Richard Hofstadter's characterization of
the era as pervaded with anti-intellectualism, and undergoing,
as compared with the intellectual achievements of the preceding generation, a "great retrogression," remains the standard
one. Still more recently, William Stanton has remarked on the
era's "egalitarian contempt for learning."[8]

It might be logically expected that such contempt for intellectual labor generally would only be compounded when the
labor involved distant parts of the world. Surely the indifference with which presidents from John Quincy Adams to
Grover Cleveland attended to foreign relations, and the refusal
of Congress throughout the nineteenth century to establish a
professional diplomatic corps, bespoke an American people
preoccupied with domestic affairs. "The Union does not med-
dle in the affairs of Europe," Tocqueville observed; "American foreign policy consists much more in abstaining than
doing." In such a setting, Ralph Waldo Emerson's 1838 dec-
laration that "our day of dependence, our long apprenticeship

to the learning of other lands, draws to a close," was part fact, part boast, and part self-fulfilling prophecy.[9]

Yet both views—that early nineteenth-century Americans were hostile to learning generally and to that about foreign parts specifically—require qualification. Tocqueville himself offered testimony contrary to the first. "In Boston," he noted during his first visit, "there are already a certain number of people, who, having nothing to do, seek out the pleasures of the mind." Tocqueville subsequently encountered similarly disposed Americans among the professional classes of New York, Philadelphia, Baltimore, and Charleston, but Boston's "cultivators of liberal studies" were both more numerous and more impressively occupied. Some even had intellectual interests that extended beyond the geographical, linguistic, and cultural bounds imposed by national loyalties and origins.[10] Among these none was more impressive than John Pickering, the founder of American international studies.

II

Pickering was in his early fifties when Tocqueville visited Boston. Unlike his more famous father, Colonel Timothy Pickering, who served both Washington and Adams as Secretary of State and then spent his declining years unsuccessfully trying to launch various Federalist plots by which New England might secede from the Union, he remained throughout his life indifferent to politics or public office. His passion, which he discovered as a schoolboy, was for languages, or, more broadly, the study of comparative philology. After graduating in 1796 from Harvard, where he studied Greek, Latin, and French, he put off settling on a career by taking a junior position at the American legation in Lisbon. During three years there he acquired a thorough command of Portuguese, Spanish, and Italian. Forty years later Pickering's Portuguese remained such that his friend William Hickling Prescott depended on it in the course of writing his various histories of Spain and Spanish America.[11]

While still in Lisbon, rumor of a diplomatic opening in Smyrna prompted Pickering to take up Turkish, "which I am informed is far from difficult." It also occasioned his confession to his father that "nothing is more pleasing to me than the study of languages; but a person cannot devote all his life to that alone." The colonel emphatically concurred with the second point, even to dismissing his son's wishful thinking that a diplomatic career might allow him to turn his linguistic interests to gainful employment. "Consider the nature of the employment," wrote the elder Pickering, his own position as Secretary of State about to end with Jefferson's election, "the changes in the administration of a government, the outs as well as the ins, the precarious tenure of public offices, and, above all, the misery of a state of dependence on court favor for one's bread." [12]

Dreams of a diplomatic career quashed, Pickering returned to Boston, apprenticed himself to a lawyer, gained admission to the bar, and labored diligently before it for four decades until his death in 1846. Language studies were relegated to after-business hours but no less passionately pursued for that. During his lifetime he acquired a working knowledge of "all the European and Semitic languages, plus Arabic, Turkish, Syriac, Persian, Coptic, Sanskrit, Chinese, Cochin-Chinese, Russian, Egyptian, hieroglyphics, Malay in several dialects, and Indian (American and Polynesian)." Usually modest about his scholarly accomplishments, as when he described them to a Russian academic as "the fruits of those few hours which I have been able to spare from the business of the laborious profession of law in which I am engaged," he was not above comparing himself with another lawyer-scholar, Sir William Jones, who, as a member of the Imperial Service in Calcutta in the 1780s, had introduced Sanskrit studies to England. [13]

Pickering's scholarly writings, which included a translation of Sallust, "A Memoir on the Pronunciation of the Greek Language," and dozens of technical papers in comparative philology, won him respectful notice both at home and in Europe.

His daughter's insistence that "he spent his days declining honors" notwithstanding, Pickering accepted a fair number, among them the presidency of the American Academy of Arts and Sciences, memberships in the Massachusetts Historical and American Philosophical Societies, and honorary memberships in the Berlin Academy of Sciences, the French Society of Universal Statistics, and the Royal Asiatic Society. Such recognition both flowed from and resulted in an active scholarly correspondence. In addition to formal exchanges with philologists abroad, Pickering maintained close ties with both the Philadelphia and New York intellectual communities through personal friendships with their respective leaders, Peter DuPonceau and Albert Gallatin.[14]

DuPonceau had come to America from France as a military aide to Baron Steuben in 1778, and after the war he took up residence in Philadelphia. There he became a successful lawyer specializing in international matters and one of the city's intellectual ornaments. His election to the presidency of the American Philosophical Society in 1828 reflected both his local standing and his international recognition as a linguist. As with Pickering, DuPonceau first attracted European notice for his work on Indian languages, which earned him the Volney Prize from the French Institute. But, also like Pickering, DuPonceau refused to limit himself to the study of "local" languages, as his *Dissertation on the Nature and Character of the Chinese System of Writing* and his interest in Russian attest.[15]

Gallatin, though best known for his diplomatic and fiscal efforts as a cabinet member under Presidents Jefferson and Madison, passed the last third of his long life as a New York banker and civic leader. A prime mover behind the founding of the University of the City of New York and the New-York Historical Society, he devoted the bulk of his scholarly labors to the study of Indian tribes. The American Ethnological Society, which he founded in 1842 and presided over until his death in 1849, is a permanent monument to that interest. Indeed, Gallatin confided to Pickering that it was for precisely such organizational efforts and the scholarship displayed in his "Notes on the Semicivilized Nations of Mexico," rather than his efforts as a Jeffersonian politician, that he wished to be remembered by posterity.[16]

Pickering, DuPonceau, and Gallatin, as spokesmen for their respective intellectual constituencies, regularly made their views known to Washington officials. All three, for example, continually reminded the Indian Department of its responsibility to encourage the study of Indian languages. In 1836 Pickering urged officials then organizing what became the Great United States Exploring Expedition to the South Seas to include a philologist. When the organizers expressed mild interest in doing so, Pickering promptly produced Horatio Hale, a twenty-one-year-old Harvard graduate whose undergraduate work on the languages of Maine Indians had attracted his attention. Hale's report summarizing his four years of philological and ethnographic researches as a member of the South Seas expedition was published in 1846 and remained the most important field study of any foreign area published in the United States until those by Franz Boas began to appear in the 1890s.[17]

However extensive Pickering's national and international contacts, his impact was most keenly felt locally. He appeared regularly in Boston's leading cultural journals to scold Bostonians for their unwillingness to recruit classical teachers from Europe or to alert them to the latest developments in "the new science—the comparative study of languages." He used his position as a Harvard overseer to lobby for a professorship in Oriental languages and his professional connections to urge upon Thomas H. Perkins and Boston's other leading China merchants "the literary, religious, commercial, and other advantages" of underwriting the establishment of a Chinese language school in Boston. Though nothing came of these two particular initiatives, a third, undertaken in 1842, led directly to the founding of the American Oriental Society and hence to Pickering's claim to the title of "founder" of American international studies.[18]

ई॰ III

The idea that Boston should have a counterpart to London's Asiatic Society and the Société Asiatique in Paris, both established in the 1820s, originated not with Pickering but with the Reverend William Jenks, a leading promoter of civic and cultural good works and an erstwhile student of Chinese. Jenks' account of the founding of the American Oriental Society, however, makes clear that it was Pickering "under whose auspices it was formed, and to whom its principal efficiency was due." A planning meeting attended by "a few gentlemen interested in Oriental Literature" in Pickering's law offices in the summer of 1842 led to more meetings, from which a draft constitution emerged. On April 7, 1843, the General Court of Massachusetts approved the constitution and granted a charter to the American Oriental Society "for the cultivation of learning in the Asian, African, and Polynesian languages," thereby bringing into being the first American learned society primarily devoted to humanistic studies.[19]

In addition to Pickering, who presided until his death in 1846, and Jenks, who served as vice president, the first board of directors of the AOS included seven other members. Four had ties to the Andover Theological Seminary, founded in 1808 to prepare young men for the Presbyterian and Congregational ministries. Moses Stuart, its president and professor of Hebrew literature, was easily the most distinguished, although the scholarly interests of his former student and then professor of Hebrew at the Union Theological Seminary in New York City, Edward Robinson, related more directly to the purposes of the society. After studying philology at Göttingen, Halle, and Berlin in the late 1820s, Robinson had conducted research in the Middle East for two years. Out of this came his three-volume *Biblical Researches in Palestine, Mount Sinai, and Arabia Petraea,* published in 1841 and promptly translated into German, the first significant American contribution to Biblical and Middle Eastern studies.[20]

Barnas Sears was another Andover man on the first AOS

board who had studied in Germany, though his subsequent
energies were deflected from Biblical scholarship upon becoming president of Brown University in 1851. Bela B. Edwards,
the fourth board member with Andover ties, was an accomplished linguist and the editor of *Bibliotheca Sacra,* then the most
learned theological journal in America.[21] The remainder of the
board consisted of Rufus Anderson, secretary of the American
Board of Commissioners of Foreign Missions, and two Harvard professors, Sidney Willard and Cornelius C. Felton, about
whom more in the next chapter.

That six of the first nine board members of the AOS were
ministers only slightly exaggerated their representation within
the society's general membership. Nearly half (32 of 66) of
those included in the first extant membership list, that of 1846,
were ministers. In 1849 a new membership category, "corresponding member," was created specifically to accommodate
American ministers residing "beyond the bounds of Christendom." By 1860 the fifty-two ministers enrolled in that category constituted 20 percent of the entire membership. Between 1849 and 1863 one of every three papers read at the
society's meetings or later published in the society's *Journal*
was contributed by a missionary in the field or temporarily
home on leave.[22]

Pickering, a Unitarian of the most nonproselytizing sort,
long before the founding of the AOS had acknowledged his
debt—"and the debt of philology"—to his many missionary
correspondents. In 1820 he had urged Hiram Bingham, about
to set off from the Foreign Missions School in Cornwall, Con-
necticut, for Hawaii, to record all he could of the native dialects encountered. Such information, Pickering assured
Bingham, would serve "both for the instruction of the heathen
and for the information of the learned." As Pickering's order-
ing of these priorities suggests, it is truer to the historical realities of the early nineteenth century to consider the organizational beginnings of American international studies as an aspect
of the American missionary enterprise, rather than the other
way round. In the absence of an overseas empire to imbue

such studies with the national purpose they enjoyed in Europe, Pickering and his colleagues found in the missions its functional equivalent.[23]

‚» IV

The American missionary movement began in earnest with the founding of the American Board of Commissioners for Foreign Missions in 1810. Based in Boston, the ABCFM coordinated the overseas commitment of the Presbyterian, Congregational, and Dutch Reformed churches of the United States. Baptists, Methodists, Episcopalians, and still later American Roman Catholics would eventually create their own boards, but for much of the nineteenth century the ABCFM was the American missionary effort's principal organizational arm.[24]

In 1812 the Board dispatched its first missionaries to India; in 1819 it established a mission in Smyrna; in the 1820s it opened Hawaii to Christian evangelization; in the 1830s it began its long presence in China by placing missionaries in several treaty ports. The ABCFM failed to penetrate Africa and achieved only a modest presence in Latin America. Still, the American missionary movement encompassed more parts of the world than did that of any other country and by the 1850s was largest in terms of personnel in the field and financial resources. By the eve of the Civil War the ABCFM had placed 1,250 missionaries abroad and raised $8,000,000 to sustain them. "The American Board was more than a benevolent enterprise," its most recent historian has concluded. "It was a big business."[25]

The impact of this religious diaspora upon American intellectual life was both immediate and long lasting. On the most personal level, it exposed hundreds of Americans to parts of the world which they or their countrymen had previously had little reason to be curious about and no opportunity to examine firsthand. They, in turn, through letters back home, lectures while on leave, and still later reminiscences, provided their countrymen with their first glimpse of "the heathen

world." Families with relatives in the missions closely attended news from that quarter of the world as reported in the
Missionary Herald and the published annual reports of the
ABCFM, and so presumably did the thousands of churchgoers
whose contributions and prayers sustained the missions. In
sum, the missionary enterprise created a substantial American
audience for information about parts of the world that were
for another century to remain outside America's strategic and
economic reach.[26]

Before missionaries could prech the Christian message they
had to learn to communicate in the languages of the heathen.
Often it fell to American missionaries to give those languages
their first written form. Justin Perkins for example, did so with
modern Syriac in the 1820s, at the outset of his ministry in the
Middle East. Similarly, among his labors during three decades
in India, David O. Allen produced the first Marathi translation
of the Bible, while Elias Riggs advanced the missionary cause
by preparing *A Brief Grammar of the Armenian Language*.[27]

Missionaries were encouraged to go beyond developing their
language skills and to examine local customs and political and
economic arrangements. "There," Rufus Anderson, secretary
of the Board, advised a missionary setting out for the Middle
East, "you will be on Classick ground, and whatever contribution or service you can afford to Literature, or to Taste,
with fidelity to your higher objects, will be interesting to many,
and useful to the general cause."[28]

The resultant contributions were many and varied, not least
in terms of scholarly value. Most took the form of anecdotal
reminiscences, like Hiram Bingham's *Residence of Twenty-One
Years in the Sandwich Islands* (1847) and Asahel Grant's *The
Nestorians; or, The Lost Tribes* (1847). Others, such as William
Goodell's *The Old and the New; or, The Changes of 30 Years in
the East* (1845) and the first edition of Samuel Wells Williams'
*The Middle Kingdom: A Survey of the Geography, Government,
Education, Social Life, Arts, Religion, etc., of the Chinese Empire
and Its Inhabitants* (1848) were hastily prepared sketches in-
tended for fund-raising purposes back home. But others,

among them the collaborative effort of Harrison Gray Dwight and Eli Smith, *Researches in Armenia* (1833), Francis Mason's *The Natural Productions of Burmah* (1850), and David O. Allen's *India, Ancient and Modern* (1856), were substantial scholarly undertakings and represent permanent contributions to the literature of Middle Eastern and South Asian studies.[29]

Not everyone in the missionary movement shared Anderson's easy optimism as to the compatibility of scholarship and proselytism. Among those who did not was Adoniram Judson. The son of a Massachusetts Baptist minister, Judson had gone to Brown and then to Andover, where he contracted "missionary fever." Already promised by his father to a Boston congregation, Judson informed his family in 1810: "I shall never live in Boston. I have much further to go than that." In 1813 he joined the first missionaries sent by the American Board to India; a year later he migrated to Burma, where he remained for thirty years.[30]

Throughout his tenure in Burma, Judson warned the Board against sending out intellectuals. "He who has undertaken to deliver a nation from the thralldom of sin," he insisted, "has objects in view more important than the researches of antiquaries or the companionship of *savans.*" Judson's first biographer, Brown University's president Francis Wayland, wrote of him: "Fully aware of the temptations to which missionaries are exposed when the treasures of a new language and a peculiar form of literature are presented before them, he therefore guarded himself with peculiar strictness." Accordingly, despite a natural facility for languages and a scholarly disposition, Judson "acquired no language of the East, except the Burman [and] discouraged a taste for such pursuits among the missionary brethren."[31]

Judson was not the only missionary who feared that literary researches would "lead him away from the peculiar work to which God had called him." Passing through Paris on his way back to the United States in 1847 after fifteen years as a missionary in China, Samuel Wells Williams found himself besieged by France's leading sinologists. Their scholarly enthusiasm he took as a warning. "How singular to see those French savans digging with such zeal after the treasure in all the languages found in the literature," he observed, "while so far as I can see, hardly one of them troubles himself about a religion for his own soul." Even Moses Stuart, the most learned of clergymen and academic administrators, feared compromising Andover's commitment to recruiting ministers for the missions by extending its intellectual activities. When approached about whether Andover would be interested in sharing an Arabic teacher with Harvard and Yale, he responded tartly: "Who needs to speak Arabic here?" [32]

These reservations notwithstanding, missionaries of a scholarly bent had the most practical and compelling reasons for their studies. Language skills were needed if the heathen were to be converted; accurate field reports on local customs and conditions were needed by headquarters for planning purposes and the training of recruits; elaborate and entertaining accounts of life among the natives were needed if the interest of church-going Americans in the missionary enterprise was to be sustained. Accordingly, missionary "literati," as their less scholarly colleagues dubbed them, were on reasonably safe gound as long as they could demonstrate that their scholarly activities were not an end in themselves. Only rarely, as in the instance of George Bowen, who abandoned his missionary post in Bombay in the 1850s to devote himself to Indian studies, did missionaries confuse scholarly means with conversionary ends. [33] On the contrary, the psychological costs exacted of those pursuing studies in the field were less likely than they would have been back home where the same pursuits put them at risk of being "set down a drone." In opting not "to live in Boston," missionary literati located themselves beyond the reach of the principled anti-intellectualism of their business-doing countrymen.

&ₑ V

But what of Americans like Pickering, DuPonceau, Gallatin, and other early members of the AOS who were not missionaries, and did not expatriate themselves, but who took up international studies because, as Pickering put it, they were "highly gratifying to a liberal curiosity"? Here the problem of justifying such studies could be formidable. "We are as yet so circumstanced, in our young country," Pickering reminded the AOS in his inaugural address, "that the imperative necessity of gaining a livelihood will not allow, even to the most resolute and zealous student, much leisure for any pursuits which do not directly tend to secure to him that indispensable object." Add to this general problem of pursuing intellectual labors in America the specific one that those Pickering and his audience cultivated set them apart from "the community of literary men, at large," and they risked being dismissed as the most dilettantish of dilettantes.[34]

Pickering advised his audience to respond to the question, "Of what utility is all this knowledge?," by appealing to their questioners' patriotism—more specifically, to their sense of national intellectual inferiority. The United States could not expect to enjoy the full respect of other nations until it earned the respect of their scholars. "At the present day, Europe and the United States constitute but one literary community," he declared, "and the reputation of our country demands the continued efforts of every American, to perform his proportion of the common duties as a member of the republic of letters."[35]

Pickering had been making the same argument for years. In 1835, when urging upon the organizers of the Great United States Exploring Expedition the appointment of a philologist, he pointed out that the United States had "already derived no little reputation from what we have accomplished by expeditions of this character on the continent of America . . . , however inconsiderable the results may appear in the general mass of science." Four years later, in arguing on behalf of the establishment of a chair in Oriental studies at Harvard, he told the university corporation that with it "a new impulse will be given to Oriental Studies generally, which have been too long in a feeble and languishing state in our country, though cultivated in Europe with more zeal and ardor than at any former time." In memorializing DuPonceau upon his death in 1844, Pickering could pay no higher tribute to his fellow philologist than that his "labors in the noble but boundless field have, among the profound scholars of Europe, contributed more to establish our reputation for solid erudition, than those of any other individual in this country."[36]

Other early members of the AOS sought legitimation for their studies less through appeals to the national pride of their countrymen than to their racist prejudices. Interest in Africa, for example, and other parts of the nonwhite world generally, could be put to the most practical uses by a generation that was, as a Southern politician crudely put it in the 1830s, "morbidly excited about the nigger business." The researchers of two charter AOS members, Drs. Samuel G. Morton and Josiah C. Nott, provide cases in point.[37]

Once established in the late 1820s, a thriving Philadelphia medical practice provided Morton with the financial resources and occupational cover to pursue his passion, paleontology. Field reports based on digs in western Pennsylvania and published in the *Proceedings* of the American Philosophical Society in 1835 secured him a modest reputation in Europe. By then he had begun to collect human skulls, eventually acquiring several hundred from all over the world. One European visitor declared the collection "alone worth a trip to America."[38]

The first results of Morton's skull studies appeared in his *Crania Americana,* published in 1839, in which he argued that cranial shape and size were racially determined. He further argued that the interior capacity of Negro skulls was substantially less than that of the skulls of whites and slightly less than that of American Indians' skulls. These findings provoked considerable criticism, less because they supported the notion of the mental inferiority of Negroes than because they lent credence to the then-circulating theories of multiple and racially distinctive genesis, which the religiously orthodox of Morton's day found unacceptable.[39]

In the course of widening his search for evidence to silence his religious critics, Morton entered into correspondence with

George Robbins Glidden, then United States vice consul at Cairo, later a charter member of the AOS, and still later the first American to offer lectures in Egyptology. Glidden gladly provided Morton with cranial measurements supposedly acquired during visits to Egyptian tombs, and with skulls from Ethiopia, while urging upon him his own racist theories. Out of this meeting of minds came *Crania Aegyptia,* published in 1841, in which Morton and Glidden argued that all ancient Egyptian leaders had been white, all their slaves black. Ancient Egypt, in effect, became the first conclusive test case for innate Negro inferiority.[40]

Such views found ready acceptance in the American South. Politicians like South Carolina's John Calhoun, put on the defensive by Northern abolitionists, seized upon Morton as a disinterested defender of the South's "peculiar institution." At Morton's death in 1851, a South Carolina medical journal eulogized him as "our benefactor, for aiding most materially in giving to the negro his true position as an inferior race."[41]

Among the early members of the AOS most impressed by Morton's researches was the Mobile, Alabama, physician and occasional "professor of niggerology" at the University of Alabama, Josiah C. Nott. Nott's *Two Lectures on the Natural History of the Caucasian and Negro Races,* published in 1844 and then serialized in *DeBow's Review,* drew heavily upon Morton, yet went further in asserting that contact between the races would render both extinct. Nott teamed up with the ubiquitous Glidden to publish *Types of Mankind* in 1854 and, two years later, *The Indigenous Races of the Earth,* both of which drew on ethnological materials from all over the world in making their elaborate apology for racial subordination.[42]

Whatever else may be thought of the work of Morton, Nott, and Glidden, which since has come to be referred to as "the American school of anthropology," it hardly constituted scholarship for the sake of scholarship. Read today, their findings are as scientifically spurious as their motives ideologically reprehensible. Yet they do provide an early and by no means unique instance of Americans drawn to international studies for reasons that contemporaries found wholly acceptable but later Americans no less powerfully attracted to the same intellectual enterprise would find embarrassing.

The reasons nineteenth-century Americans gave for pursuing international studies often masked others of a more personal, even subconscious, character. Pickering's linguistic researches, for example, afforded him an escape from his professional labors. "A lawyer whose days were worn in the faithful and uninterrupted practice of his profession," a colleague remembered him at his death, "he found less delights in the hoarse strifes of the bar than in the peaceful conversations of books." Unlike DuPonceau, who retired early to devote himself to his studies, Pickering maintained his practice to the end. He may have been financially obliged to do so, though more likely he feared being "set down a drone" if he made scholarship a full-time pursuit. "The prejudice against people who do nothing," which Tocqueville noted "has still great strength in Boston," was one Pickering may well have shared. Like Adoniram Judson determined early on not to live entirely "in Boston," he rigidly limited his travels to after hours.[43]

Antebellum New York had its professional malcontents, too, among them John Lloyd Stephens, a Columbia graduate who abandoned the bar in his early thirties to give full play to his wanderlust. His first book, *Incidents of Travel in Central America, Chiapas, and Yucatan* (1843), provided Americans with their first accounts of the remains of the Aztec and Mayan civilizations. Like those of his fellow New Yorker, Herman Melville, who fled a banking apprenticeship to sail the South Seas and then recounted his adventures in *Typee* (1846) and *Omoo* (1847), Stephens' travel books sold well. That they did suggests the existence of many job-bound Americans who shared with Melville's Ishmael "an everlasting itch for things remote" and at least vicariously responded to the appeal of distant travel which a more recent American traveler, Paul Theroux, has described as "flight and pursuit in equal parts."[44]

Less constrained by the work ethic than Pickering, though

less peripatetic than Stephens, the Concord transcendentalists openly acknowledged escapist motives behind their interest in and identification with Asian, and especially Indian, thought. Ralph Waldo Emerson, introduced to Indian writings by an aunt in the missionary movement, informed his journal that "*Nala and Damayanti* is nearer to my business and bosom than is the news in today's *Boston Journal*. I am admonished and comforted as I read. It all very nearly concerns me." On another occasion, however, he did acknowledge that his capacities to transcend his own culture were finite, when he confessed, "only so much of Arabian history can I read as I am Arabian within."[45]

Emerson's occasional boarder and neighbor, Henry David Thoreau, identified even more completely with the antimaterialism and quietism of Indian thought. "Thus it appears," he wrote upon observing ice being removed from Walden Pond for shipment to India,

> that the sweltering inhabitants of Madras and Bombay and Calcutta drink at my well. In the morning I bathe my intellect in the stupendous and cosmogonal philosophy of the Brahmin, priest of Brahma and Vishnu and Indra, who still sits in his temple on the Ganges reading the Vedas.

Thoreau never went within nine thousand miles of Asia, yet he boasted that "farthest India is nearer to me than Concord and Lexington." Of the *Vedas,* which he and his fellow transcendentalists read in translation, he said that "one wise sentence is worth the state of Massachusetts many times over."[46]

Nineteenth-century America's knowledge of the languages and cultures of the rest of the world would have been greater had the lawyers Pickering and DuPonceau devoted themselves to their studies as a full-time occupation. Had missionaries like Judson and Williams viewed their scholarly opportunities and inclinations as primary and legitimate rather than secondary and suspect, their contemporaries would have become better informed about Burma and China. Had Morton and Nott pursued their anthropological enthusiasms freed from their medical practices—and their racial biases—Africa might have become for nineteenth-century Americans something more than "the Dark Continent." It would also have increased the country's stock of knowledge had Emerson been obliged, as are graduate students in Middle Eastern studies today, to read more Arabian history than he was "Arabian within." More effort all round would likely have produced more results.

Yet precisely because early nineteenth-century Americans did not pursue international studies within an institutionally bound and occupationally exclusive setting, but rather as part of an open and nonprofessional community of "gentlemen and scholars," these first cultivators of international studies were arguably better situated to communicate their knowledge to and share their enthusiasm with a larger and more diverse audience of Americans than have been their academic successors. One need not resort to comparing the best of the past with the worst of the present to suggest that the rapid expansion of American specialized knowledge of the rest of the world that followed upon the displacement of these "mere amateurs" by their academic successors has had its costs.

ENCLOSURE DEFERRED

It is not necessary for anyone to be a professed Orientalist in order
to become a member of the Society. All persons—men or women—
who are in sympathy with the objects of the Society and willing to
further its work are invited to give it their help.

AMERICAN ORIENTAL SOCIETY, 1891 [1]

The social structure of American intellectual life underwent
fundamental transformation during the second half of the
nineteenth century. The most conspicuous and arguably the
most crucial element in this transformation was the emergence
of a new set of institutions—graduate universities—which for
the first time provided a substantial number of Americans with
the economic wherewithal, social incentives, and regenerative
capacity to undertake on a full-time and salaried basis what
had previously been part-time and self-financed intellectual
pursuits.

Three distinct but related sets of changes attended what has
since come to be designated the "first academic revolution."
In the first, which occurred within institutions of higher education themselves, the recognition and status conferred upon
research-oriented professors came to exceed that accorded those
committed to undergraduate instruction. In the second, which
occurred within the intellectual community, amateur cultivators were displaced from positions of influence and leadership

by those deriving their living from their intellectual pursuits. In the third, which occurred within American society, it came increasingly to be assumed that intellectual activity was primarily if not exclusively the business of universities and those employed therein.[2]

At a century's remove, all three sets of developments appear part of a single process which has only recently shown signs of leveling off: the academic enclosure of American intellectual life. Already by 1900, intellectual enterprises such as philosophy, anthropology, history, economics, even English literature, which three decades before had been institutionally unbounded and occupationally inclusive, were well on the way to becoming what they are now, either wholly or preponderantly academic enterprises. That nothing at all comparable occurred to the international studies enterprise, this chapter intends to demonstrate. Its larger purpose is to discuss several factors present during the first academic revolution that helped prevent international studies from undergoing academic enclosure. This discussion, in turn, should better enable us to appreciate what was distinctive about the situation when, fifty years later in the midst of the "second academic revolution," international studies proceeded with a rush to follow its predecessors.

ะ๛   I

The beginnings of academic instruction in subjects now encompassed by international studies very nearly coincide with the beginnings of American higher education. Within a decade of its founding in 1636, Harvard College provided instruction in three non-Western languages—Hebrew, Aramaic, and Syriac. Two of its first presidents, Henry Dunster and Charles Chauncy, were recognized Hebrew scholars. Yale required Hebrew from its opening in 1701, as did Columbia when it opened in 1754 as King's College. In 1764, three-quarters of a century before similar status was accorded to history or political economy, the Harvard Corporation established the Hancock professorship of Hebrew and Other Oriental Languages. Yale created a professorship of Arabic and Sanskrit in 1841, its first in the humanities. In 1854 a separate professorship in Sanskrit was established, eleven years before modern European history acquired professorial status in New Haven.[3]

Thus, early American college authorities were not wholly indifferent to international studies. On the contrary, as long as colleges accepted as a primary mission the recruiting and training of ministers, which all but a few did through the Civil War and many for a generation thereafter, courses bearing on the ancient Middle East and the languages of the Old and New Testaments retained a conspicuous place in their curriculum. So too would the persons providing such instruction retain a central place within their faculties.

It was less, then, that international studies subjects had a marginal place in pre-Civil War American colleges, than that American colleges were themselves marginal institutions within American society which accounts for the marginality of international studies academics. College-going counted for little not only among Americans generally—and they attended in proportionally smaller numbers in the 1850s than in the 1820s—but even among members of the American intellectual community. If during Henry Adams' undergraduate days "no one took Harvard College seriously," the same could be said of its faculty.[4]

"Our practice is to give the different professorships away to young men," a foreign visitor to Boston was informed in the 1830s,

in order to induce them to devote themselves to the branch they are to teach. Our country is as yet too young for old professors; and, besides, they are too poorly paid to induce first rate men to devote themselves to the business of lecturing. . . . We consider professors as secondary men.[5]

The two Harvard professors represented on the first board of the American Oriental Society, Sidney Willard and Cornelius C. Felton, are fair examples of the type.

Willard, the son of a Harvard president, lingered on in

Cambridge after graduating from Harvard in 1798, ostensibly to pursue theological studies but in fact to await a faculty opening. When the Hancock professorship fell vacant in 1806, Willard, then twenty-six and with no more training in Hebrew than any Harvard undergraduate, was elected to it. For the next quarter-century he taught Hebrew, English, and Latin. During these years he managed to publish one book, *A Hebrew Grammar, Compiled from Some of the Best Authorities* (1817), which he assigned to his students. In his autobiography, written during his retirement, Willard modestly and accurately described his duties as a Harvard professor as providing "the permanent instruction of youth."[6]

Felton, reared in impoverished circumstances, had graduated from Harvard in 1827, only two years before joining the faculty as an instructor. In 1832, at the age of twenty-six, he became Eliot professor of Greek, a position he held until 1860, when he was drafted into the presidency of the college. Two years later, as he had feared, the responsibilities of the office killed him. No less so than for Willard, Harvard for Felton was home, and academic life, with "its regular tasks, its tranquil uniformity," was very much to his liking. He published nothing.[7]

Others who taught at Harvard prior to the Civil War regarded it differently. Some, like Felton's predecessor, John Snelling Popkin, who had earlier been dismissed from a distinguished Boston pulpit, viewed Harvard as a permanent refuge from the wider world in which early promise had gone awry. Neither an accomplished classicist nor an inspired teacher—students remembered him "wading through Homer as if *The Iliad* was a bog"—he took his parietal responsibilities seriously, lived in college rooms, and seldom ventured beyond the Yard. "If he failed of distinction," a memorialist wrote of him at his death in 1852, "he at least attained peace. He was free from the tyranny of restless ambition."[8]

Then there were the Edward Everetts and George Ticknors for whom a Harvard professorship served only until something better came along. For Everett that meant, after five years on the faculty teaching Greek, a chance in 1824 to run for Congress; for Ticknor, after fifteen years teaching Romance languages, the realization in 1835 that at forty he might now indulge his aesthetic and literary interests without need of further occupational cover. Even Henry Wadsworth Longfellow, who started out to become a professor and who had taught six years at Bowdoin before going to Harvard in 1836 as Ticknor's successor, soon wearied of his duties and, following a second marriage that freed him of his dependence upon a Harvard salary, resigned in 1854 at age forty-seven. Expressions of disenchantment from those marooned on the antebellum Harvard faculty are plentiful, but perhaps that of the consummate careerist Everett is the most telling. "I find the whole pursuit," he confessed to his father-in-law in 1821 after two years on the faculty, "not respectable enough in the estimate they bring with them and lead too much into contact with some little men and many little things." [9]

The leading members of the Boston intellectual community, however willing to serve as Corporation fellows or overseers, regularly declined professorships throughout the antebellum era. John Pickering did so at least twice: in 1806, when nominated for the Hancock professorship, and in 1814, when the Eliot professorship fell vacant. "Although my attachment to the place of my education," he wrote in response to the first offer, "strongly urges me to accept the appointment, considerations of a higher nature demand that I should decline it." To the second: "I have consulted one or two friends, and regret to say that I cannot persuade myself it would be advisable for me to accept the professorship." [10]

Pickering knew, as did his friend the mathematician-astronomer Nathaniel Bowditch, who declined science professorships with even greater regularity, that Harvard Yard was no place for a scholar. Both succeeded in accomplishing more in their respective fields during lulls in business at their respective State Street offices than did any of the professors out in Cambridge, who acknowledged as much. "Rather than leading a life of ease," Sidney Willard wrote in 1819 in defense of his colleagues' lack of publishing productivity, "they are generally employed with their classes to the exclusion of any great literary undertakings to which their choice might lead them." [11]

Other early nineteenth-century colleges differed from Harvard in burdening their generally smaller faculties with even heavier teaching, parietal, and proselytizing duties. All colleges worried about survival and many failed financially. Accordingly, they were less inclined than the relatively solvent Harvard or Yale to attract committed scholars to their faculties, in international studies or any other field. Nor were they prepared, discovering a would-be scholar in their teaching ranks, to provide him with the time and support to advance his studies beyond the point required for elementary classroom instruction. "The prime business of American professors in this generation," Charles William Eliot announced upon assuming the Harvard presidency in 1869, "must be regular and assiduous class teaching." "This being the case," Eliot had confessed to a friend at Yale earlier that same year, "how is it possible that our colleges can secure first class men as professors?" [12]

Yet well before Eliot began his presidency, some Harvard faculty saw their prime business as taking place outside the classroom. Technically correct that, as of 1869, Harvard "does not hold a single fund primarily intended to secure men of learning the leisure and means to prosecute original researches," Eliot could hardly have been unaware that original research was going on in Cambridge. Indeed, it had been his own insufficient promise as a research chemist that had obliged him to resign his position on the Harvard faculty six years earlier. [13]

The first Harvard professor to occupy himself principally with research was the entomologist William Dandridge Peck, Massachusetts professor of natural history from 1805 to 1821. By the 1840s there were at least three Harvard professors who, like Peck, regarded occasional teaching as the price exacted for being allowed to devote the bulk of their time to research: the mathematician Benjamin Peirce, the botanist Asa Gray, and the geologist Louis Agassiz. It was the opposition of Peirce and Agassiz that had denied the Rumford professorship to Eliot in 1863, and it was their support of the outsider Wolcott Gibbs, whom even Eliot acknowledged to be "undoubtedly the first chemist in the country," that secured it for another of their own kind. By then Peirce and Agassiz had become conspicuous forces in the American Association for the Advancement of Science, which they had helped organize in 1847, and in the National Academy of Sciences, to which they had been elected at its opening in 1863.[14]

In both organizations Peirce and Agassiz aligned themselves with those committed to science as a career, as against its gentlemanly cultivators. Meanwhile, Gray, also among the first elected to the National Academy, had established himself on both sides of the Atlantic as the most reasoned defender of the evolutionary theories of his friend Charles Darwin. Through such extra-university efforts, Peirce, Agassiz, and Gray secured for themselves and for academic scientists thereafter a commanding place in the American scientific community. They were anything but, by their own estimate or that of their contemporaries, "secondary men."[15]

ৡ II

American academics in any numbers who defined themselves primarily by their research interests rather than by their institutional affiliations or instructional responsibilities began to make their presence felt within college faculties in the 1840s and 1850s. They were almost all in the sciences. The further spread of the research ideal to academics in other fields occurred only after the Civil War, as part of what Edward Shils has described as "a fundamental change in the institutional structure of the order of learning in the United States."[16]

Besides Shils, Richard Hofstadter, Walter Metzger, Frederick Rudolph, Hugh Hawkins, Laurence Veysey, and others, including myself, have described this change as a whole or in part.[17] Accordingly, consideration here will be restricted to just two aspects, both of which bear importantly (albeit negatively) on the history of American international studies during the opening decades of modern American intellectual life.

The first relates to the domestication of the German PhD degree. In modest but growing numbers from the second decade of the nineteenth century, Americans had been pursuing doctoral studies at German universities, principally Göttingen, Berlin, and Halle. By 1870, according to a recent estimate, over 600 Americans had completed the trek to what one of the earliest of them called "the holy land of the scholar." It was in part to stem this flow, which consisted largely of Harvard and Yale graduates, that the Yale faculty in 1861 launched its own program in graduate studies and conferred the first American PhDs.[18]

This crucial event in the history of American learning aroused little interest at the time, even in New Haven. After conferring three in 1861, Yale conferred only a dozen more PhDs in the following decade, during which time it retained its monopoly. In 1872 Cornell awarded its first PhD, but it then went several years without awarding any more. Harvard conferred its first PhDs in 1873, though in Cambridge, too, interest remained fitful into the late 1870s.[19]

The opening of The Johns Hopkins University in 1876 transformed the American PhD into something more than an academic curiosity. The Hopkins trustees and president-elect Daniel Coit Gilman were determined to establish in Baltimore an institution that would "give a higher degree of education than had heretofore been done in this country." They proceeded to do precisely that, assembling a faculty of international distinction and then providing them with research facilities that instantly made them the envy of academics elsewhere.[20]

In addition, Hopkins used twenty annual graduate fellowships to bring to Baltimore some of the ablest and most ambitious graduates of the leading American colleges. Included among these were the economists Henry Carter Adams and Richard T. Ely, the sociologist Albion Small, the political scientist Woodrow Wilson, the historian John Franklin Jameson, and the philosophers John Dewey and Josiah Royce. Most who came stayed to complete their degrees, then proceeded to an appointment at a college or university, where they promptly began recruiting their best students for Hopkins. Between 1878 and 1900, when Harvard displaced it as the largest producer, Hopkins conferred 549 PhDs, about a third of all those produced by the six leading American universities.[21]

During the late 1880s more than half of those receiving PhDs from Hopkins, Yale, Harvard, Cornell, and Columbia went on to become academics; by the mid-1890s, now with Chicago PhDs included, the proportion of American PhDs securing academic employment approached two out of three. The rapidity to which this first generation of American PhDs laid claims to places at leading American universities is startling, both in view of the prestige previously attached to a PhD acquired abroad and in view of the relatively modest growth American higher education experienced during the 1880s and 1890s. Yet between 1880 and 1892, the proportion of Harvard faculty members with American PhDs doubled, while that with European PhDs increased only slightly. President William Rainey Harper's first faculty at the University of Chicago, organized in 1892, contained half again as many American PhDs as European.[22]

"I foresee, just ahead," a Harvard PhD wrote back from his first teaching assignment at the University of Kansas in 1892, "a period of great advance in the University proper in this country." A year earlier, Josiah Royce, the first Hopkins PhD to teach at Harvard, had similarly noted "the increase of the number, of the hopefulness, and of the academic ambitions of graduate students here in Cambridge." And well they might be hopeful. Even at such colleges as Oberlin, which had no graduate program nor plans to introduce one, the number of American PhDs on its faculty of twenty had gone from none in 1891 to five in 1900. By then any university with even modest national ambitions, and many colleges as well, had already adopted the rule William James would decry six years later in "The PhD Octopus": "No instructor who is not a Doctor." [23]

Meanwhile, graduate students at Yale, Columbia, and Harvard organized a nationally federated Union of Graduate Clubs in 1894 to protect the integrity of the earned (as opposed to honorary) PhD and to promote the hiring of those who had earned it. Their doing so illustrates the most fundamental change that occurred in American intellectual life during the second half of the nineteenth century: the transformation of academic life from a selfless but marginal calling—one that appealed to the bashful and the beaten—to a rewarding but demanding profession capable of attracting, in President's Eliot's words, "men of capacity and ambition." That it had already become so by the 1890s was acknowledged by those whose own sympathies remained at least in part with the earlier generations of professors who put classroom teaching and institutional loyalties above research and professional standing. "Many of the young professors," George Santayana wrote of his Harvard colleagues in the 1890s,

are no longer the sort of persons that might as well have been clergymen or schoolmasters; they have rather the type of mind of a doctor, an engineer, or a social reformer; the wide awake young man who can do most things better than old people, and who knows it. [24]

The second aspect of this overall change to be considered here flows from the first: the effective takeover by Santayana's "wide awake young men" of parts of the institutional structure of American intellectual life that had hitherto existed without substantial academic involvement. The earliest learned societies, such as the American Philosophical Society (1743), the American Academy of Arts and Sciences (1790), and the American Antiquarian Society (1812), had few academics in their ranks and rarely drew upon them to provide leadership. When the American Academy of Literature and Belles Lettres was organized in New York City in 1820, no academics figured among its original twenty-five members. [25]

More than four decades later, in 1863, when Congress briefly considered chartering a National Academy of Literature and Art and a National Academy of Moral and Social Science, apparently to complement the just authorized National Academy of Science, only four of the forty proposed members were academics. Two years later, when the American Social Science Association was founded in Boston, lawyers, doctors, ministers, and businessmen dominated its ranks, while a journalist, Franklin B. Sanborn, provided its leadership. That academics figured among the founders of the ASSA at all, its most recent historian has written, "was a sign of the future. In 1865 college professors did not try to monopolize the whole subject of man and society."[26]

Twenty years later professors regularly dominated ASSA meetings, when not using them as occasions to launch organizations of their own. The first secession occurred in 1883, when several Hopkins-trained historians led by Herbert Baxter Adams left to form the American Historical Association. The second came a year later, led by another Hopkins PhD, Richard T. Ely, and it resulted in the founding of the American Economic Association. Academic sociologists and political scientists followed in turn, founding the American Political Science Association in 1903 and, two years later, the American Sociological Society. By then the ASSA was moribund.[27]

While none of these new associations excluded nonacademics as such, all were committed to advancing the interests of those pursuing their respective subjects within the universities. "We should remain a scientific body," insisted a Columbia University professor of economics in 1899 upon being informed that a businessman was being considered for the presidency of the American Economic Association. "I may be wrong, but I dread any yielding to the view that economic wisdom resides outside the schools and inside the counting house." Even within the American Historical Association, which during its first years occasionally elected a nonacademic to its presidency, academic enclosure proceeded apace. By 1907 the effective leadership of the association, its Hopkins-trained secretary John Franklin Jameson could report, had been wrested from those referred to as "elderly swells who dabbled in history" or, more simply, "the nobs," and was safely in the hands of those holding history professorships at the leading graduate universities. There it has since remained.[28]

ࣔ   III

The crucial point about these changes in the structure of late nineteenth-century American intellectual life, in terms of their impact on American international studies, is that they had so little. Unlike other intellectual enterprises, equally open to amateur cultivation prior to the Civil War, international studies remained thus open into the twentieth century, enclosing itself neither within Veysey's "emergent" nor within Shils' "ascendant" university. The handful of academics in international studies did not attempt to monopolize international studies, as did Thomas Haskell's academic social scientists the social sciences and Bruce Kuklick's academic philosophers philosophy. Instead, the study of foreign cultures and societies remained well into the next century what it had been from its organizational beginnings in the 1840s: an intellectual enterprise pursued by amateur enthusiasts most of whom were without relevant university credentials. The difference was that by then such persistent nonprofessionalism had made international studies an anachronism.[29]

Why international studies remained unaffected by changes that transformed other intellectual enterprises is not immediately obvious. It had, as already described, made an early appearance in the offerings of American colleges and figured among the interests of antebellum academics. Moreover, insofar as the rapid rise in the intellectual standing of academics after the Civil War is related to the growing acceptance of graduate training abroad and the possession of a PhD as the crucial credentials for ascertaining intellectual seriousness, the international studies enterprise had its share of both.[30]

Perhaps the most popular field for Americans doing graduate work at German universities until about 1870 was comparative philology. Considered the capstone of a thoroughly humanistic education—and in Germany a promising field for academic employment—comparative philology involved extensive work in Indo-European languages generally and in Sanskrit particularly. So too, among the first half-dozen PhDs conferred by Yale in the early 1860s, one was awarded for

TABLE 2.1. PhDs Awarded by Six Universities in All Social Sciences and Humanities and International Studies, 1861–1900

	PhDs in All Social Sciences and Humanities	PhDs in International Studies	Percentage
Yale	218	51	23
Chicago	113	19	17
Columbia	117	16	14
Harvard	143	12	8
Johns Hopkins	274	20	7
Cornell	77	4	5
Total	942	122	13

Sources: YALE. *Doctors of Philosophy, 1861–1960* (New Haven: Yale University Press, 1961); CHICAGO. *General Register of the University of Chicago, 1892–1902* (Chicago: University of Chicago Press, 1903); COLUMBIA. *A Bibliography of the Faculty of Political Science of Columbia University, 1880–1930* (New York: Columbia University Press, 1931); HARVARD. *Doctors of Philosophy and Doctors of Science, 1873–1909* (Cambridge: Harvard University Press, 1910); HOPKINS. *Graduates and Fellows of The Johns Hopkins University, 1876–1913* (Baltimore: Johns Hopkins University Press, 1914); CORNELL. Alumni Files, University Archives, Cornell University, Ithaca, N.Y. Designation as international studies PhD based on dissertation titles.

work in Sanskrit. By 1900, of the 940 PhDs that had been produced in the social sciences and humanities by the six principal graduate universities, 122, or 13 percent, had been for dissertations that would now be regarded as being in international studies (table 2.1). Though substantially fewer than in history, this nearly equaled the combined totals for political science and economics.[31]

While international studies made a respectable enough numerical showing among the first generation of American PhDs, the showing was skewed on several counts. First, the production of international studies PhDs was concentrated at just two

TABLE 2.2. International Studies PhDs, 1861–1900, by Field
and Discipline

	Number of PhDs Awarded	Percentage
Humanities	93	76
Ancient languages [a]	84	69
Modern languages [b]	3	2
Religion	3	2
Philosophy	3	2
Social sciences	29	24
History	8	7
Political science	8	7
Economics	6	5
Anthropology	3	2
Sociology	3	2
Other	1	1
Total	122	100

Sources: see table 2.1.
[a] Hebrew (66) and Sanskrit (18).
[b] Arabic, Canadian French, and Latin-American Spanish.

universities, Yale and Chicago, which together accounted for
over half the number. Hopkins, Harvard, and Cornell awarded
half of all nonscience PhDs but less than a third of the PhDs
in international studies.

The distribution was still more skewed by field and discipline (table 2.2). More than three of every four were in the
humanities; of these, over 90 percent were in language and
literature studies. Dissertations in Hebrew studies alone accounted for just over half of all the international studies PhDs
awarded up to 1900, while those in Sanskrit studies exceeded
the combined total in history, economics, and modern language studies. By area, most of these early international studies PhDs had as their focus the Middle East, with South Asia
a respectable second. Whereas these together accounted for 73
percent of the total, the next two most studied areas, Canada
and East Asia, accounted for 14 percent; Latin America and
Africa, 8 percent (table 2.3).

By combining these distributions a statistically "typical" first-generation international studies PhD can be approximated. He (there were only 3 women among the 122) was from Yale or Chicago and wrote his dissertation on some aspect of the language or literature of the ancient Middle East or South Asia. To be outside these institutional and disciplinary circumstances was to make an encounter with another graduate student interested in—much less with a professor knowledgeable about—"your" part of the world a highly unlikely event. The Harvard PhD candidate in political science studying the Canadian feudal system, the Hopkins candidate in modern languages study-

TABLE 2.3. International Studies PhDs, 1861–1900, by Area Focus

	Number of PhDs Awarded	Percentage
Middle East	68	56
South Asia	21	17
Canada	9	7
East Asia	8	7
Latin America	6	5
Africa	4	3
International or other	3	3
Russia and East Europe	3	2
Total	122	100

Sources: see table 2.1.

ing the phonology of Mexico City, and the Cornell candidate in anthropology studying the "Dying Out of Uncivilized Tribes" necessarily worked in isolation, with neither peer interests nor faculty expertise to sustain them. Whatever their motives, intellectual fashion and academic careerism seem not to have figured among them.

Whether institutionally scattered or disciplinarily bunched, early international studies PhDs differed from other PhDs in another respect: they did not, typically, become professors (table 2.4). The differences in the relative frequencies of subsequent academic careers varied according to institution and field but held at all six institutions in both the humanities and the social sciences. Even at Hopkins, whose international studies PhDs were unique in that a bare majority of them did become academics, the proportion of PhDs not in international studies doing so was substantially higher. At Harvard, where three out of every four first-generation PhDs became academics, the ratio among international studies PhDs was one out of three. Overall, nonscience PhDs not in international studies were twice as likely to become academics as were those in international studies.

TABLE 2.4. International Studies PhDs, 1861–1900, by Subsequent Occupation

	Number of PhDs	Percentage
Academic	43	35
Ministry or missions	37	30
Professions or business	9	7
Government	6	5
Writing	6	5
Other or early death	12	10
Returned foreign national	9	7
	122	99

Sources: See table 2.1. Post-PhD careers determined by checks of alumni registers and other biographical indexes.
Note: Percentages do not add up to 100 because of rounding.

This markedly lower incidence of subsequent academic employment among early international studies PhDs may be accounted for in two ways. First, international studies PhDs were less inclined to undertake academic careers than were other PhDs; and second, universities were less inclined to hire them. Personal considerations undoubtedly played a part, though how much is impossible to know. It is at least plausible, however, that given the exotic reputation of much comprehended by international studies in the late nineteenth century, it attracted more than its share of the constitutionally unemployable. This is to suggest that John Norton Johnson, an 1883 Harvard PhD in Sanskrit, was less an anomaly among early international studies PhDs than among PhDs generally. "His ambition, probably, was to have been a professor of Sanskrit," a classmate wrote of Johnson, "though certain marked eccentricities of manner prohibited him from appointment to positions of this sort. Probably he would not have succeeded as a teacher." Acknowledged to be "one of the most brilliant students in the class," Johnson ended up as the librarian of the Crescent Athletic Club in Brooklyn.[32]

More substantial evidence exists to suggest that other international studies PhDs who did not proceed to academic careers had no intention of doing so when they entered graduate school. Many were already committed to careers in the church, or so the facts that nearly half had had prior ministerial training and a third subsequently became ministers or missionaries would suggest. Even among those with ministerial training who did not subsequently return to the church, graduate school may have been undertaken more with the idea of easing out of an old career than starting a new one. In either case an academic career was probably not a primary desideratum.

Prior commitments also help account for the low incidence of subsequent American academic employment among the twenty-seven international studies PhDs who came from the world areas they studied. Most of these "foreign nationals," upon receipt of their PhDs, went back home. Of the eight dissertations on East Asian subjects, for example, five were written by Japanese nationals, four of whom returned to Japan.

For many early international studies PhDs, personal identification with a particular world area appears to have been more important than professional identification, and this priority was not limited to foreign nationals. It applied to Americans as well. William I. Chamberlain, born of missionary parents in India, returned there to help found Vorhees College in Vellore upon completing his Columbia PhD on "Education in India" in 1900. So too with Cornell's Harvey DeWitt Griswold, who completed his thesis on "Brahmin Culture" in 1900, between two missionary tours in India, the second extending into the 1920s.[33]

Personal considerations were also crucial in prompting W. E. B. DuBois, an 1895 Harvard PhD in history, to write his thesis on "The Suppression of the African Slave Trade." They also likely, after a few years of college teaching, led him to abandon whatever earlier plans he might have had for an academic career. Instead, in 1910 he helped found the National Association for the Advancement of Colored People and became its director of publicity and research. Thereafter, as editor of *Crisis* and a civil rights activist and polemicist, DuBois continued to write about the conditions of Afro-Americans and about Africa, where he ultimately took up residence and died in 1963.[34]

For Isaac A. Hourwich, an 1893 Columbia PhD in economics, personal considerations were no less determinative. He entered Columbia in 1890, having been expelled from his native Russia for political reasons. Three years later he submitted his dissertation on "The Economics of the Russian Village," and he then proceeded to a productive career as a lawyer, statistician, and public expert on East European immigration. His *Immigration and Labor* (1911, 1921) was a blistering exposé of the shallow scholarship and racist stereotyping that permeated the forty-one volumes of the report of the United States Immigration Commission (Dillingham Report), published in 1910 and subsequently successfully exploited by advocates of immigration restrictions. For Hourwich, DuBois, Chamberlain, and Griswold, the same promptings that drew them to the university to study what remained for most Americans strange and alien parts of the world drew them, once those formal studies were complete, back into the world beyond the university.[35]

Besides factors affecting the supply of academic candidates, market considerations limited demand. Initially, however, the academic market looked promising. Yale, Johns Hopkins, and Harvard all had established professorships of Sanskrit by the early 1880s. Shortly thereafter, they were joined by Columbia and Chicago. By 1900, Cornell, Pennsylvania, and the University of California had also acquired Sanskritists, thus declaring themselves among the handful of American universities inviting comparison with those of Germany. Indeed, few things so distinguished those late nineteenth-century American universities with international aspirations from the others than their coveting of each other's Sanskrit professor.[36]

Even before Hopkins opened, president-elect Gilman had tried to get Yale's William D. Whitney to come to Baltimore. Failing to dislodge him, he settled for Charles Rockwell Lanman, a student of Whitney's who was about to return to Yale after additional studies in Germany. In 1880, when Harvard's president Eliot awakened to the challenge posed by Hopkins, he responded by offering Lanman a full professorship, whereas Gilman had been unwilling to provide him with more than an associate professorship. When Lanman accepted and went off to Cambridge, Maurice Bloomfield, a promising graduate student at Yale, was brought to Baltimore with a graduate fellowship and the assurance that, upon completing his PhD, he would be Hopkins' Sanskrit professor. Columbia's first Sanskrit instructor, Edward Washburn Hopkins, left New York in 1885 for a professorship at Bryn Mawr, which he later left to become Whitney's successor at Yale.[37]

This brisk early seller's market notwithstanding, the supply of would-be Sanskrit professors produced by American universities quickly outstripped demand. Between 1900 and 1940 the number of Sanskrit professorships in the United States increased from eight to twelve, a 50 percent increase during a period when the American professoriate as a whole increased 600 percent. The scarcity of new positions was exacerbated by the fact that those who filled the old ones proved to be extraordinarily durable. Lanman's tenure at Harvard and Bloomfield's at Hopkins both spanned five decades, while A. V. Williams Jackson, who began teaching Indo-European languages at Columbia in 1892, was still doing so in 1935.[38]

If prospects for academic employment in Sanskrit were poor because the field expanded so slowly, they were worse in Hebrew and Semitic studies, where academic positions were being downgraded and eliminated altogether. As institutions like

Harvard and Columbia proceeded in the 1870s and 1880s to transform themselves into universities along the German model, they underwent a conscious, even calculated, secularization. Both seemed intent upon eliminating whatever remained of earlier ties with organized religion. Eliot, for example, spent an enormous amount of personal energy securing a Sanskritist for Harvard in 1880, but left the filling of the then vacant Hancock professorship of Hebrew to officials at the Divinity School. In 1887 the financial responsibility for maintaining Hebrew studies in the Columbia curriculum effectively passed from the university trustees when New York's Temple Emanu-El agreed to fund a chair in rabbinical literature, to which the son of the temple's rabbi was appointed. Not long thereafter nearly all of what had been since the first presidency of Samuel Johnson a Columbia tradition in Hebrew studies had devolved upon its Morningside Heights neighbors, the Jewish and Union Theological Seminaries.[39]

By the 1920s Hebrew had become optional at even the leading Protestant theological seminaries. "This change," Harvard's Hancock professor acknowledged, "has had the effect of greatly diminishing the number of those who study any other Semitic language." But having also observed that "the number of Semitic scholars has grown more rapidly than the number of teaching positions and not a few of them have been obliged to turn to other subjects," he could hardly fault graduate students wanting academic careers for seeking them in subjects more likely to provide them.[40] This meant subjects other than those encompassed by international studies.

ƨ IV

Both contrary personal inclinations and the very limited capacity of American universities to provide the inclined with jobs contributed to the occupational diaspora of the first generation of international studies PhDs. Yet even the few who did secure academic positions in the late nineteenth century likely could not totally escape the feeling that they were ornamental, insufficiently appreciated, and peripheral to the driving concerns of the universities that employed them. Certainly Yale's William Dwight Whitney did not.

According to his student Lanman, Whitney was the first American humanistic scholar to overcome what Lanman's generation still perceived to be "a certain condescension in foreigners" with respect to American scholarly efforts. From his student days in the early 1850s, when he worked with Franz Bopp in Berlin and Rudolph Roth at Tübingen, until his death in 1894, Whitney was considered one of the three or four leading Indologists in the world. He held memberships in the Oriental societies of Great Britain, Japan, Germany, Bengal, and Peking, as well as the Royal Academies of Denmark and Berlin, the Institute of France, and the Imperial Academy of St. Petersburg. "I only re-echo the opinion of all fellow laborers in the same field," a leading European Sanskritist wrote at his death; it "has been a heavy loss not only to his country, but to the republic of letters in general."[41]

Yet however exalted Whitney's international standing, his place in New Haven was for many years marginal and never wholly secure. His joining the Yale faculty had been not the trustees' idea but that of Edward E. Salisbury, Yale's unsalaried professor of Sanskrit and Arabic, who insisted on it when, in 1854, he divided his chair and personally funded that half to which Whitney was appointed. Salisbury continued to be Whitney's patron, most notably in 1869 when he gave Yale funds to reduce Whitney's teaching load, the price Whitney demanded to keep from going to Harvard. But because he had so few students in his Sanskrit courses, sometimes none, he was obliged to teach introductory German and French in the Sheffield Scientific School, which he did until failing health in the 1880s forced Yale authorities to relent.[42]

Whitney did such teaching begrudgingly and with mixed success. Unlike his colleague William Graham Sumner, who gave first priority to undergraduate teaching "because that's what I'm paid for," Whitney insisted upon "doing something every working day upon that really important thing, and above all, of doing that something first." Such thoroughgoing professionalism enabled Whitney to produce some 360 publications in the form of books, articles, translations, and edited works, to preside over several learned societies, and to maintian a voluminous correspondence with scholars all over the world. It also earned him the resentment of some of his colleagues and the studied indifference of others. His position was much like that of the physicist Willard Gibbs, as described by the historian George Pierson: "revered by scientists abroad, to students and alumni hardly even a name—an almost unnoticed figure crossing the campus." An alumni dinner just after Whitney's death took no notice of the fact, though some of his neighbors did. "All he knew was Sanskrit," went one local estimate. "What did he ever do for New Haven?"[43]

More to present purposes, "What did Whitney ever do for American international studies?" To be sure, his contributions to the technical literature of his subject assured him permanent standing while providing American international studies with its first academic of world rank. On the other hand, his indifferent performance as an undergraduate teacher did little to increase interest in Sanskrit, comparative philology, or international studies generally. On two other counts as well, his record is mixed.

In the broadest sense, it is true, as a German scholar said at his death, that "all American Sanskritists either directly or indirectly are pupls of Professor Whitney." Yet more narrowly construed, Whitney's performance as a "mentor"—an academic who takes upon himself the selection, training, and early professional sponsorship of those who perpetuate his field— was not particularly impressive. During four decades at Yale he sponsored ten PhDs in Sanskrit, only one of whom, Lanman, went on to become a Sanskrit professor.[44]

One might count among Whitney's protégés at Yale in the early 1870s William Rainey Harper, whose dissertation, "A Comparative Study of Prepositions in Latin, Greek, Sanskrit and Gothic," was accepted by Whitney in 1873, still several months short of the candidate's twentieth birthday. During a subsequent five-year tenure at Yale as professor of Hebrew, immediately prior to becoming president of the University of Chicago in 1892, Harper produced as many PhDs in Semitic studies as Whitney had in Sanskrit in twenty. Harper's interest in doing so, however, seems to have been less in turning out professors than in providing credentials for those staffing his varied enterprises in adult education. Chief among these was the Chautauqua College of Liberal Arts, with its thirty summer programs and correspondence courses which in 1890 enrolled more than a thousand ministers. A few of Harper's students did become professors, but even these, like their mentor, soon gravitated toward the financial and administrative side of higher education. There is not a little irony in the fact that Whitney, who resisted joining his father's bank so that he might be "all in all given to Philology," should have as his most famous student the very model for Thorstein Veblen's "captain of erudition."[45]

If Whitney's role as a producer of scholars has been overstated, his role as a popularizer has been slighted. Little was made of this facet of his career by either his European or American memorialists, probably because the former did not know of it and the latter regarded it as beneath notice. Yet throughout Whitney's long career he wrote articles for *Appleton's New American Cyclopedia* and the *Century Dictionary* and reviews for such nonacademic publications as *New Englander, North American Review,* and the *Nation.* Besides those on comparative philology, Oriental religion, and ancient India, he regularly reviewed books as far afield as R. A. Wilson's *New History of the Conquest of Mexico* and J. P. Brown's *Ancient and Modern Constantinople.* At so much a line, no part of the alien world was beyond his ken.[46]

But, like the time he gave to undergraduates, Whitney begrudged that spent on what he called "hack work." Had Yale salaries been higher or had outside support been available for "that really important thing," he almost certainly would have abandoned his popular audience in favor of one made up exclusively of his fellow academic specialists. But with a wife and three daughters to provide for, he could not afford to be as dismissive of the opportunities for popularization that came his way. Efforts at what a later generation have called "outreach" were for him not a sop to the egalitarianism of philanthropic or governmental bureaucrats but an economic imperative. It is not clear that these efforts were any the less beneficial for being so.

ᣔᣲ V

Besides his writing for nonacademic publication, Whitney maintained contact with amateur cultivators of international studies through his involvement in the American Oriental Society, which he joined in 1850. From 1853 to 1873 he served as the society's librarian; from 1857 to 1884, as its corresponding secretary; and from 1884 to 1890, as its president. By his own estimate, half the contents of the society's *Journal* during his twenty-eight-year editorship (1857–1885) came "from his pen." Whitney was clearly the American Oriental Society's most distinguished member, and his extensive involvement in its affairs did much to enhance its intellectual standing. What it did not do, however, was herald its imminent academic takeover.[47]

Compared with other pre–Civil War learned societies, the American Oriental Society had a substantial contingent of academics among its early members. Moreover, the American Philological Association (1869), the Modern Language Association (1883), and the American Historical Association (1884), all of which either at their founding or shortly thereafter were dominated by academics, can trace their origins to and drew some of their founding members from the AOS. Whitney was a member of both the APA and the MLA, as were other AOS members. Yet for all these ties and the cordial relations among the organizations, the AOS and the newer associations represented two fundamentally different and ultimately incompatible views as to the primary purpose of a learned society. They also represented two different epochs in American intellectual life. The AOS typified what American intellectual life had been, the newer associations what it would become.

The difference is partially conveyed in the terms "cultivation," used in the AOS charter, and "promotion," which found favor among the organizers of the newer associations. It is also reflected in their membership policies: occupationally inclusive in the case of the AOS, more and more exclusive in that of the newer associations. Though proportionally fewer than in the 1850s, churchmen continued to make up more than a quarter of the AOS membership into the 1890s. The American Philological Association, by contrast, had divested itself of its small initial contingent of clergymen by 1875. None of the thirty-five organizers of the Modern Language Association or the forty organizers of the American Historical Association was a minister. Clergymen constituted 12 percent of the membership of the American Economic Association at its founding in 1885; a decade later they constituted only 5 percent.[48]

Although approximately half the membership of the AOS in the late 1880s were professors, most of these taught at theological seminaries. The newer associations drew their professors primarily from the universities. Indeed, so conscious were they of their status within the hierarchy of American education that both the APA and MLA soon after their founding moved to exclude secondary teachers from their ranks. In 1905 the MLA abolished its Pedagogical Section altogether, thus fulfilling its founders real purpose—the creation of what outside the academic economy might be called a protective trade association.

Such developments within these newer associations did not escape the notice of AOS members. In 1890 a reform caucus organized by some of its young academic members attempted to bring the society's purposes and procedures into conformity with those of the newer associations. Led by Cyrus Adler, a recent Hopkins PhD and an instructor of Hebrew there, and Morris Jastrow, then professor of Semitics at the University of Pennsylvania, the reformers proposed several changes for the membership to consider at the society's spring meeting.

Some merely relfected dissatisfaction among members outside New England with the requirements that meetings be held in Boston and that the *Journal* be based in New Haven. But others, such as the proposal that meetings be scheduled so as not to conflict with university calendars, indicated the occupational impetus for the insurgency.[49]

Other proposals went directly to what their academic sponsors considered the unprofessional character of the society. The most radical of these called for the creation of committees of specialists who would screen all submitted papers, rather than have them automatically read at meetings and published in the *Journal*. It was also proposed that the *Journal* become officially affiliated with a university, Jastrow's University of Pennsylvania being mentioned as a possible—and willing—candidate. Finally, it was proposed that the society seek a national charter that would enable it to follow the lead of the newer associations in seeking federal funds for society-sponsored research.

The insurgency came to little. Except for agreeing to vary the location of future meetings, the membership rejected all the reforms proposed. Rather than accede to the proposal that the society divide into specialties, they voted to do away with the one special group they did have, the Classical Section, which had long since lost most of its academics to the American Philological Association. As if to avoid any doubt as to the outcome of this attempted academic coup, the society's leadership restated its membership policy in the next number of the *Journal*:

It is not necessary for anyone to be a professed Orientalist in order to become a member of the Society. All persons—men and women— who are in sympathy with the objects of the Society and willing to further its work are invited to give it their help.[50]

Although "professed Orientalists" have figured more prominently in AOS affairs since the 1890s, the society has retained much of its nonprofessional character. Nonacademics still constitute about half its membership, which now numbers some 1,750 "professional and amateur Orientalists." Unlike other members of the American Council of Learned Societies, which it joined in 1919, the AOS did not thereafter directly engage in lobbying, on behalf of either Oriental scholarship or academic research generally. Not surprisingly then, when after World War Two academic promoters of international studies recognized the need for organizational support, they did not turn to the AOS but instead created a half-dozen area associations, of which the American Association for the Advancement of Slavic Studies was the first (1948). These area associations are precisely what the "wide awake young men" had wanted the AOS to become in the 1890s. That its less professionally minded majority chose instead to reconfirm its amateur character helped put off the academic enclosure of at least one part of American intellectual life for another half century.

CYCLES OF CATHAY

Milwaukee held no charms for me.
GEORGE KENNAN, 1925[1]

Probably by 1900 and certainly by 1920, universities had become the central institutions in American intellectual life. Earlier competitors—private learned societies, libraries, government agencies, research institutions, informal networks of
independent scholars—proved to be unable to match the universities' ability to combine research and teaching. Once established, their dominance was easily maintained. As intellectual
labor became increasingly specialized, it divided into "disciplines," which, in the form of departments, became the crucial
organizational units of the leading universities. Within these
departments certain kinds of ideas found favor and became institutionalized, thereby assuring to both the ideas of the academics identified with them what Edward Shils has called "an
intellectual afterlife." These same developments also increased
the likelihood, as Bruce Kuklick has argued in the case of
"doing philosophy," that intellectual pursuits would become
less "a matter of life and death" and more "a job."[2]

Yet for all the progress universities made by the opening
decades of the twentieth century toward the enclosure of large
parts of American intellectual life, the study of the outside
world, particularly its contemporary forms, remained beyond
their purview. The few positions universities provided in international studies were confined to the study of the languages

and religious cultures of the ancient Middle East and South Asia. Until more positions materialized that involved other parts of the world and other disciplinary approaches, international studies was to remain a nonacademic pursuit, though no longer necessarily a nonpaying one. That this persistence of nineteenth-century arrangements well into the twentieth worked to the detriment of international studies, of the universities, of American society, or of all three, as most chronicler-promoters of American international studies have implied, is arguable. What is not arguable is that the "failure" of international studies to secure itself a home within the early twentieth-century university was attended by its efflorescence without.

৯৯ I

In the half-century after the Civil War, Protestant missionaries remained the principal generators and disseminators of American knowledge about the "non-Christian world." In 1911 some 7,000 American missionaries were stationed abroad. Most were in East and South Asia, but substantial numbers were also in the Middle East, Africa, and Latin America. Only Russia and Eastern Europe, of the major world areas as currently designated within the international studies community, fell outside the early twentieth-century American missionary reconnaissance.[3]

The intellectual byproducts of this contact varied from area to area. In Africa, where few American missionaries ventured until late in the nineteenth century, intellectually inclined missionaries like William McCutchan Morrison, Robert Hamill Nassau, and Adolphus Clemens Good concentrated on establishing a means of communicating with the West African tribes among whom they settled. Morrison's *Grammar and Dictionary of the Buluba-Lulua Language as Spoken in the Upper Kasai and Congo Basin* (1906) and Good's preparation of a Bulu primer are representative products. Nassau's *Fetishism in West Africa*

(1904) and Good's work on "Superstitions and Religious Ideas of Equatorial West Africa" suggest, however, that early African missionaries were not totally consumed by the immense linguistic tasks confronting them.[4]

Comparable tasks continued to be undertaken by American missionaries in South Asia, as Jacob Chamberlain's translation of the Bible into Telegu in the 1880s and Samuel Henry Kellogg's *Grammar of the Hindi Language* (1875, 1893) indicate. But in the Middle East, particularly in Turkey and Syria, where by the 1890s the American missionary presence was into its second and even third generation, the intellectual labors of the missionary literati included botanical surveys, such as George Edward Post's *Flora of Syria, Palestine, and Egypt* (1890), and social commentary, as in Henry Harris Lessup's *The Women of the Arabs* (1891) and Cyrus Hamlin's *Among the Turks* (1878). Political analyses of "the Eastern Question" by missionaries in the field or back at headquarters also found their way into print. One such effort, *Turkey and the Armenian Atrocities* (1878), by Edwin Munsell Bliss, who spent twenty years in the Near East as a missionary before becoming an editor of the *New York Times,* consciously sought to influence American foreign policy. Whether it did or not, books like Bliss' insured that American missionary interests in the Middle East were not overlooked by Washington.[5]

The shift of the major American missionary effort from the Middle East to East Asia, which occurred in the 1880s, was promptly reflected in the writings by missionaries about China and Japan. Samuel Wells Williams' *The Middle Kingdom,* the second and much enlarged edition published posthumously in 1884, was the best known of these works, but W. A. P. Martin's *A Cycle of Cathay* (1896) and *The Awakening of China* (1907) both enjoyed substantial readerships, as did Arthur H. Smith's *Chinese Characteristics* (1890) and *Village Life in China* (1899). What distinguishes these books from earlier ones emanating from the missionary enterprise was that they were less directly addressed to the heathen or to missionaries entering the field than to the larger audience of churchgoing Americans upon whom the missions depended for moral, financial, and political support.[6]

In addressing this audience the missionaries often, as Samuel Wells Williams did in the 1830s, disparaged "the torpor of mind in heathen countries." Yet they could not do so all the time without bringing into question the capacities of these same heathen to be, as Williams defined his mission, "fitted for the duties and privileges of a civilized nation." Indeed, having left the United States, typically in their early twenties, many missionaries eventually came to feel more comfortable with them than with the Christians they had left behind. "I do not want to go to the U. S., where I can do nothing and have nothing to do it with," the forty-six-year-old Williams informed headquarters after a quarter-century in China. "[I] prefer to stay here, where at least, I can assist in preaching and where I am at home." Only blindness and approaching death forced him to leave China two decades later.[7]

Williams' experience of spiritual expatriation following on extended physical removal was no isolated phenomenon. If few missionaries actually "went native," many had their American loyalties and Christian certainties qualified by their experiences abroad. "He had come to the Far East with a message that he was on fire to give," Earl Herbert Cressy wrote of his own experience as a missionary prior to World War One, "but in the process of transmission the East had spoken its message to him. He had gone out to change the East and was returning himself a changed man." He had become, Cressy wrote, "not only a missionary but an internationalist, an intermediary between the two great civilizations that inhabit the earth."[8]

The American missionary enterprise peaked in the first half of the second decade of the twentieth century and never fully recovered from the disruptions of World War One. The Student Volunteer Movement, which was founded in 1888 and which stimulated the second great surge of American missionary activity with its call to college students to help bring about "the evangelization of the world in this generation," declined in the 1920s into a mere shadow of its former self. Having dispatched more than 8,000 "sailed volunteers" during the preceding three decades, SVM. recruiters proved to be conspicuously unsuccessful on college campuses in the 1920s. Results were particularly disheartening at Yale, which twenty years earlier had 200 of its graduates in the missions, but little better at mid-Western colleges like Beloit, Grinnell, and Oberlin, which had earlier provided the bulk of the missionary recruits.[9]

A crisis of confidence among Protestants who had traditionally supported the missions accompanied this decline in recruitment and organizational vitality. In 1932 a group of prominent laymen, with Harvard philosopher Ernest Hocking as their spokesman, expressed "a growing conviction that the missionary movement is at a fork in the road, and that momentous decisions are called for." Other Protestant churchgoers went further and stated that "the missions had become an irrelevant and intrusive method of furthering the highest spiritual interests of mankind."[10]

Support for the missions did not completely dry up in the face of these defections. In the depression year of 1931 alone, some 10 million American Protestants gathered into 57,000 churches contributed $15 million to Protestant missions abroad. Nonetheless, among many liberal Protestants the idea of missions had become an embarrassment, a carryover from more confident days when it was easier to distinguish the political and economic forms of imperialism from the spiritual and cultural ones. Better to leave the heathen, their actions implied, to the Catholics and the Protestant Evangelicals, who have, in point of fact, provided most of the American missionary presence abroad since the 1920s.[11]

But if few recruits went into the Protestant missions after World War One, and fewer books were written by those who did, there remained in the United States thousands of Americans who had, as the result of a tour as a missionary or of being the child of missionaries born in the field, retained a residual but nonetheless proprietary interest in "their" part of the world. Many of these "returned volunteers" or "mish' kids" became academics, as I shall later have occasion to note, but by no means all. Arthur W. Hummell, after fifteen years in China and Japan as a missionary, returned to the United States in 1927 to become chief of the Division of Chinese Literature at the Library of Congress, a post he held until 1954. Edwin Bliss, the son of missionaries in the Middle East, became a lobbyist for the Armenians. Pearl Buck, the daughter of missionaries who lived in China into her twenties, became a writer. Her novel, *The Good Earth,* perhaps did more to shape a favorable view of the Chinese in the 1930s than any other American publication, excepting only the cumulative coverage of China provided by *Time* and *Life,* both published by Henry R. Luce, whose first fourteen years were spent with his missionary parents in China. As Luce's career attests, the missionary injunction "to go forth and teach ye all nations" recognized no occupational bounds.[12]

Whatever distortions were introduced into the writings of missionaries, missionary offspring, and others identified with the missionary enterprise, they typically possessed credentials which today are not easily dismissed. They were better educated than most other Americans of their generation, had long personal contact with the part of the world they wrote about, were conversant in a native language, and, not least important, assumed the prospective equality of those who spoke it. None of these qualifications guarantee disinterested appraisals, but they do hold out the possibility of informed and accurate ones, which is all any credentialing system can do, including that presently provided by our graduate universities.

ॐ II

Unlike American missionaries, whose defensiveness following World War One bespoke their identification with a faltering enterprise, American journalists brought to their overseas assignments between the wars the assurance, even brashness, of those knowingly participating in their calling's golden age.

"The 1930's," John Gunther reminisced three decades later, "were the bubbling, blazing days of American foreign correspondence." Even for Cyrus Sulzberger, who in the 1960s discouraged young men from becoming foreign correspondents by likening it to "becoming a blacksmith in 1919—still an honorable and skilled profession; but the horse is doomed," confessed that to have been a foreign correspondent in the 1930s was "a fine time and fine place to be."[13]

American journalistic coverage of distant events antedates the twentieth century. Reports filed by Eugene Schuyler describing atrocities during the Turkish-Bulgarian War in 1876, published in both England and the United States, had had a considerable impact on English policies in the Balkan region— and had rendered Schuyler thereafter *persona non grata* in Turkey. Fifteen years later, the accounts of George Kennan (an uncle of *the* George Kennan), published first in *Century* magazine and then as *Siberia and the Exile System* (1891), were hailed as the most informed reporting available on the workings of the Romanov regime. Yet it was not until the late 1890s and the war with Spain that foreign correspondence became a recognized career for Americans. Of these first professionals, Richard Harding Davis, who accompanied Theodore Roosevelt and his Rough Riders up San Juan Hill for *Harper's Weekly* and then went on to cover five more wars on three continents, was undoubtedly the best known.[14]

American journalistic coverage of foreign events did not long remain limited to military encounters. In the immediate wake of World War One several American newspapers, among them the *New York Times,* the *Chicago Daily News,* the *Philadelphia Ledger,* the *St. Louis Globe-Democrat,* the *Baltimore Sun,* and the *Christian Science Monitor,* set out to displace the moribund *New York Herald* as the American newspaper with the most extensive foreign coverage. To do so they opened offices in several foreign capitals and established news services such as the United Press, the Hearst-directed International News Service, and the North American Newspaper Alliance. Beginning in the 1920s and on through the 1930s, *Colliers,* the *Saturday Evening Post,*

Reader's Digest, and *Time* regularly assigned correspondents abroad.[15]

Of Floyd Gibbons, who wrote for the *Chicago Tribune* and covered events as removed in space and time as the Pancho Villa raids into New Mexico in 1914 and the Italian invasion of Ethiopia in 1935, it was said no war could properly begin until he arrived on the scene. But if he perpetuated the flamboyant tradition of Richard Harding Davis, others brought to foreign correspondence more contemplative ways. William Henry Chamberlain represents this second type. After graduating from Haverford in 1916 and shortly thereafter abandoning plans to become a professor—"I had come to consider the American student rather stony soil for instruction in the subjects in which I was interested"—Chamberlain drifted into newspaper work in Philadelphia and New York. In 1922, having married a Russian and decided it was better "to see Russia from Moscow and not from Union Square," he took the first job that would enable him to do so, Moscow stringer for the *Christian Science Monitor.* During the next fourteen years he regularly provided *Monitor* readers with the kinds of detailed accounts of Soviet life that only extensive research, frequent trips outside of Moscow, and a command of spoken Russian made possible. The fact that his editors were not "beat conscious" and favored lengthy, descriptive reports also helped Chamberlain to become a respected authority on the Soviet situation. His reportage was several cuts above what Edmund Taylor, a younger but no less scholarly reporter in the 1930s, disparaged as "I was there" journalism.[16]

Not all American correspondents between the wars were as linguistically equipped or as contextually familiar with their beat as Chamberlain. John Gunther, for example, wrote *Inside Europe* (1935) and in the process invented "book journalism," without command of any foreign language, though he had by then spent five years in Europe as a reporter for the *Chicago Daily News.* His *Inside Asia* (1939) was the product of two short trips to the Middle East in 1937 and a two-month visit to East Asia the following year; in both instances he was totally dependent upon English-speaking sources. *Inside Latin America* (1942) was based on still less exposure and, as he later admitted, less interest on his part.[17]

Yet Gunther's books were widely read, favorably reviewed, and, when supplemented by his freelance work for the *New Republic* and more reflective pieces for *Foreign Affairs,* provided his intended audience—"the intelligent reader"—with timely accounts of political developments and personalities in parts of the world where America's interests exceeded its comprehension. As for the inevitable charge of superficiality, Gunther's own rejoinder cannot be totally disregarded: "I would be more highly regarded than I am in some academic circles if it were not for the fact that many people seem to find me readable."[18]

American foreign correspondents in the interwar years were considerably better educated than their domestic counterparts. Anna Louise Strong, who covered revolutionary developments in Russia and later in China for the *Seattle Daily Call,* had a PhD in philosophy from the University of Chicago. Vincent Sheean put to use his undergraduate work in Arabic studies at the University of Chicago in covering North Africa and the Middle East for the *Chicago Tribune.* George Sokolsky had studied journalism at Columbia before going to China, where he became a correspondent for the *New York Times* and several other newspapers. Similarly, Edgar Snow, who was on assignment from the *Saturday Evening Post* during the preparation of *Red Star Over China* (1937), was a graduate of the University of Missouri School of Journalism, while Dorothy Thompson, who covered Eastern Europe for the *Philadelphia Ledger* in the 1920s before becoming a columnist for the *New York Herald Tribune,* was a product of the Syracuse University School of Journalism.[19]

Two Harvard graduates who became foreign correspondents in the 1930s, Cyrus L. Sulzberger and Theodore White, brought to their respective overseas assignments skills of a decidedly scholarly sort. Sulzberger, a Phi Beta Kappa graduate in the class of 1934, fancied himself in college a budding poet, then an art critic, before turning to foreign correspondence.

His facility with languages soon enabled him "to burble in Serbian, Albanian and Bulgarian," first in the employ of the North American Newspaper Alliance and then in that of the *New York Times*. White, a *summa cum laude* graduate in the class of 1938, had studied Chinese history with John K. Fairbank as his tutor, and he had seriously considered becoming a professor before misgivings about the possibility of a Jew's succeeding in academic life, an opprtunity to go to China on a traveling fellowship, and the enroute sale of a "mailer" to the *Boston Globe* turned him to journalism.[20]

Besides impressive educational credentials, American foreign correspondents brought to their assignments a willingness to accept life outside the United States as they found it, even a preference for it. No less than his father, a newspaperman "for whom the pace of American urban life was too hectic and too violent," Chamberlain "instinctively shrank from the America of mechanical progress, commercial shrewdness, boisterous boostering which I saw around me." Estrangement from their own country helps explain why Chamberlain and Sulzberger, once posted abroad, chose to remain abroad, and perhaps why Vincent Sheean identified so readily with Moroccan revolutionary Abd el-Krim and Anna Louise Strong first with the Russian Bolsheviks and later, as did Edgar Snow and Theodore White, with the Chinese Communists (or still later Herbert L. Matthews with Fidel Castro). It also gives fuller and more universal meaning to Chamberlain's rendering of a career in foreign correspondence as "an unconscious process of spiritual emigration."[21]

Such careers are harder to come by today than they were in the 1930s. "When young men ask me for advice on how to become a foreign correspondent," Sulzberger wrote in his *Memoirs*, "I tell them today: 'Don't.' " According to a 1979 Rand Corporation study, only seven American daily newspapers then had a staff of more than three foreign correspondents (*Baltimore Sun, Christian Science Monitor, Los Angeles Times, New York Times, St. Louis Post-Dispatch, Wall Street Journal, Washington Post*). In all, the study's authors estimated that there were probably 500 American foreign correspondents and foreign desk editors working for the daily and weekly press, wire services, and television news.[22]

Of these, few stay in one place long enough to develop more than a superficial familiarity with it, much less to bring to it the relevant language skills. By another count, of the twenty American correspondents assigned to Moscow in 1982, only four spoke Russian with ease. Among the factors regularly cited as contributing to the decline of this once vital intellectual enterprise are the advent of television and supersonic transportation, the high cost of maintaining foreign bureaus, the increasing dependence upon global wire services, and the declining number of American newspapers. Yet to the extent that by the early 1970s American journalism had come "to function as a kind of lesser clergy for the academic elite," the postwar decline of American foreign correspondence as an intellectual enterprise may also have been in part related to the simultaneous rise of American international studies as an academic enterprise.[23]

ટ• III

If the interwar years were a golden age for American foreign correspondence, they seemed also to be the dawn of a new era for American diplomacy. It was then that what George Kennan vaguely wished for upon graduating from Princeton in 1925—"an intellectual career in the foreign sevice"—first became a possibility. How realizable a possibility did not become clear even to him until, after two years in the Foreign Service had convinced him that what he really wanted to do was to go to graduate school, Kennan submitted his resignation. He was then informed that "if I was prepared to undergo training as a specialist for one of the rarer languages—Chinese, Japanese, Arabic, or Russian—I coud have three years of graduate study at a European university without leaving the Foreign Service at all." Kennan chose Russian and was on his way.[24]

The American diplomatic service had not always been so

accommodating to bookish and footloose young men who looked to representing the United States abroad because, as in Kennan's case, "I did not know what else to do." Throughout the nineteenth century diplomatic posts had been so entangled in the domestic political patronage system that election-year turnovers in personnel were the rule. Accordingly, junior positions went to young college graduates ready to work without salary for the experience of living abroad, while the senior positions were reserved for politicians between elective offices or wealthy backers of the incumbent party in search of a holiday from money-making. To hold two diplomatic posts in succession was unusual; to string a sufficient number together so as to fashion even an ad hoc career in nineteenth-century American diplomacy was virtually impossible.[25]

Among those who tried, Eugene Schuyler has particular relevance here. A Yale graduate and one of its first PhDs, Schuyler was admitted to the New York bar in 1864, "not because the profession especially attracted him," his sister recalled, "but rather because he had not as yet found anything that seemed to him more desirable." That same year he began to study Russian, and in 1867, he published the first American translation of Turgenev's *Fathers and Sons*. By then thoroughly bored with the law, and anxious to extend his studies, he obtained through New York Republican connections an appointment as American consul in Moscow.[26]

The change in Republican administrations in 1869 cost Schuyler his Moscow post, but during the next eight years a series of temporary postings throughout Eastern Europe allowed him to continue his Russian studies, to publish *Turkestan: Notes of a Journey in Russian Turkestan, Khokand, Bukhara and Kuldja* (1876), and to begin work on a biography, *Peter the Great*, which he published in 1883. In 1884 his position as American minister to Greece, Serbia, and Rumania was legislated out of existence, leaving Schuyler without a diplomatic position just as the Democrats were winning the White House.[27]

In search of a posting, Schuyler returned to the United States in 1885 and delivered a series of lectures at Johns Hopkins, which were subsequently published as *American Diplomacy and the Flourishing of Commerce* (1886), only to retreat empty-handed back to Europe, where he did occasional reporting for the New York *Herald* and the *Nation*. In 1890, while his appointment as minister to Cairo was stalled in the Senate, he died.[28]

To be sure, Schuyler's published views on the policies of the governments with which he had official relations, like those on the conduct of American foreign policy, were sufficiently provocative to cost him support abroad as well as at home. Nor did his personality, which his sister characterized as having "an occasional coldness of manner which was at times even repellent," ease his way. But whatever prompted his failing to combine regular diplomatic employment with the pursuit of international studies, it can hardly be said to have been want of sustained effort.[29]

The closest approximation to "an intellectual career in the foreign service" before Kennan's day was fashioned by America's first professional interpreter of Asia, William W. Rockhill. Born in Philadelphia in 1854 in prosperous circumstances, Rockhill spent his youth in Europe in the company of his widowed mother. He became interested in Oriental languages and Buddhism as a schoolboy in Paris. In 1876, at age 22, he returned to the United States and for five years engaged in a series of business ventures, none to any result. He then returned to France to resume his studies, now committed to making them his life's work. By the time his first book, *The Life of Buddha*, appeared in 1883, Rockhill had secured the position of second secretary at the American legation in Peking, which he intended to fill until he became proficient in Chinese and gained permission to visit Tibet.[30]

Rockhill's insistence that his studies take precedence over his official duties cost him his appointment in Peking in 1888, but by then he was ready to set out for Tibet. An account of his eight months of travels, some through areas never before visited by a Westerner, was published in 1891 as *The Land of the Lamas: Notes of a Journey Through China, Mongolia, and Tibet,* after earlier being serialized in *Century* magazine. Royalties financed a second trip, which led the Royal Geographical Society in 1893 to cite him as "one of perhaps three men in the world who know both Chinese and Tibetan, and the only man who is known to have waded through the enormous masses of Buddhist literature in Tibet, an absolutely unknown land to all but himself."[31]

From 1893 to 1913 Rockhill was more or less continuously employed by the State Department, first in Washington as chief clerk at the department and then, failing to get a China posting, as minister to Greece. His most important service occurred as Secretary of State John Hay's chief adviser on the Far East from 1899 to 1905, when he helped formulate the Open Door policy. Then followed four years in Peking as American minister, two years in St. Petersburg, and finally two years in Constantinople as ambassador to Turkey. During all these years and through all these assignments, Rockhill's first priority remained his scholarship, as Secretary of State Philander C. Knox well knew when he reminded Rockhill upon the latter's arrival in Constantinople "that the Embassy's energies be constantly directed to the real and commercial rather than the academic interests of the United States in the Near East." In 1913 he was replaced as ambassador by Henry Morgenthau, whose principal claim to the post was his having contributed heavily to the presidential campaign of Woodrow Wilson. Rockhill died a year later.[32]

Unlike the missionaries, of whom he was openly contemptuous, Rockhill studied Asians and Asian culture with no notion of converting the one or subverting the other. On the contrary, his interest seems to have stemmed in part from a reaction against things American. He resided in the United States for only thirteen of the fifty years of his adult life; when abroad and asked about matters relating to the United States, he invariably became "snippy." Diplomatic work provided a useful cover for both his scholarship and his expatriatism. "I am endeavoring to get another diplomatic appointment," he wrote in 1889, then just back from Tibet. "I hear I am thought of for Korea. So be it, better a cycle of Cathay or Korea than fifty years of America for me."[33]

What made possible for the generation after Rockhill's a career in the foreign service, "intellectual" or otherwise, was the passage in 1924 of the Rogers Act. In addition to combining the diplomatic and consular corps into a single Foreign Service, it effectively insulated the service from the vagaries of partisan politics. Even before formal enactment of this legislation, the State Department proceeded to make two appointments which made clear its intentions to employ those whom Kennan called "scholars by instinct and dedication."[34]

The first such appointment was of Robert F. Kelley, a Harvard graduate who had studied Russian at the Sorbonne before joining the State Department, where from 1924 to 1938 he served as chief of East European Affairs. It was Kelley who saw to it that Kennan and the department's other Russian area specialists-in-the-making—Charles Bohlen, Loy Henderson, Llewellyn Thompson, and Eldridge Durbrow—first secured postings to Berlin or Paris for formal studies. From there it was to Riga or another listening post along the Soviet border, and then, when the United States recognized the Soviet Union in 1933, to the embassy in Moscow, where they could confront their subject matter firsthand. During infrequent postings back at State, Kelley's protégés had access to his private library of Russian materials, "the best in the United States." Otherwise, Kennan recalled, they "whiled away the official doldrums with the continuation of the philosophical and political discussions we had inaugurated as college sophomores."[35]

The second appointment was of Stanley K. Hornbeck, Kelley's counterpart at the Far Eastern desk. Hornbeck had done graduate work at the University of Wisconsin, where he earned a PhD in international relations in 1909, and had then taught in China for four years before returning to Madison as a member of the political science department. In 1921 he declined an appointment to Harvard to accept his position in the State Department, where he promptly set about to enhance its capacity to comprehend Asia, particularly China.[36]

"In the 1920's," O. Edmund Clubb, who joined the State Department in 1929 after studying Chinese at the University of Minnesota, later recalled, "American Sinologs were given a high standing and China experts of the Foreign Service constituted a corps of acknowledged ability and high spirit." Clubb's first assignment after Foreign Service School was to Peking, where his principal duties were to improve his Chinese. Subsequently he became director of the language school in Peking, through which passed such budding China specialists as John Paton Davies, John K. Emmerson, James K. Pennfield, Edward E. Rice, and Everett F. Drummright. No less than Clubb, or John Carter Vincent and John S. Service, two other "China hands" in the Foreign Service, they seemed to have their careers well in hand.[37]

Although area specialization as a career strategy was most fully developed in the interwar Foreign Service, it also found favor in other parts of the federal government. Under Herbert Hoover in the 1920s, the Commerce Department developed a cadre of career bureaucrats attentive to and knowledgeable about the political economies of Latin America and the Middle East. Similarly, during the New Deal, the Department of Agriculture employed several economists who had a close interest in—and in some instances an ideological affinity for—the Soviet Union. Even the Army, as the interwar careers of Joseph Stilwell and David D. Barrett attest, was careful to maintain within its ranks at least one legitimate "expert on China affairs."[38]

Unquestionably, there were serious gaps in the knowledge American government officials in the 1920s and 1930s possessed of the world beyond Western Europe. If events in China and, after 1933, Russia were reasonably closely followed, those in Africa and South Asia were largely ignored. And even among those who paid attention to developments in these areas, there was the problem of trying to get someone in Washington to read their reports. Indeed, it was not until 1946 that Kennan broke through with his celebrated "Long Telegram" on Soviet postwar intentions and, as he acknowledged, "my reputation was made."[39]

Ironically, it was only when Washington got around to reading the reports of its China hands that their troubles began in earnest. Whereas Kennan and his generation of Kremlinologists, seemingly vindicated in their harsh view of Stalin, succeeded in turn after World War Two to the principal ambassadorships in Eastern Europe and the key policy posts in Washington, Clubb and his generation, no less accurate in their harsh view of the governing capacities of Chiang Kai-Shek, found themselves in the late 1940s either dismissed from the Foreign Service for security reasons or shunted off to minor posts well removed from Asia where they waited out their retirements.[40]

During the Congressional debates in 1951 over "who lost China," practically any Foreign Service officer who had had the foresight to see the Chinese Communists as a force to be reckoned with, and the foolhardiness to commit such views to paper, was fair game. "In those circumstances," Clubb remarked with perhaps more ingenuousness than his retrospective view should have allowed, "one could not be certain that innocence and a fine record would be enough." Twenty years after Clubb had been forced out of the Foreign Service and Barrett had been denied his general's star, John K. Fairbank expressed the view that "these men were real Chinese specialists. . . . We have none like them today."[41]

But whether their careers ultimately prospered or withered, the area specialists of the interwar Foreign Service and military shared with one another and with their predecessor Rockhill at best ambivalent feelings about the United States. As Kennan put it in listing his reasons for joining the Foreign Service, "Milwaukee held no charms for me." Ten years later, a visit back to his home town only confirmed that "I was no longer a part of what I had once been part of—no longer, in fact, a part of anything at all. . . . I, like all other expatriates, simply had been left behind." His friend Charles Bohlen, who described himself as the son of "a gentleman of leisure who had inherited a little money," had been no more interested in following his Harvard classmates "into the stock market, banking or the law, with the overriding purpose of acquiring a fortune," than Clubb had been inclined "to stay at home and work for Quaker Oats or something." But it was Stilwell who most nearly echoed Rockhill's sentiments when, finding himself temporarily stationed back in the United States in 1925, he wrote in desperation to his superiors, "How about sending me as far away from home as possible?"[42]

⟡ IV

"One of the most important observations that can be made about unattached intellectuals in contemporary America," Lewis Coser observed in 1965, "is that there were so few of them."[43] Their disappearance did not occur simultaneously throughout American intellectual life. Someone seriously engaged in physics who lacked an institutional affiliation embodying that engagement had become a rarity as early as 1870, as had by 1900 someone seriously engaged in philosophical speculation or economic theorizing who lacked a similar affiliation. Yet someone seriously engaged in international studies without such an affiliation remained a commonplace as recently as 1940.

Two types of unattached intellectuals concern us here: those with independent means that permit them to pursue intellectual activities irrespective of their potential to provide a living, and those without such means who hope to earn a living by presenting the product of their intellectual labors directly to the public. In practice, of course, these ideal types lose much of their definitional sharpness. Those without economic need to present their intellectual wares in the public marketplace may do so in order to communicate with others and to achieve some recognition. Similarly, those dependent upon the marketplace may be able to take up studies of no expected commercial value but of great personal interest by having salable topics subsidize the intellectually compelling ones. Thus, it is not one's relationship to the marketplace but the extent to which one operates outside of an institutional matrix, such as those provided by the church, the government, corporations, universities, or even a staff position over a long period of time with the same publication, that qualifies an intellectual as "free lance": "a person who acts on his own responsibility without regard to authority."[44]

The first nineteenth-century American who took up international studies as a free lance and made it pay was William Hickling Prescott. His two best known histories, *The Conquest of Mexico* (1843) and *The Conquest of Peru* (1846), both sold well enough to sustain the partially blind Bostonian in the comfortable circumstances that royalties from his earlier *Ferdinand and Isabella* (1837) and a sizable inheritance had accustomed him to. The California bookseller Hubert Howe Bancroft also succeeded in making a living out of his interest in the history of the American West and Latin America. In addition to royalties on his thirty-four-volume *History of the Pacific States of North America* (1882–1890), Bancroft realized a profit selling parts of his collection of Americana, which included several thousand items from Latin America. "History-writing," Bancroft declared, was "among the highest of human occupations," though he obviously saw no reason why it should not be among the more lucrative ones as well.[45]

The commercial success enjoyed by books like Katherine Mayo's *Mother India* (1928), a searing account of conditions in modern India, Pearl Buck's *The Good Earth* (1931), and Agnes Newton Kath's account of Borneo, *Land Below the Wind* (1940), attest to the persistence well into the twentieth century of a sizable American audience that had earlier set out with the young Melville "to sail forbidden shores and to land on barbarous coasts." On a more modest scale, Isabel Florence Hapgood found an audience for her translations of Tolstoy and Gogol in the 1880s, her sixteen-volume edition of *The Novels and Stories of Turgenev* (1903–1904), lectures such as those delivered to the Chautauqua Literary and Scientific Circle on

Russian literature, and occasional reviews in the *Nation*. Such efforts were sufficient to her economic needs and made her name at her death in 1928 "as well known to American lovers of good literature as that of many a popular author."[46]

Just as Hapgood fashioned a literary career out of her love for the Russia of the Holy Orthodox Catholic Apostolic Church, whose *Service Book* she translated in 1906, other American writers did the same out of their ideological fascination with the Russia that displaced Hapgood's in November 1917. John Reed was the first to do so, with his *Ten Days That Shook the World,* but others followed in his wake, among them the Marxists Max Eastman and Bertram Wolfe, and, in the late 1930s, the literary critic Edmund Wilson. All carried on their investigations of Russia without the aid of any permanent institutional affiliation, unless Wolfe's membership in the Communist party can be so described. All could say, as Wilson did shortly after what became *To the Finland Station* began to appear in serialized form in the *New Republic,* that they "made my living by writing in periodicals. There is a serious profession of journalism and it involves its own special problems." Indeed, as E. B. White, later Wilson's colleague at the *New Yorker,* apprised them, among the special problems was the writer's need to maintain his "amateur standing."[47]

As compared with the institutionally unaffiliated intellectuals who took up the study of Russia before 1940, all of whom seemed anxious to get their views in print, those who studied Asia seemed less determined to communicate their findings and less financially dependent upon doing so. For every Ernest Fenollosa, who put his knowledge of Japanese art and culture to use as a curator at the Boston Museum of Fine Arts and as a platform lecturer, Boston in the 1890s and early 1900s had several wealthy Trumbull Stickneys, William Sturgis Bigelows, George Cabot Lodges, and Percival Lowells, who kept their interest in Asian religions within their select circle. Thomas Sergeant Perry, the grandnephew of Matthew Perry and a Boston Brahmin of independent means, was similarly disposed. Perry spent three years in Japan, 1898 to 1901, and then declined to take up offers to comment on what he had learned there. "Whether or not he might have been a great writer," the poet E. A. Robinson wrote of Perry at his death in 1928, "is more than one can say, for he never took the trouble to find out." His long and close study of Russian literature he also kept to himself and to those with whom he corresponded.[48]

Perry's silences, as much as his scholarly subject matter, suggest the depths of his alienation from his own society and culture. For him to have sought to communicate the pleasure he derived from a consideration of Asian religions or Russian literature to his fellow Americans was to subject "his" Asia or "his" Russia to the same forces that had corrupted "his" America. Like others of his generation and class, Perry subscribed to the view of an earlier Massachusetts student of Asia, Ralph Waldo Emerson, who, when asked if he might undertake to have parts of the *Bhagavad-Gita* reprinted, responded to this proposed "sally into orientalism" with considerable coolness:

I shrunk back and asked time, thinking it not only some desecration to publish our prayers in the *Daily Herald,* but also that those students who were ripe for it would rather take a few pains, and search for it, than find it on the pavement.[49]

But of all Americans to have seized upon the study of another culture as a means of transcending their own, perhaps none has done so with fewer institutional constraints or economic reservations than George Kates. Kates traveled throughout Europe and Latin America as a child, earned degrees from Columbia, Harvard, and Oxford, and made a comfortable living as a Hollywood writer. "Feeling minor enthusiasm only, regarding conventional life in my own country," he decided in 1932, "for no practical reason whatsoever," to go to China, "the largest missing area in the atlas of my wanderings." Upon arrival in Peking he enrolled in a language school and began auditing courses in Chinese history and literature at Peking University. He lived in a manner as if "reconstructing the vanished setting of the scholar class, of the old literati, with objects for elegant if unpretentious domesticity." Not without cause did other Americans and even his own servants refer to Kates as "the Oyster," and not without truth did Kates, referring to the resident American diplomats, missionaries, and "professional sinologues," conclude that "China, to them, was not in any way what it had become to me."[50]

Kates stayed on in Peking until 1940, when the imminence of World War Two prompted him to return to the United States. In his memoir of his Peking years, *The Years That Were Fat* (1952), he tried to explain why, once back "home" (the quotation marks are his), he abandoned his studies and made no attempt to make his experiences in China "pay off." "To continue back in the West to 'Sinify' myself," he wrote, was "to evade responsibility in the pretended interests of some spiritual custodianship, while actually fleeing from reality." Thus, Kates felt more akin to the English amateur sinologist Arthur Waley, whose *Travels of an Alchemist* he greatly admired, than to the American graduate students he encountered in Peking in the 1930s, at least some of whom saw China not only as one of the great civilizations but, potentially at least, "a great field for academic enterprise."[51]

In the twelve years between Kates' sojourn in China and his coming to write about it, not only American Chinese studies but American international studies generaly underwent a fundamental transformation. Whereas well into the 1930s the enterprise continued to attract these who sought escape from American society, by the early 1950s it was attracting those in search of a permanent and rewarding, albeit academic, niche within it. Even those who regard the change as a beneficial one, or as essential for the life of international studies as an intellectual enterprise, might agree that in the process something important was also lost.

ACADEMIC AMBASSADORS

After all, it is a great thing to be a Harvard instructor, but it is not the only thing in the world.

ARCHIBALD CARY COOLIDGE, 1892[1]

The effective founders of international studies as an American academic enterprise did not belong to the first generation of professional academics that in the late nineteenth century brought the modern American university and its constituent disciplines into being. They belonged to the second, that which took up their positions between 1900 and 1920 and relinquished them around 1940. Specifically, it was the generation of the Harvard Slavicist Archibald Cary Coolidge, the Yale East Asianist Kenneth Scott Latourette, the Berkeley Latin Americanist Herbert Eugene Bolton, and the Chicago Egyptologist James Henry Breasted.

To depict four decades of an academic enterprise by a consideration of the careers of just four individuals, each with his own personal motivations, each in his own institutional setting, and each involved with the study of a different world area, is to risk personalizing and localizing the early history of academic international studies to such a degree as to deprive it of any general value. It also departs from the current trend among American intellectual historians, who tend to define their subject less in terms of a few individuals than in terms of collectivities, of social aggregates. "Professions are collective enterprises," Thomas L. Haskell has insisted, "so their emergence and growth must be gauged in terms of collective, not individual criteria." In his view the pioneering figures in the rise of professional social science in the late nineteenth century, such as Richard T. Ely, James Franklin Jameson, Edward A. Ross, and Jeremiah Jenks, were merely "instrumentalities" in the much larger process affecting the whole of American society. Other students of academic professionalization, myself among them, reacting against the traditional interpretation of American academic history, have consciously tried to depersonalize the process by rendering quantitatively what Arnold Thackray and Robert K. Merton have called its "sociological regularities," with the effect of conferring upon it a predetermined and irreversible character.[2]

Yet a characterization that minimizes the role of human and local contingencies may also thereby distort the process by which an intellectual enterprise becomes academically enclosed, particularly during its early stages, before the sociological regularities take over, if indeed they ever wholly do. This would seem to be especially the case in international studies where its first effective academic promoters would have been likely to view its prospective transformation into yet another academic enterprise with considerable ambivalence. Thus, a consideration of the individual motives, the institutional circumstances, and the particularities of area that shaped academic international studies during its first generation is also a consideration of alternatives to academic enclosure that have been not so much discredited by subsequent events as mislaid.

⁖ I

Archibald Cary Coolidge might as easily have done less with his life than introduce modern international studies at Harvard and found Slavic studies as an American academic enterprise. Born in Boston in 1866 into a family of wealth and social standing, he graduated *summa cum laude* from Harvard College in 1887 with neither occupational plans nor the financial need to develop them. After touring Europe for two years and spending a third as an unpaid secretary at the American legation in St. Petersburg, where he took up Russian, his future remained undecided. "I long ago came to the conclusion," he informed his father in 1890, "that if I had not been an American, I should have gone into the diplomatic career as a profession, but for an American it is not worth while." A year later, having at least concluded that he did "not care to travel for the fun of it indefinitely," yet aware "to go home to America now would be a confession of failure," he decided to return to the University of Freiburg, where he had studied briefly before going to St. Petersburg, "until that degree is got."[3]

Coolidge received his PhD from Freiburg in 1892 for a dissertation entitled "Theoretical and Foreign Elements in the United States Constitution." He then gave diplomacy a second try, this time as secretary at the legation in Vienna. But as in St. Petersburg, lack of political connections with the incumbent administration precluded his reappointment. "Once again I am a globe trotter wandering over the face of the earth," he wrote home. "My glory as a diplomat is over and I have gone back to my old life of sightseeing and study." Despairing of "further office-seeking," Coolidge returned to Boston in 1893, whereupon president Eliot of Harvard, a friend of the family, arranged for him to teach a section of Edward Channing's History I, while waiting to see what might turn up.[4]

During his second year of teaching, Coolidge assumed full responsibility for History I. Thereafter he began introducing courses into the Harvard curriculum focusing on what he called "the unhealthy countries." In 1894 he began teaching a course on the history of Northern and Eastern Europe, the first in an American university to deal with the Slavic world; in 1897, a course on contemporary Balkan and Near Eastern affairs; in 1907, "The Far East in the Nineteenth Century" and a full course on Russian history. In addition to these offerings, some of which Coolidge continued to teach into the 1920s, he sponsored the introduction of Slavic languages into the Harvard curriculum in 1896 and, a decade later, Latin American history.[5]

Coolidge's efforts to internationalize the Harvard curriculum led him to take an early and abiding interest in the Harvard library. Even before he was made director of the library by his cousin Abbott Lawrence Lowell, who became president of Harvard in 1909, he had assumed personal responsibility for its non-Western holdings. "For the Far East," he informed Lowell in 1910, "we have perhaps the best working library out of Washington; for Russia and other Slav countries the best (not in Slavic Languages) in the United States; for the Ottoman Empire and the Near Eastern Question perhaps the best in the world."[6]

Along with Leo Wiener, a Russian emigré whom he brought to Harvard in 1896, and Robert H. Lord, one of his early PhDs, Coolidge helped to train virtually all Slavicists produced in the United States up to 1925. Among these were Frank A. Golder, who introduced Russian studies at Stanford; George Rapall Noyes and Robert J. Kerner, who together developed Russian studies at Berkeley; and Samuel Hazzard Cross, who, after serving in government, returned to Harvard in 1930 to succeed Wiener as professor of Slavic languages, a position he held until 1946. Coolidge's successor was one of his last students, William L. Langer, who in turn helped train several of the leading figures of postwar American Slavic studies.[7]

The success that Coolidge enjoyed in internationalizing the Harvard curriculum, strengthening its library resources in non-Western materials, and establishing Slavic studies as a graduate program was due in large part to his willingness to finance these initiatives out of his own pocket. Taking only a nominal salary himself, he drew on personal resources to provide Wiener's salary, to establish graduate scholarships, and to underwrite the Harvard Historical Series, in which the dissertations of several of his PhD students appeared. He also gave generously to the Harvard library, providing all the funds for acquisitions relating to Polish history, India, the Dutch East Indies, Morocco, Algiers, and China.[8]

In addition to his own funds, Coolidge regularly called upon those of family and friends. His father, after declining his son's suggestion that he help in "getting up a collection" for books on Arctic and Antarctic travel in 1898, later contributed several thousand dollars for the purchase of books on the Ottoman Empire and the Crusades. Similarly, after Coolidge himself provided funds to begin instruction in Latin American history at Harvard, he secured an endowment to establish a chair (to which Clarence H. Haring was appointed in 1913) from his friend and ex-student, Robert Woods Biss.[9]

Coolidge's considerable skills as an academic politician also contributed to the success of his efforts on behalf of the international studies at Harvard. He maintained close ties with both President Eliot, with whom he was aligned on most issues, and with President Lowell, with whom he shared uncles, as well as with prominent fellows of the Harvard Corporation and overseers. He also held the respect of his fellow faculty members, as evidenced by his successful negotiation of the separation of political science from history in 1911, and of disciplinary colleagues, as evidenced by his election to the presidency of the American Historical Association in 1924. To question the wisdom of extending Harvard's intellectual interests and financial resources to encompass "the unhealthy countries" was to take on a formidable antagonist.[10]

Yet in pressing Coolidge's claim as founder of American Slavic studies and of international studies generally at Harvard, one can easily rate his accomplishments as mentor and academic promoter more highly than he did. While he carefully monitored the subsequent academic careers of his PhDs and took pride in their professionel accomplishments, he had as lively an interest in the careers of undergraduates who did not become academics. Having admonished himself back in the midst of his own career-deciding throes that "it is a great thing to be a Harvard instructor, but it is not the only thing in the world," Coolidge seems not to have hesitated to advise undergraduates accordingly.[11]

That undergraduates sought Coolidge's advice on such matters is understandable. A bachelor, who lived in a college dormitory throughout his years on the faculty, Coolidge enjoyed the company of undergraduates; they, in turn, appreciated his interest in them, perhaps especially because most other faculty members showed little. Moreover, many turn-of-the-century Harvard undergraduates saw in Coolidge something of themselves. Like him, they came from wealthy families, had traveled as children, and were on the lookout for, as one later put it, "a good enough occupation for a young fellow with a certain amount of money and no particular interests." For such individuals, public service seemed much preferable to what another called "the pallid career of family trustee," yet they were unwilling or unable to accommodate themselves to the realities of elective politics. Faced with such a dilemma, many jumped at Coolidge's suggestion that they consider the foreign service.[12]

Joseph C. Grew, Harvard College 1902, is a case in point. After six years at Groton and four at Harvard, Grew set out following graduation—accompanied by twenty-two pieces of luggage and a Japanese valet—on a eighteen-month world tour. The trip was to give him time to decide what to do with his future. He had already decided that he did not want to follow his father and two brothers into banking and real estate. His trip taught him that he liked to travel and did not mind in the least being away from Boston. Nevertheless, his decision to "serve my country abroad" was not made until he received a telegram from Coolidge informing him of an available secretaryship in Cairo. "It is to you that I owe the original opportunity of entering the foreign service," Grew later reminded Coolidge, just as it was Coolidge's example that allowed Grew to "overcome a stubborn New England conscience which assured me that to stray from the ancestral fold of State Street was to be damned to all eternity."[13]

In addition to his willingness to serve as an informal recruiting officer for the foreign service, there are negative indications that Coolidge saw himself less as an academic scholar than as an ambassador between the worlds of scholarship and public service. Compared with his departmental colleagues, Edward Channing and Albert Bushnell Hart, Coolidge wrote little, and what he did write was seldom based on the extensive archival research that had become the hallmark of the professional historian. If Roger B. Merriman's assessment of his approach to history as that of "the drum and trumpet school" was a bit harsh, one cannot imagine Coolidge saying, as did Channing, that he wrote his books for his graduate students to read. Two of the books he published, *The United States as a World Power* (1908) and *Origins of the Triple Alliance* (1917), originated as public lectures delivered to foreign audiences, while the third, *Ten Years of War and Peace* (1927), was a posthumous collection of magazine articles. Other books had been planned, and two, a biography of Suleiman and a study of the expansion of Russia, were partially written but so often put aside that they remained uncompleted at his death. Then again, he may have simply lacked the powers of concentration needed to see a book through to completion. "While wellstocked and perfectly reasonable," Santayana characterized Coolidge's mind, it "seemed somehow thin, as if there were no central sun in it, no steady light and center of gravity."[14]

The calls that most dependably diverted Coolidge from his scholarship originated in Washington. Though not the first academic to have his advice solicited by government officials— economists like Harvard's Frank Taussig, Columbia's E. R. A. Seligman, and Chicago's J. L. Laughlin began appearing regularly before congressional committees in the 1890s—Coolidge was, along with the Wisconsin political scientist Paul S. Reinsch, the first to be regularly consulted on matters of foreign policy. Originally wishing to be a diplomat and coming from a family that included Thomas Jefferson Coolidge, a leading figure in the shaping of American opinion about foreign affairs in the 1890s and early 1900s, Coolidge welcomed such requests for his advice and assiduously cultivated the personal relationships that prompted them.[15]

In addition to his ex-students in the foreign service, several of whom by World War One had reached ambassadorial or undersecretarial rank, Coolidge maintained semiofficial friendships with Theodore Roosevelt, William Howard Taft, Charles Evans Hughes, Elihu Root, Henry Cabot Lodge, and Herbert Hoover. As one of America's most traveled men—he made thirty-two separate trips abroad—and one determined to stay abreast of world affairs, Coolidge was hard to ignore. It was a matter of pride, both to him and to his students, that the State Department doorman knew him by name.[16]

The best-known incident in Coolidge's career as a foreign-policy adviser was his participation in "The Inquiry," a research group conceived by President Wilson's confidant Colonel Edward House in the fall of 1917. Headed by House's brother-in-law, Sidney E. Mezes, president of the City College of New York, it was charged with producing reports, collecting documents, and otherwise preparing the American case for the peace settlement. Although drawn into the organization at its inception and placed in charge of its Eastern European and Near East problems group, Coolidge played a minor role in The Inquiry's proceedings. His own work on its behalf was interrupted in the summer of 1918 by a secret mission to Russia for the State Department, and his area was then transferred to others during an organizational reshuffling in his absence. He did manage, however, through aggressive recruiting, to see that his alma mater was well represented in this early attempt at academic foreign-policy making. More than one-third of those who made significant contributions to The Inquiry had either educational or professional ties to Harvard.[17]

However one judges the effectiveness of Coolidge's efforts as a member of The Inquiry, as a special envoy to Moscow, as a member of the Paris peace delegation, and as "the political adviser and diplomatic go-between" during the American Relief Administration's involvement in Russia in 1921–22, they all reflect his desire to make his knowledge of international politics and familiarity with Eastern Europe available to those outside the university. This same disposition prompted his involvement in the Council on Foreign Relations and, in 1922, his agreeing to become the first editor of the Council-sponsored quarterly, *Foreign Affairs*.

The Council on Foreign Relations as constituted in 1921 represented a merger of two organizations of similar interests but differing composition: the New York Council on Foreign Relations, a discussion group of Wall Street bankers and industrialists formed in 1914 to keep abreast of the war in Europe; and the American Institute of International Affairs, formed in 1919 and composed of Americans who had attended the Paris Peace Conference in one "expert" capacity or another. When the council decided in 1922 that it "must publish or perish," Coolidge was asked to assume the editorship of the proposed journal. He accepted, despite its necesitating weekly trips to New York, where the council insisted on basing its journal, and a reduction in his teaching. Coolidge concentrated his remaining energies upon launching *Foreign Affairs,* and from its success derived many of his final satisfactions.[18]

While consciously "following a highbrow policy and not running too much after the latest thing," but also insisting that "we must have plenty about Russia first and last," Coolidge and his associate and successor at the council, Hamilton Fish Armstrong, saw *Foreign Affairs* not as a professional journal addressed to an academic audience but as an instrument "to guide American public opinion by a broad hospitality to divergent ideas." Academics have subsequently figured more prominently among the contributors to *Foreign Affairs* than they did in the 1920s and 1930s, but, like the public officials and journalists who remain its principal contributors, they have used its pages to address the same "international-minded" audience of Americans that Coolidge's career, inside and outside the university, had been devoted to nurturing.[19]

Coolidge died of cancer in January 1928 at the age of sixty-two. He left $450,000 to Harvard, $150,000 of which became the endowment for a professorship named in his honor. His colleague, the medieval historian Charles Homer Haskins, speaking for the Harvard faculty, said that Coolidge's death "has snapped a link between us and the world of big affairs."

But that link once forged could, as the subsequent careers of McGeorge Bundy and Henry Kissinger have amply demonstrated, be forged again.[20]

·ε· II

The case for Kenneth Scott Latourette as the founder of American East Asian studies and of international studies generally at Yale can be in neither instance based on simple precedence. Seven years before he joined the Yale faculty in 1921, Harvard, Clark, Columbia, Wisconsin, Stanford, Berkeley, and the University of Washington each had at least one faculty member offering courses relating to East Asia. Yale itself had three.[21]

Of Latourette's ten forerunners, eight had lived in the Orient and six spoke either Japanese or Chinese. Three—Paul Reinsch of Wisconsin, George Blakeslee of Clark, and Kan-Ichi Asakawa of Yale—had American PhDs, but only Asakawa, born in Japan, had done graduate work on East Asia. Reinsch and Blakeslee did not speak Chinese or Japanese, nor did Payson Treat, who taught Asian history at Stanford, or Langdon Warner, who taught Japanese art at Harvard. Harlan P. Beach, Latourette's immediate predecessor at Yale, had learned Chinese during six years residence as a missionary, and, like John Fryer at Berkeley, a longtime member of the British consular service in Hong Kong, and Frederic Hirth at Columbia, a retired member of the German consular service in China, he took up university teaching only after completing another career. Henry H. Gowen of the University of Washington, an Englishman by birth, combined his professorial duties with those of rector of a large Seattle church. Thus, only with Latourete's appointment at Yale in 1921 did an American university acquire the full-time services of an American-born, linguistically equipped, PhD in East Asian studies.[22]

Both Beach and Asakawa, the latter a member of the Yale history department from 1906 to 1935, had offered courses on East Asia prior to Latourette's arrival but had failed to spark interest in the field among either undergraduates or graduate students. Asakawa, finding few takers for his "Japanese Art, Thought, and Customs," redirected his teaching and research interests to become a recognized authority on European feudalism. Meanwhile, Beach occupied himself in building up Yale's Day Missions Library and preparing elaborate statistical studies on behalf of the missions.[23]

What student interest in East Asia existed at Yale prior to 1921 was attributable to Frederick Wells Williams, whose father, Samuel Wells Williams, had joined the Yale faculty in 1877 as an unsalaried professor of Chinese. Whereas the elder Williams had lived in China for forty years, spoke Chinese, and had made several scholarly contributions to the study of Chinese history, his son had not been to China since childhood and did not read Chinese. This struck his more exacting colleagues, notably William Graham Sumner, as a disqualification for a teaching position in the field. Yet it was generally conceded that "Oriental Bill" had his uses. His undergraduate course on modern Asian history drew large enrollments, a testimony to Williams' engaging manner as a lecturer and to the course's reputation as a "gut."[24]

Graduate students regarded Williams as an undemanding and genial mentor, as the case of his most distinguished PhD, Kenneth Scott Latourette, illustrates. Shortly after arriving at Yale in 1906 to begin graduate studies, Latourette abandoned his original plan to pursue a PhD in geology or economics, his undergraduate interests, in favor of getting a PhD in history with Williams. He did so, he later acknowledged, because "I could get it more quickly."[25]

Latourette's impatience stemmed not from any desire to get on with an academic career but from his desire to honor a pledge that he had made as a senior at Linfield College in his native Oregon: "It is my purpose if God permits to become a missionary." In so pledging, Latourette joined 3,000 other collegians who, between 1886 and 1920, had enrolled in the Student Volunteer Movement to bring about "the evangelization of the world in this generation." In many ways Latourette typified the SVM recruit. Unlike the American Board of Commissioners for Foreign Missions, the lay-directed SVM drew most of its recruits from the Middle and Far West. It also enjoyed greater success among Baptists, which the Latourettes were, and among Methodists and those churches identified with the fundamentalist wing of American Protestantism, than among the Congregationalists and Presbyterians who had swelled the missionary ranks earlier.[26]

Latourette went to Yale to go to China. During his three years as a graduate student he involved himself more in his work on behalf of the YMCA, in voluntary Bible classes, and in recruiting for the missions among undergraduates than in his own studies. But because the offer of a teaching position at the Yale-in-China educational mission in Changsha was conditional upon his getting a PhD, he submitted a dissertation, "The History of the Early Relations Between the United States and China, 1784–1844," to Williams in the spring of 1909. It was accepted, and after a year as traveling secretary for the SVM, he sailed for China.[27]

At the end of his first year in Changsha, Latourette wrote back to friends in New Haven:

The opportunity grows on me daily. It is the chance to help lay the foundations of an institution which will influence the educational standards of an entire nation, and which will train men to carry out in China those ideals of Christian service which have so characterized the Older Yale. I can think of no place where I would rather be.

A year later he contracted amoebic dysentery and was sent home. Latourette left China intending to return the following year, but doctors in Oregon advised against it. He thus became, as the SVM designated cases like his, a "detained volunteer," a respectable if vague status.[28]

In the fall of 1914, still recuperating at home, Latourette began teaching a course on the Far East at nearby Reed College. In 1916, he accepted an offer from Denison University in Ohio because, as he later indicated, he found Reed intellectually stimulating but evangelically torpid. At Denison he "quickly felt at home," accepted the position of college chaplain and the ordination required, and renewed his recruiting efforts. "My primary concern," he later wrote of his first year's teaching, "was students, not a subject." But it was also at Denison that Latourette seems to have resolved his occupational dilemma by committing himself to an academic career. Accordingly, he quickly revised his dissertation for publication and wrote three more books in rapid succession: *The Development of China* (1917), *The Development of Japan* (1918), and *The Christian Basis of World Democracy* (1920). Yet as the last title implies, Latourette did not abandon his earlier loyalties in the process of buttressing his academic credentials. In 1920 he declined a professorship of Far Eastern history at Wisconsin because it did not offer the opportunity to "fulfill my missionary purpose by helping to prepare missionaries" that he hoped he might find elsewhere. The Yale call came a year later.[29]

The precise position that Latourette assumed at Yale in 1921 was the professorship of missions, a chair endowed in 1906 by the family of D. Willis James, a prominent New York Presbyterian and supporter of the missionary cause. During Beach's tenure the chair had been primarily identified with the Yale Divinity School. It remained so until 1927, when its title was broadened to professorship of missions and Oriental history and Latourette became a member of the Yale history department. Though he retained his membership in the history department until his retirement in 1953, he took a more active part in the affairs of the Divinity School.[30]

Latourette functioned during his thirty-two years on the Yale faculty primarily in two academic roles: as a publishing scholar and as the principal link between Yale and what had earlier been one of its major outside constituencies. By writing about what he did—the history of Christian missions worldwide—he sought to combine these roles. "He covered mountains of sources, and produced manuscript," it was said, "every morning except Sundays." His *History of the Christian Missions in China* (1929) and still more his monumental *History of the Expansion of Christianity,* published in seven volumes between 1937 and 1945, were addressed less to fellow East Asian scholars than to a more general audience: "those who form the main-stay of the churches in the Anglo-Saxon world from which the major part of the support in personnel and money has come and continues to be drawn for the Protestant wing of the missionary enterprise."[31]

Latourette's contacts with this audience went beyond writing for it. The year he joined the Yale faculty he also joined the American Baptist Foreign Mission Society. The following year he became a trustee of Yale-in-China and was elected to the executive committee of the World Student Christian Federation. In 1929 he assumed editorial responsibilities for the International Missionary Council. Three years later, upon the appearance of *Re-Thinking Missions,* a critical inquiry into the missionary enterprise undertaken by liberal churchmen and edited by the Harvard philosopher William Ernest Hocking, Latourette responded with a spirited defense of the missions. "It scarcely needs to be said," he wrote in the preface to his *Missions Tomorrow,* "that the author is the mouthpiece of no organization or group."[32]

Latourette's efforts as an ambassador and his awesome productivity as a scholar—in all he published eighty books—were not matched by comparable success in other academic roles. As an undergraduate teacher he was, by his own estimate, "reasonably good but certainly not one of the great ones." He lacked the drawing power of his predecessor Williams and of East Asianists elsewhere. In 1928, for example, when H. H. Gowen had 214 University of Washington undergraduates enrolled in his History of Asia course and Payson Treat had 139 Stanford undergraduates in his course on the Far East, Latourette's course in Chinese history drew 22 students, his course on the Christian church in China, 18.[33]

Nor was he a conspicuous success as an academic mentor. During his thirty-two years on the faculty, Yale produced twelve PhDs in East Asian studies, all but one in religious studies. Of these, seven went into the missions, two became professors at theological seminaries, and one returned to his native China to teach. Two of Latourette's students, Eldon Griffin (PhD 1937) and John M. H. Lindbeck (PhD 1937), did take up academic careers; but Griffin had been teaching at the University of Washington before coming to New Haven and Lindbeck's subsequent career at Harvard and Columbia was primarily that of an administrator rather than of a publishing scholar or a producer of PhDs.[34]

Ironically, Latourette's tenure at Yale coincided with its loss of preeminence among American universities in Oriental studies. Where it had been in the late nineteenth century the only university to offer regular instruction on the Far East, and in 1914 was the only one to have more than one faculty member doing so, by 1928 it had fallen behind eight other universities in course offerings, enrollments, and disciplinary coverage in East Asian studies. In that year, Washington offered twenty-six courses on East Asia, California twenty-five, Stanford fifteen. Among East Coast universities, Columbia offered fifteen courses. Harvard also had fifteen courses, but was about to expand with the opening of the Harvard-Yenching Institute that year and the resulting surge of interest in East Asian studies in Cambridge. By comparison, Yale offered only five courses, four of them taught by Latourette.[35]

The situation was worse still in terms of language courses. Whereas Berkeley offered eleven courses in East Asian languages in 1928, and Columbia five, Yale offered none. This remained the case until the appointment of the linguist George Kennedy in 1937, an appointment Latourette applauded but had no part in initiating. Even in library holdings relating to East Asia, Yale had slipped behind Columbia, Harvard, and California.

Of Yale's involvement with international studies generally and East Asian studies specifically in the interwar years, George Pierson has recorded the widely held view that "the whole movement was a mistake: just a flight of scholarly curiosity and an academic failure."[36] Surely part of the problem turned on the enterprise's persistent identification with the Protestant missionary movement, which had already peaked and entered a period of economic and organizational crisis. Meanwhile, promoters of academic international studies at such West Coast institutions as Berkeley, Stanford, and the University of Washington had begun to stress the economic importance of East Asia, just as those at Columbia, Harvard, and Chicago were urging its importance to the study of international politics.

Thus, for all Latourette's off-campus efforts to promote East Asian studies, both among historians through regular surveys of the field in the *American Historical Review* and scholars generally through his helping to launch the Committee on the Promotion of Chinese Studies in 1929, he was viewed by colleagues as a throwback to the "Old Yale," where scholarship was thought properly to be in the service of Christian proselytizing. Latourette, while denying the imputation, nevertheless acknowledged it: "to many on the Yale faculty and elsewhere in academic circles, missions seemed to be associated with propaganda and valid scholarship in the field was deemed unlikely."[37]

But if Latourette's ties with the missions may actually have slowed the development of East Asian studies at Yale, his personally having made the transition from missionary to academic pointed the way for other ex-missionaries, without whom East Asian studies would have lacked the personnel necessary to effect even the modest growth it experienced elsewhere. Among the "sailed volunteers" who went to China between 1906 and 1923, and who subsequently played an important role in American academic Chinese studies between the wars, were John Lossing Buck, George B. Cressey, Homer H. Dubs, Henry Courtney Fenn, L. Carrington Goodrich, Daniel H. Kulp, Harley F. McNair, Ida C. Pruitt, John K. Shryock, and Nancy Lee Swann. Another academic whose parents had been missionaries in Japan, Evarts B. Greene, though an American historian at Columbia, made certain that Japanese studies would not be neglected on Morningside Heights. His brother, Jerome D. Greene, as a Fellow of the Harvard Corporation, performed a like function in Cambridge. So long as such individuals figured prominently in the ranks of American East Asian studies, the enterprise would retain some of the evangelical fervor and decidedly nonacademic concerns that Latourette brought to its founding.[38]

ॐ III

Unlike Coolidge and Latourette, Herbert Eugene Bolton, the effective founder of Latin American studies as an American academic enterprise and early leader in the development of international studies at the University of California, spent virtually his entire academic career west of the Mississippi and teaching at public institutions. Born in rural Wisconsin in 1870, he went to the University of Wisconsin, where he also did most of his graduate work (before securing his PhD from the University of Pennsylvania in 1899). His first six years of teaching were at the University of Texas, his last thirty at the University of California. Not only was Bolton's career influenced by these two circumstances, so too was the academic enterprise he helped launch.[39]

Bolton's efforts on behalf of Latin American studies in the United States were preceded by those of others. In 1883, Daniel De Leon, later better known as a radical activist, initiated a series of lectures on Hispanic diplomatic history at Columbia University, the last of which he delivered in 1889. Bernard Moses taught a course on Latin American history at the University of California off and on in the 1890s. Course work in Latin American history was begun at Yale by Edward Gaylord Bourne in 1900 and at about the same time by L. S. Rowe at Pennsylvania. Columbia renewed its interest in Latin American history when William R. Shepherd took up the subject in 1904, the same year Bolton introduced his course on Spanish colonization at Texas and two years after Roger B. Merriman began his course on the Spanish empire at Harvard. Of these, Bourne was the most clearly identified with Latin American history; his volume in the American Nation Series, *Spain in America* (1904), has since been regarded as marking the point where the canons of professional historiography were first applied to the subject. His death, at the age of forty-eight in 1908, came before he had been able to train a successor.[40]

Besides by Moses, Bolton had been anticipated at Berkeley by Henry Morse Stephens, who joined its history department in 1902. Three years later he acquired for the university the library of Hubert Howe Bancroft, which contained, in addition to 60,000 items of Western Americana, the world's largest and most diversified collection of books and manuscripts relating to Spanish America. Stephens' entrepreneurial energies also led to the founding of the Native Sons of the Golden West, a California equivalent of the Mayflower Society, which provided research fellowships for Berkeley graduate students working in Western or Latin American history. As both Stephens and later Bolton never tired of reminding Californians, to be interested in their state's past was by definition to be interested in its Spanish antecedents and its ties with the rest of Spanish America.[41]

Bolton began his academic career as an American historian. His dissertation, started under Frederick Jackson Turner at Wisconsin and completed under John Bach McMaster at Pennsylvania, was on "The Free Negro in the South Before the Civil War." Only after securing his first academic job at Texas, and finding his teaching opportunities blocked in American history, did he take up Spanish in order to exploit the Mexican archives during his summer vacations. In 1906 he was commissioned by the Carnegie Institution to prepare what eventually became his *Guide to Materials for the History of the United States in the Principal Archives of Mexico,* perhaps his most enduring scholarly contribution to Latin American historiography. By the time the *Guide* appeared in 1913, Bolton had left Texas, spent two years at Stanford, and was in his second year at Berkeley.[42]

A crucial element in Bolton's success at Berkeley as a promoter of Latin American studies was his intuitive grasp of both the ideology and the economics of public higher education. Although Bolton understood the difference between quality and quantity, he never let pursuit of the first take precedence over the second. If a scholarly enterprise hoped to survive in a public university like Berkeley, it had to pay its way. Nor did Bolton ever show any doubt about the negotiable coin of the public university realm—student enrollments. "He was," as his student John Caughey said of him, "a teaching machine, a one-man assembly line, a tax-payer's dream of efficiency in the degree factory."[43]

Few academics have ever approached Bolton as a processor of students. In 1920, his first year as chairman of the Berkeley history department, he introduced a new course, "History 8a-b: History of the Americas," which he then offered virtually every year for the next quarter-century. Consisting of a twice-a-week lecture supplemented by discussion sections, History 8a-b regularly enrolled a thousand undergraduates. Bolton usually coupled this course with one on the History of the West that dependably drew two hundred upperclassmen and graduate students.[44]

Bolton's position as department chairman, which he held for two decades, made it easier for him to arrange departmental schedules and university requirements to encourage such huge enrollments. He easily dismissed occasional complaints from colleagues that History 8a-b was so heavily subscribed "as to shift the whole structure of the department" by pointing out that it encompassed nothing less than the history of the entire Western hemisphere, from Alaska to Patagonia, from the fifteenth to the twentieth century. Whatever the analytic merit of the so-called "Bolton thesis," an extrapolation of Turner's frontier thesis to all the countries of the Western hemisphere, its curricular possibilities were manifold.[45]

Bolton's statistics as a graduate teacher were equally impressive. His graduate seminar regularly enrolled upwards of thirty students. One reason he had so many is that he never seems to have turned anyone away. Though a Methodist, Bolton attracted more than his share of Catholic students, including a large number of priests and nuns, by his sympathetic rendering of the role of the Catholic church in the history of Latin

America. Moreover, once Bolton took on a graduate student, he nearly always saw that student through to a degree. In thirty-three years at Berkeley, he produced 350 MAs and 105 PhDs, 54 of the latter in Latin American (as distinct from Western American) history. Even an admirer acknowledged the possibility that these "perhaps were somewhat too many."[46]

Bolton provided for intellectually unimaginative students by assigning them parts of a larger topic, such as missionary-government relations, which, if likely to produce a pedestrian dissertation, made good use of the Bancroft library's Latin American resources and presented few theoretical obstacles. He seems never to have failed to find something in a student's work to commend, interpreting his role as mentor "to first of all give encouragement." And for graduate students needing financial assistance, Bolton had at his disposal the twenty or so assistantships generated by History 8a-b. Finally, for students who lacked confidence in their literary abilities, there was Bolton's own example. "He could not write worth a damn," one of his last students has since recalled, "but he went ahead and wrote and wrote."[47]

A Bolton bibliography that appeared in a Festschrift (the second) published by his students in 1945 runs to ten pages and contains 120 entries. Between its publication and his death in 1953 another dozen pieces appeared, including his *Coronado, Knight of Pueblos and Plains* (1949). Among his publications are guides to Latin American archives, collections of documents, translations, editions of diaries, and several biographical studies of missionaries, including a 600-page account of his "favorite Black Robe," *The Rim of Christendom: A Biography of Eusebio Francisco Kino, Pacific Coast Pioneer* (1936). Then there is his collaborative effort with his first PhD student, Thomas M. Marshall, *The Colonization of North America, 1492–1783* (1917), and perhaps his most influential book, *The Spanish Borderlands* (1921).[48]

In addition to these books and the articles and reviews that he published in such professional journals as the *American His-*

torical Review, the *Hispanic American Historical Review*, and the *Catholic Historical Review*, Bolton appeared frequently in local newspapers, travel magazines, and virtually any other kind of publication that might have readers whom he could interest in what he called "The Epic of Greater America." His writings for this popular audience include *The California Story* (1922), an account of the founding of San Francisco; *Outpost of Empire* (1931); and the text used by the thousands of Californians who took History 8a–b, *History of the Americas: A Syllabus with Maps* (1932). These writings brought him numerous awards from local and state organizations, just as his overall treatment of the history of the Spanish missionary enterprise resulted in his being made a papal knight and in his receiving the Serra Award of the Academy of American Franciscan History.

Yet perhaps because he consciously chose to do narrative history, even Bolton's most scholarly writings have found little favor among the postwar generation of Latin American historians. His own students have compared his prodigious publication record with the modest output of his Harvard contemporary, C. H. Haring, for example, only to conclude that Haring's work was the more sophisticated and the more rigorous and resulted from his "asking the right kinds of questions." In this, of course, Bolton's fate has been much like that of his cofounders, Coolidge and Latourette, neither of whom owes his retrospective prominence in his own enterprise to the enduring quality or seminal character of his scholarly contributions.[49]

Unlike Latourette in East Asian studies and to a much greater extent than Coolidge in Slavic studies, however, Bolton produced PhDs in Latin American studies who went on to become professors. Of his fifty-four PhDs in Latin American history, forty-two proceeded to academic careers. Of these, at least ten—Charles E. Chapman (Berkeley), Charles W. Hackett (Texas), J. Fred Rippy (Chicago), John L. Mecham (Texas), Lawrence F. Hill (Ohio State), George P. Hammond (New Mexico), Irving A. Leonard (Michigan), John T. Lanning (Duke), Woodrow W. Borah (Berkeley), and Jeffrey Johnson

(Stanford)—acquired professorships at universities where they in turn produced PhDs who then went into academic life. The votes of Bolton's "boys" and "girls" in the profession alone should have assured him the presidency of the American Historical Association, to which he was elected in 1932.[50]

Nonetheless, the overall distribution of Bolton's PhDs reflects some of the problems encountered by academic Latin American studies during the Bolton era. All but five of his academic placements taught at Catholic or public institutions, the great majority of these located in the Southwest. Where no regional or religious connection with Spanish colonization could be exploited, Bolton's students found jobs harder to come by. Indeed, among academics north and east of what Bolton referred to in his writings as "the rim of Christendom," his notoriety as a mass producer of PhDs, together with the uneven and disputed quality of his scholarship, only reinforced the reputation of Latin American studies as lacking in intellectual rigor. "Despite adequate resources and collections as at Yale and Harvard," Bolton's student Irving Leonard informed the American Council of Learned Societies in 1942, "Latin American studies have been neglected or reduced to a definitely subordinate position in the curriculum." Even at Bolton's own Berkeley, when it made its surge to the top of the American university rank order in the two decades after World War Two, its prewar distinction as *the* center for Latin American studies in the United States was allowed to lapse.[51]

Yet it would be patently unfair to hold Bolton responsible for the subsequent ups and downs of the enterprise for which he labored so long and so productively. However much an embarrassment he was to those who succeeded to the leadership of academic Latin American studies in the expansive 1950s and 1960s, his "living off the land" strategy has recovered some of its initial plausibility in the more recent period of budgetary restraint and what David Riesman has called "consumer sovereignty" in academic affairs.[52] As outside funding for international studies declined in the 1970s, those charged with its welfare came to see large undergraduate enrollments and local community interest less as distractions from the main business of producing scholarship than as the means by which such scholarship is to be underwritten. They discovered, in short, what Bolton knew all along: to ignore the clienteles in their midst was to put their entire enterprise in peril.

ई॰ IV

James Henry Breasted, early promoter of the academic study of the ancient Middle East and founder of the Oriental Institute of the University of Chicago, acquired a keen appreciation of the importance of money in scholarly undertakings by struggling through most of his academic career without it. His father, a Rockford, Illinois, hardware merchant, went bankrupt when Breasted was eight and thereafter was a financial burden for his son rather than a source of support. What family help he did receive came from an Aunt Theodocia, whose loans for her nephew's education and early travels left her home heavily mortgaged and Breasted permanently in her debt. Otherwise he managed by moonlighting. While attending North Central College in Naperville, Illinois, he worked as a bookkeeper and apprentice druggist; during his first two decades on the University of Chicago faculty he gave public lectures wherever and whenever "fifty and my expenses" were offered. In 1912, aged forty-seven, he was "still in constant financial anxiety."[53]

Breasted's chronic financial distress was directly tied to his unusual choice of careers. Unlike business or the ministry, both of which he considered, Egyptology carried with it no obvious means of support. Yet once he decided against accepting a call to the ministry in favor of a life of scholarship, a resolve taken while studying Hebrew at the Chicago Theological Seminary in 1889, he proceeded directly to Yale to work under its resident Orientalist, William Rainey Harper. Breasted arrived in New Haven just as Harper was preparing to leave to assume the presidency of the just-founded University of Chicago. Before heading west, however, Harper promised

Breasted the new university's professorship of Egyptology, "if you will go to Germany and get the best possible scientific equipment, no matter if it takes you five years." Four years later and deeper in debt but with a Berlin PhD and glowing recommendations from the leading German Egyptologist, Adolf Erman, in hand, Breasted joined the Chicago faculty, as an instructor rather than a professor and with a considerably smaller salary ($800) than Harper had originally promised.[54]

For the next twenty years Breasted struggled with limited success at two interlocking endeavors: to copy the inscriptions on all the surviving monuments of ancient Egypt, preparatory to writing a history of Egypt based on them, and to secure funds to accomplish this heroic project. Because students interested in Egyptology during Breasted's early years at Chicago were few, university authorities approved of his spending the bulk of his first thirteen years on the faculty in Egypt or in European museums, copying inscriptions, for they were thereby relieved of any responsibility for his salary, while still listing him on their roster. Some faculty members, however, attributing their own heavier teaching schedules to his absence, complained bitterly about his time away on leave. Yet neither backbiting from colleagues nor his always precarious health deflected him from his researches. "I cannot walk to my office," he was once heard muttering to himself during one of his infrequent stopovers in Chicago, "but I am going to Egypt, if I go on a stretcher!"[55]

Such singlemindedness came at considerable cost to his family. Breasted's wife seems to have grown increasingly distracted during the course of their marriage and his frequent absences, and years before her death in 1926 she lapsed into a state of permanent depression. Catching his father during a rare moment at home and away from his desk, Breasted's son and later biographer, Charles, then ten, engaged him in conversation only to lose his attention almost immediately. When brought back, Breasted responded to the question written on the boy's troubled face with: "Ich war in Nubien, mien Kind."[56]

Such support as Breasted's work enjoyed prior to World War One came from several sources. The Royal Academy of Berlin helped with expenses connected with his work on the Kaiser's Egyptian Dictionary Project; President Harper provided some funds for acquisitions for the university's Oriental Museum; personal savings earned by lecturing and still more loans from Aunt Theodocia provided the balance. But as none of these sources was sufficient nor, especially in the case of Harper, dependable, Breasted became increasingly preoccupied with the need to find "someone ready to invest a few thousand a year in my scientific work. I shall find him someday." [57]

That day seemed at hand in 1902 when, at Harper's suggestion, Breasted approached Frederick Taylor Gates, the "benevolent representative" of John D. Rockefeller. Unfortunately, most of the $50,000 grant resulting from Breasted's pilgrimage to 26 Broadway went to fund a Babylonian excavation project directed by Harper's brother Robert, an Assyriologist, rather than Breasted's own work on the Nile. Three years later, when Breasted asked for $455,000 to expand his Egyptian researches, Gates informed Chicago officials that he—and presumably his employer—had concluded that Egypt's contribution "to the civilization of which we are the heirs is much less important than that of Assyria and Babylonia," and therefore less worthy of exhumation. Breasted's already pronounced "pro-Egyptian bias" and his corresponding tendency to denigrate both Babylonian civilization and the integrity of its promoters were not moderated by this rebuff. [58]

Out of funds and back in Chicago in 1908, where he remained until 1920, Breasted again took to the lecture circuit. "I am lionized to nausea at every corner," he complained in 1910, "but my checkbook is as impotent as before." Two years later, so desperate was his financial situation that despite previous refusals "to turn aside from research to undertake pure popularization," Breasted signed a contract with Ginn and Company to write a textbook designed for a junior high school audience. [59]

Though grudgingly undertaken and lamented while in

progress, Breasted's *Ancient Times,* published in 1916, proved to be the crucial event in his career. Royalties from the 100,000 copies that were sold annually into the 1930s put an end to his personal economic plight. More importantly, *Ancient Times* brought the field of Egyptology to the attention of thousands of American readers, some of whom were in a position to advance it. "This is a book to read, to re-read and to read still again," a converted Gates wrote to its author, "and to commend to every lover of books, of men, and of the story of human progress." Theodore Roosevelt's review, in *Outlook,* was more discerning and less effusive, but it was Gates' reassessment of Egypt's place in "the story of human progress" that reohened the prospect of securing Rockefeller backing for his researches. This time Breasted made the most of the opening.[60]

By the time *Ancient Times* came out, Breasted had already developed considerable skill in approaching potential benefactors. He was an engaging conversationalist, physically impressive, and obviously filled with enthusiasm for his work, and he had a businessman's appreciation of a dollar. These qualities so impressed Mrs. Elizabeth Milbank Anderson, creator of the Milbank Fund and prominent benefactor of American higher education, that in 1914 she authorized Breasted to arrange a three-month trip for the two of them down the Nile, during which they could assess what projects they might undertake. The outbreak of war in Europe forced cancellation of the trip, but Mrs. Milbank did support some of Breasted's subsequent work.[61]

The University of Chicago provided Breasted with several exemplars of academic entrepreneurship. Before his death in 1906, President Harper enjoyed remarkable success in multiplying John D. Rockefeller's initial commitment to the university several times over. Similarly, Breasted's contemporaries on the faculty, Charles E. Merriam and Samuel N. Harper (son of the university's president), regularly secured support for their researches by tapping resources available among public-spirited Chicago philanthropists. But by far the greatest influence on Breasted as an academic entrepreneur was exercised by his close friend, the astronomer George Ellery Hale. As a member of the Chicago faculty in 1895, Hale had persuaded the traction magnate Charles T. Yerkes to provide the funds for what became the Yerkes Astronomical Observatory. He the went on to secure funds from the Carnegie Institution to build the Mount Wilson Observatory in California and, still later, to provide a building in Washington for the National Academy of Sciences, over which he presided during its resuscitation in World War One.[62]

During several years of correspondence, Hale and Breasted worked out an effective fund-raising strategy. Persuaded by his own experience that would-be donors must first be personally excited by a particular project, Hale suggested an excavation into the alluvial flood plains of the Nile. "Is it not probable," he wrote to Breasted in 1913,

that valuable inscribed objects may have been thrown into the river either by despoilers or merely in the natural course of loading and unloading barges, or building and expanding the great temple? Might we not strike some evidence of them by probing with a special drill? I feel sure that if sculptors' studios existed at Tell el-Amarna during its short life, there must have been many on the Plain of Thebes. Those are words to charm with!

And charm they did. Breasted's proposal in 1919 for the creation of an Oriental Institute at the University of Chicago, to stage expeditions such as that envisioned by Hale, received a five-year grant of $50,000 per annum from John D. Rockefeller, Jr. Several Chicago trustees, prominent among them Julius Rosenwald, matched the grant and the Institute was launched. In 1924 the Rockefeller-funded General Education Board gave another $250,000. A year later the original Rockefeller grant was renewed for another five years.[63]

Breasted's entrepreneurial activities became so time-consuming in the 1920s that the Chicago trustees relieved him of all teaching duties and placed the daily operation of the Oriental Institute in the care of his son. This simplified his life by making it unnecessary for him to be in Chicago at all, but it also eliminated whatever prospect Breasted had of training younger scholars to carry on his work. "I often wonder," he wrote in 1925, "where I shall land with all these argosies I am loading, with such reckless disregard of the fact that there is only one captain for the whole fleet." Comparing himself to the Hopkins classicist Basil Gildersleeve, who had died a year earlier but not before seeing a dozen of his PhDs installed in professorships throughout the country, Breasted lamented the fact that "when I am gone, there will not be much to say about me, for my students will never be scattered through all the leading universities." [64]

Despite regrets about slighting the classroom, Breasted accepted his special role in the academic economy. Throughout the 1920s he devoted himself to the task of forestalling the possibility that, as he put it, "the resources I have tapped might be shut off." In early 1929, despite poor health, he accompanied John D. Rockefeller, Jr., and Rockefeller's family on a three-month trip through the eastern Mediterranean. Prior to sailing, Raymond Fosdick, who was Rockefeller Jr.'s Gates, asked invited guests not to raise financial questions during the trip. Breasted readily agreed; his approach, he informed his son, would be more subtle. Included in Breasted's baggage were glass slides which he had used to illustrate *Ancient Society* and which he now proceeded to show as part of nightly informal presentations on the historical significance of places upcoming on the party's itinerary. Before the trip was half over, Rockefeller began raising financial questions, specifically about Breasted's own needs. By the end of the trip he had committed another $2,000,000 to the Oriental Institute, "largely because," he told Breasted, "of my belief in you." [65]

Failing health limited Breasted's activities after 1929, though he managed to complete two more books, *The Edwin Smith Surgical Papyrus* and *The Dawn of Conscience,* before his death in 1935. He also remained active in the affairs of the Oriental Institute, which by the mid-1930s was the country's largest humanistic research organization. Breasted envisioned the in-

stitute as a means by which American Oriental studies would
be transformed from what they had been, a primarily linguistic endeavor identified almost exclusively with ancient civilizations, into an historical discipline "in which art, archaeol-
ogy, political science, language, literature, and sociology, in
short all the categories of civilization shall be represented and
correlated."[66] To the extent that Breasted succeeded in this
effort, the Oriental Institute anticipated the "area center" approach that became fashionable among proponents of international studies after World War Two.

Before such a comprehensive approach to the study of the
Middle East or any other part of the world could be imple-
mented, extensive outside funding would have to be secured.
As Breasted acknowledged in 1935, the effort involved in creating and sustaining a large research enterprise "was in the first
instance financial." Nothing so well illustrated this as Breasted's own career, except perhaps the difficulties encountered by
his successor, John A. Wilson, in trying to sustain the Oriental
Institute in the late 1930s, when Breasted's "loaded argosies"
had been sunk by the depression. With the return of prosperity, however, and in the wake of World War Two, two factors
combined to ensure that the Oriental Institute was substantially funded: a growing disposition on the part of private philanthropies like the Rockefeller Foundation, the Carnegie Corporation, and, still more crucially after its reorganization in
1950, the Ford Foundation, to look favorably upon universities as supplicants; and the emergence of international studies
entrepreneurs possessed of "words to charm with." In this sense
at least, Breasted had underestimated his role as mentor.[67]

Other international studies academics of this founding generation might have been discussed here. James T. Shotwell,
for example, vigorously promoted the study of international
studies, both as a member of the faculty of political science at
Columbia University from 1905 to 1942 and as chief editor of
the Carnegie Endowment for International Peace series in 150
volumes, *Economic and Social History of the World War*. The series contained 300 monographs on eighteen different countries

and consumed $850,000 of the Carnegie Endowment's funds, which made Shotwell, as a recent biographer called him, "one of the first great entrepreneurs of scholarship." Trained as a medievalist but converted to the study of international relations by the coming of World War One, he thereafter conceived his principal function as teacher, editor, and publicist "to guide the intelligence of the world from such catastrophes."[68]

Though a half-generation younger, the Sanskritist W. Norman Brown and the anthropologist Melville J. Herskovits might also have been included; both took up their positions at the University of Pennsylvania and Northwestern, respectively, in the late 1920s, and from there proceeded to lay the groundwork for South Asian and African studies in the United States. Still, a consideration of their interwar careers would not have altered the conclusion inferable from the four considered here: that the founders of American academic international studies not only did not attempt to monopolize the study of the outside world, they sought at every opportunity to engage nonacademic audiences and extra-university participation in their enterprise. One might argue, of course, that they did not try to bring about the academic enclosure of international studies only because they lacked the resources and personnel to do so. Yet the foregoing consideration of the motives these founders brought to their own careers admits to the possibility that, apprised of the degree to which their enterprises subsequently did enclose themselves within the university, they might well protest that they had had a different outcome in mind.

≥ V

Putting hindsight aside, however, what one finds most striking about the academic international studies enterprise on the eve of World War Two is a quality best described by the term "fugitive": "apt to flee; evanescent; having to do with temporary interest."[69] To be sure, the enterprise had grown during

TABLE 4.1. PhDs Awarded in International Studies in Selected
Years, 1900 to 1940

	Number of PhDs Awarded in International Studies			
	1900	1925	1934	1940
Chicago	5	5	11	10
Harvard	2	3	11	14
Columbia	3	8	6	9
Berkeley	0	4	8	11
Yale	1	4	5	4
Wisconsin	1	1	1	1
Total of six universities	12	25	42	49
Estimate for all other American universities[a]	3	5	8	11
Estimated total for all American universities	15	30	50	60

Sources: for 1900 and 1925, annual reports of individual universities; for 1934 and 1940, Associated Research Libraries, *Doctoral Dissertations Accepted by American Universities* (New York: H. W. Wilson, 1935, 1941).
[a] Estimates arrived at by examining annual bulletins of ten other major universities (those included in the post–World War Two expanded sample used in later chapters) and annual listings of PhDs by area and discipline, such as Jesse J. Dossick, *Doctoral Dissertations on Russia* (New York: New York University Press, 1960); Michael Bratton, *American Doctoral Theses on Africa, 1886–1972* (Waltham, Mass.: African Studies Association, 1973); and Curtis W. Stucki, *American Doctoral Dissertations on Asia, 1933–1966* (Ithaca, N.Y.: Cornell University Press, 1968).

the first four decades of the twentieth century, as PhD production figures indicate. In 1900 some fifteen PhDs in international studies were conferred by American universities; in 1925, around thirty; in 1934, fifty; in 1940, perhaps as many as sixty (table 4.1). Yet this rate of growth, which represents a doubling every twenty years, was significantly below that experienced in the production of PhDs in the humanities and social sciences overall, where the doubling time was around fifteen years. In relative terms, international studies was falling further and further behind, barely holding its own even at the handful of universities where it had established some standing early in the century (table 4.2).

Another striking feature of the academic international studies enterprise in 1940 is how few institutions comprised it. Of the 150,000 academics employed by colleges and universities that year, about 200 provided regular instruction or pursued research in international studies. More than half of these taught at four universities—Harvard, Columbia, Chicago, and Berkeley—each of which had somewhere between 20 and 25 faculty identifiably engaged in international studies. Of all the other universities, only Yale and Wisconsin had as many as a dozen

TABLE 4.2. International Studies PhDs as a Proportion of All PhDs Awarded in the Social Sciences and Humanities by Six Universities in Selected Years from 1900 to 1940

	Number of PhDs Awarded		
	All Social Sciences and Humanities	International Studies	Percentage
1900	84	12	14
1925	183	25	14
1934	332	42	13
1940	374	49	13
Total	973	128	13

Sources: see table 4.1. The six universities are the same as those listed there.

faculty so engaged.[70] It is therefore only these six institutions which are represented in tables 4.1 and 4.2.

PhD production figures reveal the same pattern of institutional concentration. Of the 933 PhDs awarded in the humanities and social sciences in 1940, approximately 80 were in international studies. More than half of them (45) were awarded by Harvard, Columbia, Chicago, and Berkeley. Six other universities—Texas, Yale, Cornell, Michigan, Pittsburgh, and Stanford—accounted for most of the rest. Wisconsin, which produced forty PhDs in the humanities and social sciences, produced one in international studies. Like Yale, Wisconsin's interest in international studies was less in evidence on the eve of World War Two than it had been on the eve of World War One.[71]

Although Berkeley, where virtually all international studies activity focused on one world area, Latin America, and emanated from one department, history, represents the extreme case, area coverage and departmental participation were everywhere spotty. Africa went unexamined, except in courses on European imperialism, as did the contemporary Middle East and South Asia (table 4.3). Eastern Europe was similarly ig-

TABLE 4.3. International Studies PhDs at Six Universities, 1900–1940, by Area Focus

	PhDs Awarded in Selected Years		Estimated National Totals, 1900–1940 [a]	
	Number	Percentage	Number	Percentage
East Asia	31	24	300	25
Latin America	26	20	250	21
Middle East	25	20	250	21
Russia and East Europe	12	9	100	8
South Asia	12	9	100	8
International or other	12	9	100	8
Canada	8	6	75	6
Africa	2	2	25	2
Total	128	99	1,200	99

Sources: see table 4.1. Universities and selected years are the same as those in tables 4.1 and 4.2.
Note: Percentages do not add up to 100 because of rounding.
[a] Estimates arrived at by calculating totals for years between selected years as reflecting proportional growth in each area.

nored, except for a flurry of interest in Poland among sociologists at Chicago in the 1920s. Most of the attention given to East Asia was concentrated on China, to the relative neglect of Japan and other parts of the region.

At most of the universities where international studies had acquired a presence, it tended to be concentrated in their history departments (table 4.4). During the 1930s faculty in several history departments developed courses on East Asia, Latin America, and Russia. Not so with political science departments, whose members, aside from their interest in international relations, remained largely indifferent to the study of non-Western political arrangements. Anthropology departments, with the exception of Columbia's under Franz Boas, were only beginning in the 1930s to extend their teaching and fieldwork concerns beyond the Americas and the South Pacific. Economics departments, as a result of the depression and the New Deal economic legislation, became more domestically oriented in the 1930s than they had been in the 1920s.

Among humanities departments interest in international studies had declined relatively since the early 1900s, and inter-

TABLE 4.4. International Studies PhDs, 1900–1940, by Field and Discipline

	PhDs Awarded in Selected Years [a]		Estimated National Total, 1900–1940 [b]
	Number	Percentage	
Social sciences	90	70	850
History	43	34	400
Political science	17	13	160
Economics	14	11	140
Anthropology	11	9	110
Sociology	5	4	50
Humanities	38	30	350
Language and literature	24	19	225
Other humanities	14	11	125
Total	128	100	1,200

Source: See table 4.1.
[a] 1900, 1925, 1934, and 1940.
[b] See note to table 4.3.

est in Middle Eastern languages, literature, and religions had declined absolutely. Instruction in Russian, Chinese, and, by the late 1930s, Japanese were available at Harvard and Columbia, as was instruction in Arabic and Hindi at Chicago. Yet at these universities, graduate students who sought to acquire more than a minimal competence in any of these languages were expected to do so by further study abroad.

Even among those international studies academics with presumably the surest sense of collective identity, the China specialists, an uncertainty and tentativeness characterizes their interwar efforts at enterprise-building. Would-be promoters were faced not only with a dearth of numbers but also with the fact that those comprising the enterprise were so institutionally scattered. According to one inventory of the "China tribe," taken in 1936, it consisted of a dozen or so professors situated at ten different universities located along a line stretching from Hawaii to Harvard Square. That several members of the tribe knew little or no Chinese, and that they were further divided between those interested in contemporary China and those immersed in its ancient past, suggest that they could not depend upon internal cohesiveness to make up for their small numbers.[72]

Perhaps it is not so surprising, then, that American East Asianists as of 1940 had neither a journal of their own in which to publish their research nor a professional association to promote their enterprise. Several of those interested in contemporary China involved themselves in the affairs of the Institute of Pacific Relations, founded in 1925 as an outgrowth of the YMCA, and wrote for one of the IPR's two principal publications, *Pacific Affairs* and *Far Eastern Survey*. Those interested in ancient China were often affiliated with the American Oriental Society and availed themselves of its *Journal*. Both groups participated in the activities of the Committee on the Promotion of Chinese Studies, sponsored by the American Council of Learned Societies and supported by the Rockefeller Foundation. But like the Institute of Pacific Relations, the Committee's effective leadership was provided by nonacademics, Mortimer Graves of the ACLS and David Stevens of the Rockefeller Foundation, whose agendas were not primarily academic. In short, academic East Asianists in 1940 were in no position to assert hegemony over their field of study, even had they been inclined to do so.[73]

Surely one of the most important negative factors prompting international studies academics in the 1930s to maintain cordial ties with nonacademic organizations and their audiences was their persistent inability to find academic jobs for more than a minority of their PhDs. In 1934, only sixteen of the forty-two international studies PhDs (38 percent) produced by the six principal international studies universities secured permanent academic positions; in 1940 only twenty of forty-nine (41 percent) did so. (See table 4.5.) Academic employment of PhDs in the humanities and social sciences as a whole during these same years was at least half again as high.

The principal obstacle to the growth of international studies as an academic enterprise, as Mortimer Graves acknowledged

TABLE 4.5. International Studies PhDs, 1900–1940, by Subsequent Occupations

| | Receiving PhD in Selected Years [a] | | Estimated National Total, 1900–1940 |
	Number	Percentages	Number
Academic	54	42	500
Ministry or missions	10	8	100
Government	10	8	100
Writing or research	5	4	50
Other	19	15	180
Returned foreign national	30	23	270
Total	128	100	1,200

Sources: See tables 4.1 and 4.3. Occupations determined by consulting alumni directories; directories of disciplinary associations; *The Directory of American Scholars,* 1st, 2nd, and 3rd eds. (New York: R. R. Bowker, 1942, 1951, 1957); and *Who Was Who in America,* vols. 1–3 (Chicago: Marquis Who's Who, 1897–1960). Occupations of those receiving PhD in 1940 determined as of 1950, to control for disruptions of war years.

[a] 1900, 1925, 1934, and 1940.

in 1936, was not the lack of supply of young Americans ready and willing to pursue such careers, but a lack of demand for them to do so. Throughout the 1930s the Committee for the Promotion of Chinese Studies, which in 1939 became the Committee on Far Eastern Studies, acted as an academic placement bureau, anticipating openings wherever they might occur and trying to keep unemployed PhDs in the field through stopgap fellowship support. Yet despair often attended these efforts. "It is useless to train personnel," a committee report concluded in 1937, "if no provision is made for their employment." [74]

Until such provision was made, and in vastly greater numbers than seemed possible in the 1930s, academic international
studies would be obliged to struggle along as best it could and
with little prospect of dramatic change. "My career," the forty-
eight-year-old Harvard historian William L. Langer informed
his twenty-fifth class reunion in 1940, "has been the rather
unruffled one of university teacher, proverbially ensconced behind the ivory towers."[75] Having succeeded to his mentor
Coolidge's position in 1926, and with it to the primary responsibility for Harvard's offerings in both Slavic and Middle Eastern studies, Langer seemed at least reconciled to the prospect
that the second half of his career would match the tranquility
of the first. Were it not for the entry of the United States into
World War Two only months later, it might have.

THE YEARS THAT WERE FAT, 1941–1966

The first needeful thing for a Garden is water.
The nexte to that is enclosure.

BARNABY GOOGE,
Heresbach's Farm Bookes of Husbandry, 1577

In the case of almost all these enclosures the interests
of the poor have been systematically neglected.

HENRY FAWCETT,
Manual of Political Economy, 1863

WAR, BLESSED WAR

War, blessed war, had come to my generation,
and nothing ever would be the same.
ALFRED KAZIN, 1977[1]

In Part One I sought to establish the origins of American international studies as an intellectual enterprise and, more narrowly, an academic enterprise prior to 1940. To the extent that
these enterprises were indeed initiated that early, subsequent
developments are necessarily deprived of claims to being present at the creation of either one, still less to have created them.
This is not at all to dispute the importance of such developments in the overall history of American international studies,
only to insist that their putative impact must be understood as
transforming ongoing enterprises rather than creating new ones.

Part Two consists largely of an extended consideration of
three such developments: World War Two and the global implications of its outcome for the United States; the reorganization of the Ford Foundation in the late 1940s and its assumption of the principal responsibility for funding academic
international studies; and the expansion of American universities in the late 1950s and 1960s. Together, it will be argued,
these three developments made possible the rapid transformation of academic international studies from the marginal enterprise that it was in 1940 into the prominent and perdurable
fixture of American university life that it had become by the
1960s. Each, at the same time, accelerated the process by which

international studies became more and more enclosed within the university. The war and the "lessons" derived from it provided a crucial and hitherto missing rationale for enclosure; the Ford Foundation provided the funds and outside endorsement; the expanded university provided the accommodations and personnel.

Yet in advancing the cause of international studies within the universities and among academics, each of these developments also hastened the decline of international studies as an American intellectual enterprise operating outside the confines of the university and engaging the energies of other than academics. Whether the benefits attributable to the academic enclosure of American international studies more than offset the costs attributable to the waning of international studies as a nonacademic intellectual enterprise, we have no real means of gauging. But that the very real benefits accruing from enclosure, not least to international studies academics, also exacted real costs, though for the most part indirect and therefore less easily calculated, the following chapters seek to make clear.

ક્ષ   I

With the possible exception of those physicists engaged in the Manhattan Project, no academics were so dramatically affected by the national mobilization following Pearl Harbor as were those in international studies. Those in Japanese studies, whether specialists in Japanese poetry of the history of the Tokugawa period, suddenly became experts on "the Enemy." Similarly, those in Russian and Chinese studies became experts on important if problematic allies. Those familiar with North Africa, the eastern Mediterranean, Southeast Asia, or the Pacific islands became valued sources of information about prospective theaters of military action. Even those specializing in the Middle East and Latin America, areas removed from the combat zone, were assumed to possess language skills and insight into alien cultures sufficiently above those of most other

Americans to put their services in demand among those responsible for staffing the war effort.

International studies academics adjusted easily to their new status. Like most other mobilized academics, as one later recalled, they were "glad of the vacation from teaching [and] enjoyed the excitement of proximity to great events and to great authority as well as the occasional exercise of power on their own." Some positively reveled in their wartime assignments, as the Harvard anthropologist Carleton Coon did in his as a secret agent in North Africa; he acknowledged in 1943 that "since childhood I have wanted to do the kind of work I have been doing for the past year." Nor did he think himself alone in doing so, thinking it "probably the secret ambition of every boy to travel in strange mountains, stir up tribes, and destroy the enemy by secret and unorthodox means. Most boys, however, grow up, and as they adjust themselves to civilized living this ambition dies."[2]

Coon's Harvard colleague William Langer had been even quicker to realize the opportunities presented by the war. Six months prior to Pearl Harbor, he took leave of Cambridge to join the Office of Strategic Services, then being organized by General William "Wild Bill" Donovan at the personal request of President Roosevelt. Once installed in Washington, as chief of research and analysis, Langer began recruiting other international studies academics for key positions in OSS. These included several Harvard colleagues, among them Coon and the international economist Edward S. Mason. From Columbia he recruited the Russian historian Geroid T. Robinson; from Chicago, the Middle Eastern archeologist John A. Wilson; from Michigan, the East Asian political scientist Joseph R. Hayden; from Pennsylvania, the Sanskritist W. Norman Brown. Not without reason did the journalist and in-house historian of OSS, Stewart Alsop, characterize Langer's first recruits as "a veritable galaxy of academic stars."[3]

These senior academic appointees in turn staffed their respective sections by recruiting from among their junior colleagues and recent PhDs. Robinson, for example, secured the services of his first Columbia PhD in Russian history, John S. Curtis. From among recent international studies PhDs produced by Harvard came the Soviet economist Abram Bergson and the Middle Eastern historians Richard P. Stebbins and Robert L. Wolff; from among Yale PhDs, the international economist Walt W. Rostow; from Chicago, the Russian geographer Chauncey Harris. Among still younger OSS recruits who later figured prominently in postwar academic life and at least peripherally in international studies were the historians H. Stuart Hughes and Arthur Schlesinger, Jr., the political scientists Evron Kirkpatrick and Roger Hilsman, and the economist Carl Kaysen. Little wonder that for all the cloak-and-dagger machinations commonly associated with the OSS, insiders remember it as having the aura of the senior common room of a distinguished Oxbridge college.[4]

If the OSS was the most glamorous wartime posting for international studies academics—Alsop called it "the last refuge for the well-connected"—other wartime agencies also sought their services eagerly. The Office of War Information had on its staff the Harvard anthropologist Clyde Kluckhohn and the Columbia anthropologist Ruth Benedict, as well as the Harvard East Asian historian John K. Fairbank and his University of Washington counterpart, George E. Taylor. Benedict's study of Japanese culture, *The Chrysanthemum and the Sword*, published in 1946, was undertaken as an OWI assignment. The State Department drew into its expanded wartime staff the Chicago political scientist Quincy Wright, his younger counterpart in international relations at Columbia, Grayson Kirk, the Harvard East Asian historian Edwin Reischauer, and the Columbia Russian historian Philip E. Mosely, as well as a recent Columbia PhD in Latin American history, Bryce Wood. Army Intelligence placed the Chicago historian of ancient China, Herlee Creel, in charge of its Far East section, while Navy Intelligence employed the services of William A. Spurr, a 1940 Columbia PhD in East Asian economics who later taught at Stanford.[5]

Members of the academic international studies community figured prominently among the 5,000 names listed in the "World File of Area and Language Specialists" maintained by the Ethnogeographic Board. The board, a Washington-based clearing house presided over by the Yale Latin American anthropologist Wendell C. Bennett, helped wartime agencies obtain information about specific foreign areas.[6] In sum, although most international studies academics spent the war analyzing data from the field rather than mining the beaches of North Africa or parachuting into the jungles of Burma, they had little reason to be subsequently embarrassed by their wartime activities, as were many academics who served in various propaganda-generating capacities during World War One. At the very least they could respond to the question posed on that earlier war's recruiting posters—"And what did you do during the Great War, Daddy?"—with an enigmatic smile.

Not all members of the prewar academic international studies community resumed membership after the war. A few, among them James H. Gaul, a 1940 Harvard PhD in East European anthropology, who was captured while on an OSS mission behind enemy lines in Austria in 1945, did not survive the war. Others, like Gaul's classmate John Campbell, who had an academic career under way as an East European historian when he joined the State Department in 1942, thereafter "somehow got derailed into government service." So, too, with Clinton Knox, who exchanged a prewar teaching career for a postwar career in the Foreign Service. For still others, among them the political scientist Evron Kirkpatrick and the historian Ray Cline, wartime intelligence service in OSS became a bridge leading from the classroom to the inner sanctum of the Central Intelligence Agency, the postwar successor to OSS.[7]

Others returned to academic careers, but reluctantly. Both Hugh Borton, an East Asianist trained at Columbia, and H. Stuart Hughes, who completed his history PhD at Harvard in 1940, seemed prepared to stay on in the State Department after the war until what Hughes called its "militarization" and what

Borton described as its "purge of almost all the people who knew anything about China" impelled both to leave. Similarly, Jacob C. Hurewitz, who served with the OSS during the war and with the United Nations for five years thereafter, lingered on in government service before returning to Columbia to complete his PhD in Middle Eastern history and join its faculty.[8]

Still others, most conspicuously Langer at Harvard and Mosely at Columbia, resumed their professorships after the war but retained close ties with the State Department, the CIA, and the intelligence community generally. Both became prototypes of the academic/government "in and outer" who came into favor during the Kennedy and Johnson administrations. On regular call to Washington, when not on temporary assignment there, Langer and Mosely no longer devoted much time to teaching, which in Langer's case was a relief, or to research, which Mosely later regretted. On campus, both were largely taken up with seeking and administering funds for international studies programs. Neither was likely to be confused with Mr. Chips and both were prime examples of, as Mosely put it, "people with experience in public service or in the social sciences, or both, who were able to feel their way and identify the needs and point them out."[9] Among post war academic enterprises, international studies had more than its share of such people.

On balance, the exigencies of the war lost far fewer academics to international studies than it won to it. To be sure, not every GI pressed into a language program or into direct contact with alien circumstances was enthralled by the experience. But many did find such unexpected exposure to another culture both exciting and worth pursuing. One way to do so was through graduate training focusing on that part of the world. The fact that such training could be acquired by veterans under the GI Bill hardly lessened its appeal. Again, not all who enrolled in graduate programs in international studies in the immediate postwar years did so because of wartime experiences with or in the area they were studying, but the number for whom this was the case supports the conclusion that World War Two was less a disruption in the history of American international studies than a mighty if redirecting catalyst.

Pursuing graduate work in the area of one's wartime experiences or where the wartime language training could be used was also a way of minimizing the time "lost" in uniform, no small matter to the members of a generation anxious to get on with their lives. As one veteran told the journalist Theodore White during the midst of the 1960 presidential campaign, "I used to think during the war that people who stayed home in their jobs were getting ahead of us. There we were overseas, losing all those years. And there they were at home getting ahead." Yet, as White's source went on to acknowledge, his— and White's—generation did not emerge from the war without its own sense of self-worth, so much so that upon returning to civilian life they found it easy to "feel sorry for the older men. I think we learned something during the war about how to do things; we learned to work in a way the generals didn't understand." [10]

Finally, World War Two did more than expose a generation of Americans to a larger world that they were never again able to ignore. By the nature of its outcome and by the temporary monopoly of nuclear weaponry attending it, the war seemed to impose on that generation a peculiar responsibility to ensure that there not be another major war, in which, unlike the case in "their" war, there would be no victors. And if that were so, did it not follow that academics who had played a significant part in deciding the outcome of the just-ended war, and who were in the process "remade" by it, should play comparably significant parts in the postwar world? Few academics of that generation doubted it, as one of them later acknowledged. "Like so many others I came out of the war effort knowing more clearly what I thought and how I could function," the Harvard East Asianist John K. Fairbank recalls in his autobiography. "This was because the war posed radically new problems of thought and organization. They required creative action." [11]

ई॰ II

The universities to which these international studies academics returned after the war had been no less remade by it. Unlike the Spanish-American War, fought "between semesters," or World War One, the American phase having extended over only one academic year, World War Two lasted long enough to provide ample opportunity for American universities to participate in it. That they enthusiastically chose to do so, despite substantial antiwar campus sentiment well into 1941, confirmed their patriotism, enhanced their standing among Americans generally, and assured them a favored place in postwar affairs.[12]

Wartime Columbia illustrates the extent to which even private universities mobilized. Besides the 500 faculty and staff in uniform or assigned to government agencies during the war, 3,000 others on the Columbia payroll engaged in war-related campus activities. The most famous of these, the Manhattan Project, alone enlisted the services of 250 faculty and a staff of 1,200. But others, drawing heavily upon Columbia's modest resources in international studies, demonstrated still other ways the university was prepared to commit personnel and resources to the task of winning the war.[13]

In addition to a midshipmen's school, which trained and commissioned over 20,000 ensigns, the Navy located its School of Military Government and Administration on the Columbia campus. The SMGA's mission was to train naval officers to administer territories in the Pacific as they were captured from the Japanese and came under American authority. Besides instruction in the technical aspects of military law and government, the school provided intensive language training in Dutch, Malay, Chinese, and Japanese, using the "intensive study" techniques developed at Columbia in the 1930s by the anthropologist Franz Boas and the linguist Edward Sapir. Courses on native institutions and prewar colonial arrangements were offered, and a series of Civil Affairs Handbooks to be used by occupying forces was produced. Faculty from several departments—language and literature, anthropology, history, linguistics, economics, political science—participated in these efforts, which in effect constituted Columbia's first area studies program.[14]

Other universities with equally modest international studies capacities were similarly called upon to expand, intensify, and update them to meet military needs. Princeton, for example, added to its prewar coverage of the ancient Near Eastern languages courses in Arabic and Turkish; Pennsylvania did much the same with respect to its earlier interest in Sanskrit studies, by offering instruction in such modern South Asian languages as Urdu and Hindi. At the Army's behest, Berkeley, Harvard, and Colorado all expanded their language offerings in Russian. At Chicago, a Civil Affairs Training School turned out many of the military administrators for the occupation of Japan; at Yale, the Cross-Cultural Survey, which had been organized in the 1930s, prepared bulletins on Oceania for the Navy. By war's end, Army Specialized Training Schools for language and area study had been established on fifty-five campuses, and Civil Affairs Training Schools, with their own language and foreign-area curricular requirements, on another ten.[15]

Although instituted at the request of various wartime agencies, the area and language programs were staffed and administered by regular university personnel. The SMGA at Columbia, for example, was directed by professor of government Schuyler C. Wallace, who later became the first director of Columbia's School of International Affairs and still later director of the Ford Foundation's Foreign Area Fellowship Program. Yale's wartime efforts in language and area training were directed by then associate professor of government, A. Whitney Griswold, later president of Yale. On the whole, the experience of these cooperative efforts was such as to persuade both the universities and the government agencies involved that similar arrangements would be mutually advantageous come the peace.

Not the least agreeable aspect of this wartime partnership was the underwriting by the federal government of university activities that could not otherwise have been sustained in the face of sharply reduced civilian enrollments. Between 1940 and 1946 Columbia signed 118 research and development contracts with a dozen different government agencies, generating $43 million in the process, no trivial amount when one considers that income from student fees never exceeded $4 million in any single wartime year.[16]

Indeed, as the war reached its final stages, not a few private university administrators who had earlier opposed federal aid to higher education came to conclude that only through a continuation of federal support could private universities hope to resume their prewar functions as institutions for civilian instruction and disinterested scholarship and research. Moreover, some administrators were prepared to argue, with all the passion of recent converts, that their universities had more than earned such support by their unstinting wartime service. "The University knows a different world is in the making," the author of *Columbia in Peace and War* put in none too delicately in 1944, "and it wants to have something to say about that world and about its place in it."[17]

ও III

No American generation has ever been more convinced that there were "lessons" to be derived from its collective experience than that which fought in World War Two. Nor has any been more determined to have the next generation avoid what it took to be its own "mistakes." The principal "lesson" was that the United States could no longer isolate itself from the affairs of other continents; the principal "mistake," that Americans in the interwar period had thought they could. "Global warfare has made plain the fallacy of isolation," Columbia University's president Nicholas Murray Butler declared in 1945, "which, if followed now, would lead the people of the United States to political, economic, and social disaster." Whether or not history was otherwise about to repeat itself, Americans emerged from World War Two, as Ernest R. May has argued, "doing those things which might have been done to prevent World War II from occurring."[18]

This determination manifested itself in several ways, perhaps most clearly in American backing of the United Nations, the International Monetary Fund, and the World Bank. Still later, it can be discerned in the Marshall Plan, the creation of the North Atlantic Treaty Organization, and the decision of the United States to intervene militarily in Korea. This determination took another form as well, that of a vast education campaign to so discredit isolationism as a national policy that the American public would never again be attracted to it. To succeed, such a campaign would have not only to reeducate the unreconstructed isolationists within the voting population but also, and more crucially, to properly instruct the upcoming generation too young to have acquired its internationalism on the battlefield.[19]

Obviously, a campaign of this magnitude could not be staffed exclusively or even primarily by academics. Yet because academics enjoyed public favor and possessed credentials as educators, they were, if they wished to participate, assured a prominent place in the campaign. This was especially the case with international studies academics, whose wartime service and specialized knowledge of those parts of the world Americans were now determined to comprehend made them particularly compelling advocates for internationalism. That they had, in addition to the patriotic promptings common to their generation, special professional considerations for joining in the campaign against resurgent isolationism only made their participation that much more enthusiastic.

Even before the war ended, academics began investing it with retrospective educational value. In 1944 a young University of Chicago diplomatic historian, Walter Johnson, published *The Battle Against Isolation,* an altogether sympathetic account of the Committee to Defend America by Aiding the Allies and its efforts in 1940 and 1941 to convince Americans of the need to intervene in World War Two. Johnson's concluding paragraph both summarized the book's message and provided an early formulation of the "realist" case for American internationalism and, in some later renderings, for American interventionism:

The American people who are suffering from the plague of war must see clearly by the grave lessons of many years that their stubborn isolationist sleep brought neglect of their responsibilities to other nations. A failure to cooperate with the other nations of the world in the years to come will imperil both the present generation and generations to come. A wide, world-embracing view, with all its responsibilities, is theirs to adopt. This is America's self-interest. It is not only her self-interest, but the interest of all peoples and all nations.[20]

Johnson and his colleagues at Chicago—including the political scientist Quincy Wright, the historian Avery Craven, and the anthropologist Robert Redfield, all of whom read drafts of *The Battle Against Isolation* and urged its publication—were well aware of the vogue a revisionist interpretation of American entry into World War One had enjoyed in the 1920s and which, in the 1930s, came to be widely accepted as the definitive interpretation. They further believed that this interpretation, harshly critical of Wilsonian internationalism, had provided much of the intellectual rationale behind opposition to American entry into World War Two. It was not necessary to hold revisionists like Charles A. Beard, Harry Elmer Barnes, and C. Hartley Gratten responsible for America's delay in entering the war—though the Yale diplomatic historian Samuel F. Bemis came very close to doing so—to welcome Johnson's book as a preemptive blow against the possibility of a revisionist interpretation emerging in the wake of World War Two.[21]

This same intent can be reasonably inferred from several of the first postwar accounts describing American entry into World War Two, and in one important instance it was explicitly stated. In early 1946, at the request of and with funding from the Rockefeller Foundation, the Council on Foreign Relations commissioned William L. Langer, then just back at Harvard, to write four volumes on the history of American foreign relations prior to and during World War Two. Langer, in collaboration with his one-time student, S. Everett Gleason, managed to complete only two volumes, the second ending with the Japanese assault on Pearl Harbor, before being diverted back into public service. Nonetheless, *The Challenge to Isolation, 1937–1940,* published in 1950, and *The Undeclared War, 1940–1941,* which appeared three years later, promptly became the standard account of American foreign policymaking during those years. As such, their purpose, as Langer later described it—"to offset any debunking of war aims"—was admirably served.[22]

Langer and Gleason specifically declined to attribute the ascendancy of isolationism in the 1930s to American ignorance of foreign affairs or lack of interest in them. "Never before in their history," they wrote, "had Americans been so well informed about events abroad and never before had they followed them so closely." Nor were they prepared to attribute such ignorance and lack of interest that did exist to failures of the American educational system. Others examining the same period, however, did both by positing an "educational gap" at the heart of their analysis of the shortcomings of American foreign policy, past and present. Among the first was the Stanford diplomatic historian Thomas A. Bailey, in his *The Man in the Street: The Impact of American Public Opinion on Foreign Policy,* which appeared in 1948.[23]

Citing as evidence public opinion polls that had since the mid-1930s contained questions relating to foreign affairs, Bailey firmly concluded that "the people of the United States are notoriously provincial." However tolerable such provincialism might have been in the absence of a creditable foreign threat, Bailey found its persistence into the nuclear age a threat both to American security and to world peace. What he called America's "appalling ignorance of foreign affairs" was not merely embarrassing but fatally dangerous.[24]

For all the evidence Bailey presented to document his contention that, with respect to foreign affairs, Americans remained "nine-tenths ignorant and one-tenth informed," *The*

Man in the Street was less a lamentation than an exhortation. Its epigraph set the book's tone: "Do not be too severe upon the errors of the people, but reclaim them by educating them." Bailey elsewhere assured his readers that their fellow Americans "fortunately can be taught when their interest is aroused."[25]

When Bailey argued, as he did at several points, that "education is our greatest hope," it was not always clear who he assumed needed to be educated. His title would indicate that any such educational effort be aimed at "the man in the street," or those he referred to elsewhere as "the purposeful public." His use of opinion polls as a gauge for calculating American understanding of foreign affairs would similarly suggest that he was calling for the education of Americans generally. He said as much in his conclusion: "We should, above all, undertake the Gargantuan task of raising the educational and apperceptive level of our entire population."[26]

Yet Bailey demonstrated little interest in the actual mechanics of launching such an educational program and not the slightest in securing for such a program the endorsement of those who might be expected to participate in it. On the contrary, his references to the role Protestant clergy and missionaries had traditionally played in informing Americans about the outside world were both critical and disparaging. Nor did his slighting references to the educative function of American journalists suggest that he held out much hope from them in the "Gargantuan task" ahead. That Bailey's only specific recommendation called upon colleges and universities to "offer more and better work on foreign languages, history, geography, foreign affairs, comparative government, international economics, international law, and international organizations" need not be construed as occupationally self-serving, but it does indicate the narrowness of his operational definition of the term "education."[27]

The disparity between the comprehensiveness of Bailey's diagnosis—that most Americans remained perilously ignorant of an impinging world—and the specificity of his remedy—that more university work be offered in international studies—was by no means peculiar to his analysis. Others writing in the late 1940s about the threat of a resurgent isolationism and how it best could be met were just as likely, once having identified the threat as national in scope, to proceed to advocate corrective measures aimed at a single audience, that found in the universities.[28]

Yet as the then vice president of the Carnegie Corporation, John W. Gardner, pointed out in a 1948 article there existed at least three different audiences, each with significantly different but equally important educational needs. They were (1) adult citizens (i.e., Bailey's "man in the street"); (2) college-age students; and (3) "experts highly trained with respect to one or another area of the world." Having performed this useful service of audience differentiation, Gardner then, however, devoted the remainder of his article to the needs of the third audience, "that pitifully small corps of experts on each of the various areas of the world."[29]

Whereas Gardner lumped all "experts" into one category, others closer to the academic scene argued that they properly fell into two. Frederick S. Dunn, the director of Yale's Institute of International Studies, distinguished between "experts as scholars," those doing research in international studies in universities, and "experts as practitioners," those formulating international policy in government and business. The distinction was not intended invidiously, at least in this instance, but was intended to show that Dunn's principal recommendation—an increase in graduate facilities in international studies—would serve the interests not only of the academic international studies enterprise but of the wider society as well. "In any case," Dunn wrote, "the number of complex international questions now facing the nation is huge and the number of people equipped to handle them is woefully small."[30]

As had Bailey and Gardner, Dunn cited the need to improve the education of the general citizenry "in the fundamentals of international relations." But unlike them, he acknowledged some misgivings on the part of his colleagues to undertake the task of "preparing the layman for effective thinking about foreign affairs. There has even been," he admitted, "some doubt about the academic respectability of public education in the field." One such colleague, Columbia's Grayson Kirk, did not so much argue against popular education as argue for the concentration of available resources upon the task of expanding graduate training opportunities, along with creating separate departments of international relations, his own speciality.[31]

Thus, as academics made finer and finer distinctions among the audiences whose needs could be met within the university proper, consideration of the needs of the general citizenry or even those of undergraduates became more and more perfunctory. Perhaps nowhere was this tendency more marked than in the series of surveys published by the Committee on World Area Research. An outgrowth of the wartime Ethnogeographic Board, the committee consisted of the Yale Latin Americanist Wendell Bennett, the Michigan East Asian geographer Robert B. Hall, the Columbia Russian historian Geroid T. Robinson, and Harvard's leading promoter of regional studies, the historian Donald C. McKay. Although the committee's self-provided mandate was nothing if not specific—the perpetuation and expansion of the area-focused, multidisciplinary arrangements adopted by their respective universities during the war—it proceeded to make the case for area studies in terms of the national interest.[32]

In the committee's report on its initial survey, published in 1947, Hall cited "the woeful lack of area experts, however defined," as having greatly inhibited the American war effort. "It is a high compliment that the job was done so well," he argued, "but few would contend that we should not have been equipped to do it much better." Nothing less than "the lesson of this experience," he continued, had prompted him and his colleagues on the committee to call for "the launching of scores of area programs." It also inspired Hall to render the argument that an expanded international studies enterprise was essential to the national interest in its most succinct form: "we must know if we are to survive."[33]

A report on another of the committee's surveys, written this time by Wendell Bennett, appeared in 1951. Like Hall four years earlier, Bennett concerned himself almost exclusively with the need to expand opportunities for graduate training and research in area studies. He had little to say about the needs of undergraduates, nothing about those of the American public generally. Unlike Hall, however, he made the case for area studies primarily on academic grounds, perhaps assuming that the national interest argument had already been established. But a case for more area studies programs which depended on the argument of continuing academic need had, as Bennett's rendering of it indicated, already begun to present problems for those who would make it.[34]

Despite the fact that he used more exclusive criteria than had Hall, Bennett identified twenty-nine integrated area programs in 1950, almost twice the number Hall had found. Approximately 500 faculty members were attached to these programs, along with more than 800 graduate students. Another 400 faculty were engaged in area studies on campuses where area studies programs did not as yet exist but were contemplated. This was a long way from 1941 when, as Hall had reported, "for all practical purposes there were no trained area specialists." Bennett acknowledged as much by stating that "area interests and facilities have increased since the war." In doing so, he confronted for perhaps the first time the problem that would confront every promoter of academic international studies during the next twenty years: How do you keep the palpable fact of the rapid expansion of academic international studies programs from undercutting the argument that, as Bennett put it, "much still needs to be done"?[35]

If Bennett was the first international studies academic to face the problem of arguing for more in the face of much, he proved to be equal to it. Rather than dwell on those parts of the enterprise experiencing the most rapid growth, which in the late 1940s included the study of Russia, East Asia, and Latin America, Bennett focused on those parts lagging behind, such as the study of South Asia, Africa, and the Middle East. By discussing growth in relative rather than absolute terms, Bennett and subsequent promoters of international studies were always able to point to parts of the enterprise that were not prospering as mightily as others and were therefore in need of compensatory attention.[36] In the military this strategy is called "pulling up the rear"; in Matthew 19:30, "The last shall be first."

Similarly, Bennett emphasized that even currently flourishing areas presented serious problems that might inhibit future growth. Difficulties in securing permission to do research in Russia and China, for example, did not bode well for Russian and Chinese studies. On the other hand, Latin American studies, which presented no shortage of research opportunities, suffered from being scattered among dozens of American universities, with the most distinguished reluctant to commit themselves to the kinds of full-fledged programs they enthusiastically supported in Russian or East Asian studies. Disciplinary coverage of a given area, being almost necessarily uneven—for example, too many historians in Russian studies and too few in South Asian studies—could be counted on to be in need of corrective attention. As for the availability of language training in a given world area, it could safely be described as inadequate as long as all the area's principal languages were not equally provided for. In the case of East Asia, for example, Bennett pointed out that while Chinese was regularly offered at several universities, Japanese was less so, Korean and Mongolian seldom, Tibetan hardly ever, and so on.[37]

Promoters of Chinese studies in the 1960s would even be able to qualify Bennett's sanguine view of the state of Chinese language studies in the United States by pointing out that American universities did not train their students to "read Chinese" but "only some kinds of Chinese." By then still more alarming gaps had been revealed in the academic international studies enterprise, such as the uncertain availability of instruction in Uzbek and Ugaritic. These gaps, too, would have to be closed, if not, as Hall argued, because the national interest required it, then, with Bennett, on grounds of academic equity. Either way, the case for academic international studies developed and advanced by the postwar generation of international studies academics proved to be sufficient to its day— and some twenty years more.[38]

§» IV

All who wrote about academic international studies in the years immediately after World War Two deemed it worthy of financial support; they also agreed that it was not ever likely to be financially self-supporting. Given the national interest with which they imbued the enterprise, their contention that, as Bennett put it, "ultimately, the federal government must furnish support for the type of training that its activities demand," reasonably followed. Bennett specifically suggested a federal program for international studies "modelled on those for studies of atomic energy," while others cited Vannevar Bush's case for federal support of science contained in his *Science: The Endless Frontier* (1945) as equally applicable to their enterprise. This was not entirely wishful thinking. President Truman's 1946 letter of appointment to the members of his Commission on Higher Education had questioned "the adequacy of curricula, particularly in fields of international affairs," and the commission's final report, *Higher Education for American Democracy* (1948), cited the need to support the study of non-Western cultures in endorsing federal support for research in the social sciences and humanities. But direct federal support for international studies, first provided by Title VI of the National Defense Education Act of 1959, was still a decade away.[39]

The international studies enterprise did, of course, indirectly benefit from other federal programs, such as the GI Bill, which financed the graduate training of hundreds of international studies PhDs in the late 1940s and early 1950s. So, too, the Fulbright Act, as passed in 1946 and amended in 1948, provided American international studies academics and graduate students, among others, with opportunities for research and study abroad. Promulgation of the Truman Doctrine in 1947 and the Point Four program in 1949, both of which committed the American government to extensive overseas technical assistance programs in which American universities would be important participants, further encouraged, among university officials looking to Washington to underwrite their international activities, the belief that help was on the way.[40]

Yet the mechanics of these programs, particularly the university contract system, had still to be worked out. In 1951, in the midst of the Korean War, a proposal made jointly by the Social Science Research Council and the American Council of Learned Societies to have American universities train 1,000 Far Eastern specialists at government expense failed to secure congressional approval. A year later, Dwight D. Eisenhower—lately president of Columbia University—successfully campaigned for the presidency on a Republican platform flatly opposed to federal aid to education.

Until federal support materialized, Bennett acknowledged, the cost of building international studies programs would have to be borne primarily by the universities themselves. Here, too, means were limited. Private universities of the size, wealth, and distinction of Harvard, Columbia, and Chicago, which together accounted for nine of Bennett's twenty-nine integrated programs, were committed to sustaining their existing programs, although they might in time make operational a few more. Similarly, smaller private universities like Princeton, Pennsylvania, and Northwestern, were not about to abandon their already distinguished programs in, respectively, Middle Eastern, South Asian, and African studies. But private universities, no matter how large, wealthy, or distinguished, all faced in the late 1940s and early 1950s the prospect of declining enrollments and revenues as the GI Bill-supported veterans gave way to a smaller generation born during the depression. However persuaded of the national need for and academic efficacy of international studies, administrators hesitated committing limited resources to expensive programs that gave no promise of ever sustaining themselves by enrollments.

Still more caution was incumbent upon administrators of public universities, with state leglislators to answer to for what might be perceived to be their curricular folly. The case for specific international studies programs based on local considerations, such as those the University of Washington could make for expanding its program in Far Eastern studies or Berkeley or Texas could make for sustaining their Latin American interests, assured those programs continuing state support. So, too, arguments put forward by administrators and faculty at Midwestern state universities that involvement in overseas technical assistance programs represented a logical extension of "the land grant service tradition" could be expected to help in persuading state legislatures of the need to internationalize their curricula. Still, it was far easier for President Herman B. Wells of Indiana University and President John Hannah of Michigan State to be convinced of the importance of developing international programs, not least because such programs represented a shortcut to institutional parity with older and more distinguished private universities, than it was for them to persuade legislators in Indianapolis and Lansing that the cost of providing graduate instruction in Serbo-Croatian, Swahili, and Telegu were fair charges on Indiana and Michigan taxpayers.

That left outside private sources. Early in the century, individual benefactors—such as General Horace Walpole Carpentier, who endowed chairs in Chinese studies at Berkeley and Columbia; Philip Crane, who subsidized the career of the Chicago Sovietologist Samuel Harper; and the Charles M. Hall estate, which provided the funds to establish the Harvard-Yenching Institute in Cambridge in 1928—had been crucial in getting academic international studies under way.[41] In the 1930s the Rockefeller Foundation became a principal financial backer of the enterprise, both by direct grants, such as those earlier to Chicago for its Oriental Institute, and by indirect support funneled through the American Council of Learned Societies.

This support, together with the effective collaboration of ACLS secretary Mortimer Graves and David Stevens of the

Rockefeller Foundation, had led directly to the establishment of six world area committees, all of which by the end of the 1930s were dispensing fellowship support, organizing summer language institutes, and generally raising the level of collective identity among those engaged in international studies. If the sums involved were modest by later standards—Rockefeller support for academic international studies between 1934 and 1942 totaled less than $1 million—they did indicate that others besides international studies academics thought their enterprise worthy of support.[42]

Rockefeller backing for international studies increased significantly during World War Two. In 1944 grants totaling $260,000 went to Stanford, Berkeley, Pomona, and the University of Washington for expansion of existing programs in Far Eastern and Russian studies. The following year, as a result of negotiations begun by Geroid Robinson, then chief of the East European section of research and analysis at OSS, the Rockefeller Foundation made a grant of $250,000 to Columbia for the establishment of its Russian Institute. By 1951 the Rockefeller Foundation's investment in academic international studies totaled $6 million.[43]

The Carnegie Corporation's interest in international studies, if slower in materializing, developed rapidly after World War Two. In 1945, Carnegie grants relating to foreign affairs totaled only $257,000, with most of this going to such nonacademic organizations as the Council on Foreign Relations and the Carnegie Endownment for International Peace. The following year, however, Devereux C. Josephs, president of the Carnegie Corporation, committed the foundation to helping "make the country more literate and more emotionally mature in international affairs," which meant, he emphasized, "we have got to learn, and to learn we have to study."[44]

In 1947 Carnegie made grants for international studies to a dozen universities, the largest of which was $125,000 to the University of Michigan for its Center for Japanese Studies. In 1948 Harvard received what was up to then the largest single grant ever made for academic international studies, $740,000, for support of its just-opened Russian Research Center. A second Carnegie grant that year, for $130,000, went to the Social Science Research Council to launch a program of national fellowships for graduate-level training in foreign area studies. Between 1947 and 1951 Carnegie grants for academic international studies exceeded $2.5 million.[45]

Yet as eager as some officials at both foundations were to expand such support, perhaps most conspicuously John W. Gardner and James A. Perkins at Carnegie, neither foundation was prepared to assume the primary financial responsibility for "the launching of scores of area programs" that the Committee on World Area Research had called for. Even had their combined resources been equal to such a task, each had no less pressing and substantially older claims on its resources which made it unwilling to concede to academic international studies more than a secondary place among its claimants.[46]

What international studies academics needed in the early 1950s, if the momentum its enterprise acquired in the wake of World War Two was to be sustained through the decade and beyond, was a new source of outside financial support. Rather than provide stopgap support tied to its own needs, this new source ought to provide support that was long-term and relatively unencumbered. Ideally, from the perspective of those within the enterprise, such a source not only should be willing and able to support the enterprise to the limits of its needs, but should allow those within it a considerable voice in specifying those needs. Another generation of academics would likely have concluded that no such ideal benefactor existed and tried to make do with less. But this generation proceeded, with an assurance perhaps given only to those "blessed" by war, to find—in the Ford Foundation—its reasonable approximation.

ॐ V

The financial uncertainties of the period notwithstanding, the half-dozen years following World War Two marked the "takeoff" of American international studies as an academic enterprise. Before then the growth of the enterprise had been irregular and often lagged behind that of the overall academic enterprise; after then it was uninterrupted and consistently exceeded overall academic growth.[47]

Consideration of the postwar growth of academic international studies requires a larger institutional sample than that used to describe the prewar enterprise. Accordingly, the earlier sample of six institutions has been expanded to include ten others. All were drawn from among the fifty largest producers of PhDs in the mid-1970s, and most contained several departments ranked "distinguished" in the various departmental-reputation rankings compiled in the last quarter-century.[48] In addition to favoring large universities with distinguished reputations, the expanded sample also favors universities where international studies constituted an important part of their graduate offering and contributed to their reputation.

A final consideration in compiling the expanded sample was historical. To provide it with a measure of generational diversity, five universities were included which began producing PhDs on a significant scale (i.e., more than 1 percent of the annual national total) before 1900; six which began to do so between 1900 and 1940; and the remaining five, only after 1945. The distinction among these three generational clusters of universities—which will be called "Ancients," "In-Betweens," and "Moderns"—makes it possible to observe relative developments within the sample, without getting down to institution-by-institution comparisons, in which local and transitory factors detract attention from those affecting the overall enterprise. The list of universities in the sample, separated by generation, is given in table 5.1.

The production of PhDs of all kinds dropped sharply during World War Two, so that by 1945 the annual output of international studies PhDs among the sample universities was less than half that of 1940—twenty-seven as compared to sixty-seven. What is significant, however, is the alacrity with which the enterprise recouped its wartime losses. The production of international studies PhDs exceeded prewar levels by 1948.

TABLE 5.1. Sample Universities by Generation

	Decade of Entry as PhD Producer[a]
Ancients (before 1900)	
Yale	1860s
Cornell	1870s
Harvard	1870s
Columbia	1880s
Chicago	1890s
In-Betweens (1900–1940)	
Wisconsin	1910s
Berkeley	1910s
Michigan	1920s
Stanford	1920s
Pittsburgh	1930s
Texas	1930s
Moderns (after 1945)	
Indiana	1940s
UCLA	1940s
Washington (Seattle)	1940s
Michigan State	1950s
Syracuse	1950s

Source: Bernard Berelson, *Graduate Eduction in the United States* (New York: McGraw-Hill, 1960), p. 93, and author's calculations.
[a] Decade when PhD production of the university exceeded 1 percent of national production.

During the next three years, the production of international studies PhDs expanded at an annual rate one-third greater than did its constituent disciplines. Even allowing for the war years, between 1940 and 1951 academic international studies increased its production of PhDs at a rate of more than 15 percent a year, rapidly enough to double output every seven years (table 5.2). The doubling time for the constituent disciplines during the takeoff of international studies was more than ten years.

For all the quantitative impressiveness of this postwar surge in academic international studies, the enterprise in 1951 looked very much as it had in 1940, only bigger. It remained, for

TABLE 5.2. Number of PhDs Awarded in the Social Sciences and Humanities and in International Studies in Selected Years from 1940 to 1951

	PhDs Awarded in All Social Sciences and Humanities by All U.S. Universities	PhDs Awarded by Sample Universities[a]		
		All Social Sciences and Humanities	International Studies	Percentage
1940	933	508	67	13
1945	517	211	27	13
1948	1,273	510	71	14
1951	1,967	1,049	181	17

Source: Association of Research Libraries, *Doctoral Dissertations Accepted by American Universities, 1939–1940, 1944–1945, 1947–1948, 1950–1951* (New York: H. W. Wilson, 1941, 1946, 1949, 1952).
[a] Sample universities are listed in table 5.1.

TABLE 5.3. International Studies PhDs, 1940 and 1951, by Generational Clusters

	Clusters			
	1940		1951	
Sample Universities[a]	N	%	N	%
Ancients	41	61	119	66
In-Betweens	25	37	54	30
Moderns	1	1	8	4
Total	67	100	181	100
Other U.S. universities (estimated)	13		44	
U.S. totals	80		225	

Source: see table 5.2.
[a] Sample universities are listed in table 5.1.

example, concentrated within the same handful of universities that had accommodated it during the previous half-century (table 5.3). If anything, the quantitative dominance of Harvard and Columbia had become even more marked; they increased their share of the sample universities' production of international studies PhDs from one-third in 1940 (23 of 67) to nearly one-half (89 of 181) in 1951. In 1940 just four institutions—

Harvard, Columbia, Chicago, and Berkeley—accounted for more than half the estimated total national production of international studies PhDs; eleven years later the same four universities still did so.

Nor had the disciplinary representation within the enterprise been dramatically altered. History remained the dominant discipline in 1951, as it had been in 1940 (table 5.4). What ground history had lost was to its immediate neighbors, political science and economics, rather than to the humanities, as reflected

TABLE 5.4. International Studies PhDs Awarded by the Sample Universities, 1940 and 1951, by Field and Discipline

	1940		1951	
	N	*%*	*N*	*%*
Social sciences	*54*	*81*	*146*	*81*
History	28	42	54	30
Political science	8	12	30	17
Economics	9	13	35	19
Anthropology	4	6	23	13
Sociology	5	7	4	2
Humanities	*13*	*19*	*35*	*19*
Language and literature	7	10	28	15
Other humanities	6	9	7	4
Total	*67*	*100*	*181*	*100*

Source: see table 5.2.

in the fact that, despite a substantial increase in the number of international studies PhDs in language and literature, the place of the humanities overall in the enterprise in 1951 was almost exactly what it had been in 1940.

The distribution of international studies PhDs among areas in 1951 also differed little from that eleven years earlier (table 5.5). In 1940, Latin America and East Asia were the two most studied areas; in 1951, Latin America had increased its lead, although Russia and East Europe had barely edged out East Asia as the second most studied area. The Middle East and South Asia attracted relatively less attention than before the war, while Africa remained terra incognita. The increase in

TABLE 5.5. International Studies PhDs Awarded by Sample
Universities, 1940 and 1951, by Area Focus

	1940		1951	
	N	%	N	%
Latin America	15	22	54	30
Russia and East Europe	9	13	31	17
East Asia	15	22	29	16
Middle East	13	19	24	13
International or other	3	4	17	9
South Asia	7	10	7	4
Canada	5	7	7	4
Africa	0	0	3	2
Total	67	97	181	95

Source: see table 5.2.
Note: Percentages do not add up to 100 because of rounding.

"international" or nonregionally-specific PhDs between 1940
and 1951 was attributable primarily to political scientists addressing topics in international relations and international organizations.

Overall, then, the takeoff of academic international studies
in the half-dozen years after World War Two was launched
from the institutional and disciplinary bases that had been long
established, and from the study of world areas that had long
attracted American scholarly interest. If anything, the enterprise entered the 1950s more institutionally and disciplinarily
concentrated, and no less narrowly focused in its regional interests, than it had been in the 1920s or 1930s. It would not
remain so for long.

CHAPTER 6

TO ADVANCE HUMAN WELFARE

We'll build this [the Ford Motor Company River Rouge plant] as well as we know how, and if we don't use it, somebody will. Anything that is good enough will be used.

HENRY FORD, SR., 1913[1]

It may be argued that it does not matter who provides a needy enterprise with its money, only how the enterprise uses it. Balanced against this "money is money" view is its opposite, "calling the tune," which holds that source determines use. If neither of these extreme positions captures the essence of the relationship between the academic international studies enterprise and the Ford Foundation in the 1950s and 1960s, each does point to an element present in that relationship. Implicit in the "calling the tune" argument is the assumption that benefactors have their own purposes to serve in giving away money and that, as a rule, they do not give money away in a manner to do violence to those purposes. Implicit in the "money is money" argument is that prospective recipients can always refuse to take money from would-be benefactors who impose, in pursuit of their purposes, unacceptable conditions as to its use. Just as there are no wholly disinterested benefactors, so there are no wholly innocent recipients.

From the above it follows that the best situation a needy enterprise could hope for is a benefactor whose purposes coincide with its own. "Next best" would be a benefactor whose initially different purposes first yield to those of the enterprise and then, in time, are set aside to permit the benefactor to adopt the enterprise's purposes as its own. The resultant relationship would not be one where benefactor turned recipient to its purposes, but the reverse. For all its complexities and evolving character, the relationship between the academic international studies enterprise and the Ford Foundation from the early 1950s to the mid-1960s was—from the enterprise's perspective—of this "next best" sort.

ะ I

The Ford Foundation began as a family charity incorporated under Michigan statutes in 1936, ostensibly to coordinate the previously ad hoc philanthropic activities of Henry Ford, Sr., and his son, Edsel. It was also intended to perpetuate family control over the Ford Motor Company after New Deal tax legislation had made family retention of all company stock financially prohibitive. The pattern of grant making during the Ford Foundation's early years belies the existence of any large philanthropic vision behind its creation.[2]

Henry Ford believed that charity began at home, or at least close by. Of the $16 million expended by the Ford Foundation prior to his death in 1947, nearly all went to local institutions in which he or members of his family had a personal interest. These included the Detroit Symphony, the Henry Ford Hospital in Dearborn, and Greenfield Village, Ford's horse 'n buggy retreat from the motorized civilization he had helped create. Whereas Rockefeller Foundation benefactions to various Chinese projects alone amounted to $43 million by 1946, and Carnegie Corporation support for such activities as the Carnegie Endowment for International Peace began with its founding in 1913, the Ford Foundation, except for a modest grant to China Relief in 1941, consistently declined to support overseas projects or American-based activities identified with the cause of internationalism.[3]

Such provincialism closely reflected, if it was not mandated by, Ford's personal views. Disillusioned by his own quixotic efforts at international peacemaking during World War One, Ford had become increasingly xenophobic (and more openly anti-Semitic) in the 1920s. In the 1930s he espoused the isolationist if not pro-German views of his friend Charles A. Lindbergh; in 1940 he aligned himself with Lindbergh and other isolationists by joining the America First Committee and opposing American aid to the Allies.[4]

The early Ford Foundation also differed from both the Rockefeller Foundation and the Carnegie Corporation by its almost total indifference to the financial needs of American higher education. Having made do himself with only a grade-school education, Ford did not send his son to college. A great admirer of Thomas A. Edison, Ford shared more than a little of his hero's principled anti-intellectualism and suspicion of the well educated. Whereas both of the John D. Rockefellers devoted vast amounts of time and committed vast sums of money in support of private universities, Ford limited himself to occasional grants to Detroit-area colleges. One can only wonder what he must have thought of Andrew Carnegie going to all the trouble involved in establishing the Carnegie Foundation for the Advancement of Teaching, the purpose of which was to ease the financial plight of academics in their retirement! The irony here, of course, is that two of the most conspicuous and no doubt intended omissions in the philanthropic agenda of the Ford Foundation during its benefactor's lifetime—international activities and support of American academics—would within a decade of his death be among its preoccupying concerns.[5]

The long-expected death of the ninety-two-year-old Ford in 1947 presented complications by its occasion. His presumptive heir, Edsel, had died four years earlier, though his estate had yet to be settled. Like his father's, Edsel's holdings of Ford Motor Company stock were to go to the Ford Foundation. Thus both estates were to be settled just when the Ford Motor Company, rejuvenated under the direction of Henry Ford II,

Edsel's eldest son, was earning spectacular profits, which meant that the stock transfer about to take place would transform a heretofore modest family philanthropy into by far the richest private foundation in the world.[6]

ɞ II

Henry Ford II, was, in addition to being head of the Ford family and president of the Ford Motor Company, chairman of the five-member board of trustees of the Ford Foundation. In this last capacity he asked Dr. Karl Compton, the president of MIT and senior nonfamily trustee, to determine how the foundation might best utilize its imminent windfall. Compton promptly turned to his wartime associate at the MIT Radiation Laboratory and then chairman of the Rand Corporation, H. Rowan Gaither, to organize a study committee that would produce an advisory report for the Ford trustees' consideration.[7]

Formally submitted to the foundation's board of trustees at its September 1950 meeting, the *Report of the Study for the Ford Foundation on Policy and Programs,* thereafter known as the Gaither Report, was the joint effort of Gaither, eight committee members, and a staff of four. Together and separately they had spent six months soliciting testimony from more than a thousand persons as to how the Ford Foundation might "most effectively and intelligently put its resources to work for human welfare." From this advice they concluded that "the most important problems of human welfare now lie in the realm of democratic society, in man's relation to man, in human relations and social organization." So persuaded, they proceeded to stake out five broad program areas for the Ford Foundation's special attention:

    I. The Establishing of Peace
   II. The Strengthening of Democracy
  III. The Strengthening of the Economy
  IV. Education in a Democratic Society
   V. Individual Behavior and Human Relations

While carefully acknowledging the established claims of other foundations, particularly those of the Rockefeller Foundation in the biomedical sciences, the agenda the Gaither Report proposed for the Ford Foundation could hardly have been faulted for narrowness of philanthropic vision of failure of philanthropic nerve. It represented, as a critical student of American foundations later acknowledged, not only "the finest statement of the case for creative philanthropy yet produced," but "the quintessence of the liberal, internationalist, socially concerned outlook of that period."[8]

In retrospect, perhaps the most distinctive feature of the Gaither Report was its pervasive internationalism. At several points it stipulated that the responsibilities of the Ford Foundation should be global in scope. The international implications of each of the five program areas were discussed at length. Among the goals assigned to Program I, The Establishing of Peace, for example, was overcoming "our own ignorance of other peoples—their traditions, institutions, and aspirations." Even Program V, Individual Behavior and Human Relations, held out the prospect of, "in addition to contributing to scientific knowledge by testing it in the various cultures of mankind," contributing "to the betterment of international relations."[9]

The internationalism of the Gaither Report reflected the outlook not only of those who wrote it but also of those for whom it was written. Henry Ford's charge to the committee that it consider problems confronting "the people of this country and mankind in general" imbued the undertaking with an internationalist perspective from the outset. Though its chairman and some other members of the foundation's board of trustees might have been made uncomfortable by some of the Gaither Report's recommendations relating to the behavioral sciences, they were to a man supportive of its internationalist thrust. Like those who subsequently joined the board in the early 1950s, perhaps most notably John J. McCloy, those who were expected to vote on the report's recommendations—Ford, Compton, dean of the Harvard Business School Donald K.

David, *Minneapolis Star and Tribune* publisher John Cowles, and the chairman of W. R. Grace and Company, Charles E. Wilson—were for the most part Republicans, but Republicans distinctly unsympathetic to the isolationist views espoused by Republicans like Ohio's Senator Robert A. Taft.[10]

The recommendations contained in the Gaither Report were unanimously adopted by the trustees at their September 1950 meeting. As if to underline their commitment to internationalism, they used the occasion of their next meeting, in December, to elect Paul G. Hoffman as president of the foundation. Prior to his election, Hoffman, earlier president of the Studebaker Automobile Company, had been the chief administrator of the Marshall Plan. In that capacity he had achieved a worldwide reputation for having "helped save Europe." Indeed, so great was Hoffman's zeal for international cooperation that some fellow Republicans judged it excessive, a view reinforced by Hoffman's assaults on Senator Taft during the 1952 Republican primaries and his championing of the presidential candidacy of General Dwight D. Eisenhower.[11]

The staff that Hoffman gathered in Pasadena, California, to where he moved the Foundation's headquarters from Detroit, shared his internationalism. Several of his earliest appointments, including Richard M. Bissell, Milton Katz, Joseph M. McDaniel, Waldemar A. Nielson, and William H. Nims, had worked with him on the Marshall Plan. Others, like Bernard L. Gladieux and John B. Howard, were self-described "Truman refugees" who came from Washington, where they had identified with the foreign policy initiatives of the Marshall and Acheson years at the State Department. Other early appointments included Melvin J. Fox, who joined the foundation after working with U.S. Citizens for U.N. Day and before that with the Carnegie Endowment for International Peace; Carl Spaeth, dean of the Stanford Law School and a State Department adviser on Latin American affairs; and George F. Kennan, a career Foreign Service officer and historian, who served as a foundation consultant in 1951 between ambassadorships to Yugoslavia and the Soviet Union. Chester C.

Davis, a banker and a member of the Gaither study committee, whom Hoffman brought in as an associate director, had long been associated with the cause of international agricultural development. The only prominent Hoffman appointee not a longtime certified internationalist was his vice president, Robert M. Hutchins, who in the 1930s as chancellor of the University of Chicago had been an isolationist. His postwar views, however, accorded with Hoffman's and were espoused with all the fervor of a recent convert.[12]

III

The prevailing consensus in Pasadena that the philanthropic responsibilities of the Ford Foundation were to be international in scope did not extend to how these responsibilities were to be given programmatic form. A reconstruction of these early policy deliberations, drawing heavily upon the subsequently recorded accounts of several participants, attests to the variety of approaches that were under consideration during those first heady months, when it seemed to some "that there was nothing, including world peace, which several hundred million dollars couldn't bring about if they were properly spent."[13]

Predictably, Hoffman's was the most ambitious proposal put forward. Hoffman envisioned the Ford Foundation doing for the rest of the world what the Marshall Plan had done for Europe: to provide it with the technical and administrative wherewithal to acquire a level of economic well-being that would allow the development of democratic institutions, thereby effectively eliminating both the threat and the appeal of communism. Hoffman had always insisted that the Marshall Plan was not an exercise in disinterested philanthropy but an imaginative weapon in the Cold War the United States was waging with the Soviet Union; his plans for the Ford Foundation contained this same strain of ideological combativeness.[14]

Hoffman proposed that the foundation begin with India,

which he designated as the "keystone" of its overseas activities. Several factors figured in the selection of India: the magnitude of the human problems there; the opportunity presented by the recent departure of the British and the expressed desire of Indian officials for American assistance; the fact that the Indian administrative class and much of its political leadership spoke English. That India also was viewed by Hoffman as "the underbelly of China" and therefore both strategically and ideologically crucial to his perception of American national interests also made the choice logical if not foregone. So it was there, Hoffman announced in his first *President's Report* to the trustees, that the Foundation would begin to meet its international responsibilities "by assisting people in some critical areas to achieve a better standard of living." [15]

If Hoffman was persuaded that world peace could be bought, others participating in these early deliberations were not. George Kennan, particularly, "didn't think there was anything that could be done in the international field, by a foundation, that could essentially change the prospects for peace." He proposed instead a much more modest program, both in global reach and cost, that would have the Ford Foundation support study projects designed "to improve the policies of our government, the degree of profundity of analysis and maturity." [16]

Specifically, Kennan had in mind the establishment of a permanent study group in Princeton—his alma mater—to assist the policy planning staff of the State Department, which he had set up and directed prior to coming to the foundation. The proposed Princeton group would undertake precisely those studies that the policy planning staff would have done, Kennan later recalled, had it "the leisure time, the detachment, and the staff facilities to do them." Out of this collaboration Kennan hoped would come what, in his 1951 Walgreen lectures at the University of Chicago, he argued the United States had lacked for more than a half-century: "an adequately stated and widely accepted theoretical foundation to underpin the conduct of our external relations." [17]

Others shared Kennan's doubts about the efficacy of Hoffman's overseas development projects without endorsing his proposal that the Ford Foundation fulfill its international responsibilities by underwriting the staff work necessary for a reformulation of American foreign policy. Similarly, some agreed with Kennan that there was a need for an educational program that would address itself to the implications of the new role the United States had in world affairs, but proposed that such a program be aimed at the American public, to which Kennan's policymakers were answerable. Among those who supported this approach, none did so with more fervor than Hoffman's vice president, Robert M. Hutchins.

As chancellor of the University of Chicago from 1929 to 1950, Hutchins was regarded by friend and foe alike as one of American higher education's leading inside critics. The dissatisfaction he expressed with the general level of undergraduate teaching which he found at Chicago—and which he assumed existed at other leading universities—and his vigorous support of a "general education" curriculum were taken by many senior faculty at Chicago and elsewhere to reflect a more fundamental disagreement with the standing order within American universities. The fact that he was also a strong advocate of such nonacademic educational ventures as the Great Books seminars, which he and his Chicago colleague Mortimer Adler had vigorously promoted, further marked him as no friend of the disciplinary specialists who ruled most university departments.

Once at Ford, Hutchins promptly proposed the creation of a Fund for the Advancement of Education and a Fund for Adult Education, which, once authorized and funded by the Ford trustees, were to operate independently under Hutchins' direction. Both were envisioned as supporting projects in education designed primarily to develop "intellectual capacity and independent judgment," not "technical, specialized, or professional proficiency." While both funds had the potential of supporting all manner of nontraditional educational initiatives in international affairs, the Fund for Adult Education was the principal mechanism Hutchins intended for the support of projects that would simultaneously "broaden the cultural horizons of the American people" and enlarge "the base of public understanding of international problems."[18]

Of the early proposals, the one closest to meeting the expressed needs of the academic international studies enterprise was that advanced by Carl Spaeth, who joined the Ford Foundation in early 1952 as its first head of overseas activities. In his previous capacity as a consultant on Latin American affairs, according to an early associate in Pasadena, Spaeth had become a critic of "quickie overseas projects" and an advocate of the "long-term" view that if the United States wanted to accomplish anything internationally, it "had better be much more thorough and long-range in the way it acquired competence about foreign countries." Without dissociating itself from the ends identified in the Hoffman, Kennan, or Hutchins proposals, Spaeth's proposal at least implied that before the competences needed by those in overseas development, by government officials, and by the general public could be extended to them, they must first be acquired by larger numbers of American academics.[19]

All these proposals were less likely put forward as competing strategies than as complementary approaches for meeting the foundation's assumed but as yet undefined international responsibilities. Moreover, when each acquired some programmatic form, considerable overlap would exist among them. Yet because each proposal recommended that the Ford Foundation meet its international responsibilities by spending money in a particular geographical and institutional context, and each had its own immediate beneficiaries, those advancing the proposals in Pasadena represented the interests of four different, and at least potentially competitive, constituencies.

Hoffman's proposal for overseas development projects would require that the bulk of the foundation's grants in the international area be made abroad, either to foreign governments directly or to private agencies staffed with foreign nationals who would administer the grants. Some funds, of course, would be expended in the United States for materiel and for the training of those foreign nationals and Americans involved in the projects. But by one account Hoffman intended that one-third of the Ford Foundation's total annual expenditures would be made overseas. Not surprisingly, a trip he made to India and Pakistan in 1951 struck some back in Pasadena as having all the appearance and some of the reality of a visit among his constituents.[20]

Kennan's, Hutchins', and Spaeth's proposals, on the other hand, envisioned the bulk of the foundation's "international" funds being spent in the United States, with American organizations administering them and Americans as their immediate beneficiaries. Kennan targeted the State Department and the Foreign Service Association as likely administrative agencies if his proposal were to be funded, with perhaps the Council on Foreign Relations handling matters relating to the nongovernmental members of the American and allied foreign policy-making communities. Hutchins had in mind his Fund for Adult Education and also such nonacademic educational organizations as the American Friends Service Committee and the Institute of International Education, both of which had long been involved in student-exchange and other "people-to-people" programs. Spaeth pushed for support of university-based international studies programs, such as that proposed by Stanford University for a Center for Asian Studies.[21]

A review of the grants approved by the Ford Foundation trustees in 1951 attests to the initial success Hoffman and Hutchins had in getting their respective approaches funded. Of that year's total grant allocation of $22 million, almost $7 million went for development projects in South Asia and the Middle East. Among those administering these grants were the Indian and Pakistani governments, the Allahabad Agricultural Institute, the All-Pakistan Women's Association, the Philippine YMCA, and the American University of Beirut. Another $10 million went to set up Hutchins' two funds, with an unspecified portion of that going to the Fund for Adult Education earmarked for programs designed "to advance international understanding." In addition, the American Friends

Service Committee received $1 million and the Institute of International Education $300,000 to support student exchange and other "people-to-people" activities.[22]

Kennan fared somewhat less well. His proposal to establish a study group at Princeton to assist the State Department's policy planning staff went unfunded, although support for Kennan's own efforts to develop a rationale for American foreign policy was provided. Another Kennan-favored project, however, the East European Fund, to assist in the resettlement of East European refugees and support contemporary research on Soviet-bloc countries, received a grant of $785,000.

Spaeth's efforts on behalf of the academic international studies enterprise met with still more limited success. Other than $75,000 to University of Chicago anthropologist Robert Redfield for a multiyear study of intercultural relations, a study that had carried Hutchins' earlier endorsement, the only grant to the academic international studies community was for $23,000 to Stanford to conduct a survey of Asian studies in American universities. Even here, the grant letter to Stanford specified that the trustees' action did not reflect any willingness on their part to approve a much larger request from Stanford's Hoover Institution to establish a Center for Asian Studies. Among grant proposals rejected by the Ford Foundation in 1951 was one submitted by four leading economists from four distinguished universities—Clark Kerr from Berkeley, John T. Dunlop from Harvard, Frederick H. Harbison from Chicago, and Charles A. Myers from MIT—to undertake a comparative study of labor movements in the underdeveloped world. Another was from Harvard University for support of its Russian Research Center and for Russian studies generally.[23]

Overseas development, student exchanges, and nonacademic undertakings again received the bulk of the Ford Foundation's international grants in 1952. Of the nearly $12 million in grants approved under the program rubric "Efforts Toward Peace," nearly $6 million went to overseas development projects in South Asia and the Middle East; another $3 million went to aid in refugee resettlement. Meanwhile, the American

Friends Service Committee, Catholic and Protestant relief agencies, and the Institute of International Education retained their positions as favored agencies through which the Foundation sought to meet its international responsibilities.[24]

But if the level of support provided to academic international studies by the Ford Foundation in 1952—about $1.5 million—fell substantially below that of other claimants, it was nevertheless in that year that the enterprise acquired programmatic recognition within the foundation. The decision of the trustees at their February meeting to assume the financial and administrative responsibility for the Foreign Studies and Research Fellowship Program, which had since its establishment in 1948 been funded by the Carnegie Corporation and administered by the Social Science Research Council, led to the creation of a Foreign Study and Research Program within the foundation. This in turn prompted the creation of an outside Board of Overseas Travel and Research to advise on the administration of the new program. In addition to Spaeth, the board included Gordon Gray, president of the University of North Carolina; John S. Dickey, president of Dartmouth College; and John Gardner, vice president of the Carnegie Corporation, all of whom Spaeth expected would look kindly upon claims from the academic international studies community for support.[25]

The trustees allocated just under $1 million for the Foreign Study and Research Program in 1952, enabling it to provide support for eighty-three Fellows to study in Asia and the Middle East. In addition, the Board of Overseas Travel and Research was authorized to expend $1 million for foreign studies projects that it deemed worthy of foundation support. Among grants made by the board in 1952 was one for $100,000 to the University of Michigan for its Near Eastern studies program, another to the American Council of Learned Societies for $250,000 to help develop basic language tools in relation to Asia.

The next year, 104 more fellowships, now called Foreign Area or simply Ford fellowships, were authorized for study in

Asia, the Middle East, and Africa; Eastern Europe was added, beginning in 1954–55. This involved an expenditure commitment of $755,000. Another $150,000 went to MIT to help set up its Center for International Studies, $35,000 to Michigan to supplement the earlier grant for its Near Eastern studies program, and $150,000 to Columbia for its Middle Eastern studies program. Stanford's Hoover Institution received $255,000 to make its holdings on Asia and the Middle East more accessible to students and researchers. Finally, $500,000 went to the American University Field Staff for a program giving American foreign-area specialists an extensive period in the field before bringing them to American universities, where they were expected to conduct seminars in which they discussed the results of their studies. In all, then, Ford Foundation grants going to the academic international studies enterprise in 1953 approached $2 million, about 15 percent of all the foundation's expenditures in the international field.

Increases in the absolute and relative levels of funding provided to academic international studies in 1953 were not the only indicators that the enterprise was becoming a recognized claimant on the Ford Foundation's resources. Equally indicative was the replacement that year of the makeshift arrangement whereby the internally staffed Foreign Study and Research Program and the external Board of Overseas Travel and Research shared responsibility for considering proposals submitted to the foundation from the academic international studies community. In its place was put the International Training and Research Program (ITR), wholly staffed by foundation personnel and reporting directly to the foundation's vice president for international programs. This change formed part of a larger reorganization in which "international activities," hitherto considered a single administrative undertaking, were divided into three separate programs: Overseas Development; International Affairs, which encompassed programs "aimed at increasing public understanding of international issues and augmenting the effectiveness of American participation in world affairs"; and International Training and Research, aimed at increasing the number of American foreign-area specialists. While even this arrangement proved to be short-lived, its tacit assumption that academic research enjoyed equal standing with overseas development and public education bespoke the brightening prospects of academic international studies as a Ford Foundation beneficiary.[26]

Some close observers of the Ford Foundation in the 1950s have interpreted the belated emergence of academic international studies as a substantial beneficiary to have been less the result of changes in foundation policy than of the time needed for those in academic international studies to develop acceptable proposals.[27] According to this view, support for academic international studies as an essential component of any comprehensive strategy by which the foundation might contribute to the world had been assumed as far back as the Gaither study committee hearings in 1949. This evolutionary view has much to commend it, perhaps not least its conflict-free depiction of the bureaucratic ways of private philanthropy. Yet it would seem to overlook, or at least to minimize, the importance of two unanticipated developments that occurred subsequent to the 1951–52 policy deliberations in Pasadena and which contributed significantly to the elevation of academic international studies from a programmatic afterthought to one of the most favored enterprises in the history of American private philanthropy.

ಶಿ IV

The first of these developments occurred wholly within the Ford Foundation and took the form of a major personnel shakeout. By the middle of 1953 all four of the officers who had advanced proposals during the 1951–52 deliberations about how the foundation might best meet its international responsibilities had departed. Kennan went first, in late 1951, to become ambassador to the Soviet Union. With him went most of the early interest in having the Ford Foundation provide direct staff support for those formulating American foreign policy. Subsequent concern that such support might overlap with activities of the CIA seems also to have eliminated whatever enthusiasm survived Kennan's departure.[28] Meanwhile, support for private organizations interested in foreign policy issues such as the Council on Foreign Relations became a concern of the International Affairs Program.

The departures of Hoffman and Hutchins were more spectacular and less voluntary. In January 1953, Henry Ford informed Hoffman of his and the other trustees' dissatisfaction with his performance as president, particularly during his long absences while campaigning for Eisenhower the previous fall. His insistence upon maintaining the foundation's headquarters in Pasadena in the face of trustee sentiment favoring New York may also have weighed against him. So too, some said, did his leaving Hutchins in charge in his absence. Hoffman stepped down in March, returned to his old job at Studebaker, and went from there to the United Nations Development Fund, where his penchant for overseas projects again found full play. Gaither became interim president.

Hutchins left a year later to become president of the Fund for the Republic, but not before the Ford Foundation trustees provided the fund with a grant of $15 million. Also out was Chester C. Davis, whom Hoffman had recruited to oversee the foundation's agricultural development projects and who, by his subsequent account, realized only after he was "dropped" that "there was a hell of a lot I didn't know about that was going on."[29]

The Ford Foundation's continued involvement in South Asia and the Middle East, and its later activities in Africa, show that Hoffman's departure did not deprive overseas development of its inside support. The shift away from direct grants to national governments toward grants administered by American agencies staffed primarily by Americans that did follow on Hoffman's departure, however, may have been related to it. So, probably, was the more considered pace at which subsequent proposals for overseas projects were undertaken. In any event, Hoffman's unscheduled removal deprived the overseas-development approach to the foundation's international activities of the singularly compelling presidential backing it had enjoyed in the early 1950s.

A clearer case can be made with regard to the programmatic consequences of Hutchins' departure. With him went much of the senior-level support that nonacademic and nontraditional educational undertakings had within the foundation. Indeed, so strong was the animosity some trustees felt toward Hutchins that his identification with the cause of adult and public education may have rendered the cause itself suspect in their eyes thereafter. What support it retained on the international side of the foundation came from the International Affairs Program. But this program, under the directorship of Shepard Stone and with the personal involvement of trustee John McCloy, was primarily concerned with sustaining support for American policies among various influential groups throughout the Atlantic Community, rather than with, as critics said of Hutchins' Fund for Adult Education, "inducing Des Moines housewives and Little Rock doctors to meet regularly in small groups to study and discuss world affairs."[30] The fund was terminated the year of Hutchins' departure.

Spaeth also left in 1953, returning to Stanford as director of international programs. His foundation responsibilities were assigned to two members of the staff, Don K. Price and John B. Howard, neither of whom had had any prior involvement with the academic international studies enterprise. Price had served on the Gaither committee staff prior to joining the foundation full time in 1951; he expected to concentrate on domestic government issues, drawing on his previous Washington experience and training in public administration. If not "hard" on overseas development as a foundation strategy generally, as some remember him being, Price did see the hectic pace at which Hoffman undertook his projects as undercutting their—and his—credibility with the trustees. Correspondingly, without ever identifying with the expansion of university-based international studies as an end in itself, he appreciated Spaeth's argument for a solidly academic component in any long-term international effort by the foundation. As vice president for international programs from 1953 to 1958, when he left the Ford Foundation to become dean of the Graduate School of Public Administration at Harvard, Price had ample opportunity to advance it.[31]

Without diminishing the importance of Spaeth's initial advocacy of academic international studies in the early deliberations in Pasadena, or that of Price's support during his tenure, neither was as crucial to the transformation of the enterprise into a principal beneficiary of the Ford Foundation as the efforts of John B. Howard. In part, Howard's greater impact was a function of his staying at the job much longer than either Spaeth or Price. Howard was, as one colleague said admiringly of him, "a survivor."[32] By training and temperament a lawyer, he had joined the Ford Foundation in 1951 after a decade of government service, his last position being special assistant to Secretary of State Dean Acheson. He accompanied Hoffman to India in 1951, worked closely with Spaeth, kept his head down during the Hoffman-Hutchins-Davis purge, and in 1953 became program director of what later became ITR. He was to hold that position for thirteen years.

Opinions vary as to what made Howard so singularly successful and long-lived a program director, but there is universal agreement as to his being so. He neither began with nor developed close personal ties with any of the three presidents under whom he worked, nor did he have direct access to any individual trustees as did his counterpart in International Affairs, Shepard Stone. He simply won over successive presidents and trustees to his program by the logic of his case for it. One colleague has characterized him as the archetypical "good staff member"; another as "great on internal politics"; still another as possessed of "an extraordinarily well-trained mind" (he had done graduate work in sociology and had a PhD in chemistry), if "not a yeasty kind of thinker." But even this last characterization attests to his self-effacing ability to direct attention away from himself and toward the ITR Program, which, as one of his staff recalled, Howard "ran like a good law firm."[33]

Perhaps more to the point, Howard ran ITR like a law firm that had only one principal client: the academic international studies enterprise. Abetted by a personal style that eschewed self-promotion, Howard likely understood more quickly and accepted more readily than others in comparable positions within the foundation that his function as program director was that of advocacy. He was never so indiscreet to have depicted the relationship between ITR and the international studies enterprise as one between lawyer and client, yet, several years after leaving the Ford Foundation, with only a slight change in choice of simile, he allowed as much. "The ITR Program operated," he told an interviewer in 1972, with respect to international studies academics, "much like an area program with a country representative; they are his constituents, he is there for their benefit."[34] For as long as Howard was there, the case for his client-country constituents could hardly have been more effectively advanced.

V

The second development of the early 1950s that had the unanticipated effect of strengthening the standing of academic international studies within the Ford Foundation was the foundation's finding itself the object of congressional scrutiny. Since their founding in the early twentieth century, the various Rockefeller and Carnegie philanthropies had never been without governmental critics. Senate opposition, led by Idaho's William Borah, to granting a federal charter to the Rockefeller Foundation in 1912 obliged foundation officials to settle for a state charter. Two years later, a Senate committee under the chairmanship of Frank P. Walsh called for the confiscation of Rockefeller Foundation funds. Just as had Progressives earlier, New Dealers in the 1930s criticized foundations as tax havens, public-relations devices, and bastions of traditional privilege.[35]

Thus, for foundations in the early 1950s to find themselves the target of two congressional investigations was not in itself a novel experience. What did distinguish this round of scrutiny from all earlier—and most later—efforts was that it was prompted not by liberal suspicions that foundations were perpetuating the status quo but by conservative fears that they were subverting it. What Georgia Democrat Edward Cox wanted to determine, he advised his colleagues in the 82nd Congress on April 4, 1952, in House Resolution 561, was "whether tax exempt foundations . . . were being used for un-American and subversive activities or for purposes not in the interests of the United States." [36]

The Cox committee investigation, convened in August, held hearings into the fall but to no particular effect. Although Hutchins appeared before the committee, it did not deal specifically with the Ford Foundation. Members did, however, closely question Dean Rusk, then president of the Rockefeller Foundation, about Rockefeller support of the Institute of Pacific Relations, which during the past year had been the subject of an extensive investigation by the Senate Internal Security Subcommittee under the chairmanship of Senator Pat McCarran. The McCarran committee report, published a month before Cox began his own hearings, had concluded that IPR activities "had been such as to serve international Communist interests and to affect adversely the interests of the United States." When asked during the Cox hearings whether the Rockefeller Foundation would be making additional grants to IPR, Rusk indicated that the prospects of its doing so were "remote." [37]

Finding no evidence to substantiate the charges implicit in its enabling resolution, the Cox committee disbanded in the wake of the fall elections, the Democrats having lost control of the House. A second investigation, launched by the incoming Republican 83rd Congress in the spring of 1953, promised to be more critically disposed and more pointedly directed at the Ford Foundation. It was headed by B. Carroll Reece, a Tennessee Republican, a minority member of the Cox committee and a backer of Senator Taft at the same Republican convention at which Hoffman had figured so prominently among those supporting the successful candidacy of Eisenhower. Reece's staff included three of Washington's most vigilant anti-Communists, Thomas McNiece, René A. Wormser, and Norman Dodd.

Staff releases prior to the scheduled public hearings in the summer of 1954 specifically singled out the Ford Foundation for its support of "empiricist" and "inherently collectivistic" projects in the social and behavioral sciences. More to present purposes, they also criticized the foundation for adopting "an internationalist viewpoint and discrediting the traditions to which [the United States] had been dedicated." One release concluded, "It seems incredible that the Trustees of typically American fortune-created foundations should have permitted them to be used to finance ideas and practices incompatible with the fundamental concepts of our Constitution. Yet there seems evidence that this may have occurred." [38]

If such unsubstantiated charges did much to impugn the objectivity of the Reece committee even before it began its hearings, they also put the trustees of the Ford Foundation on notice that they were a primary target. "I don't know if any other foundations were as panic-stricken as Ford was," one close observer of the trustees at the time later recalled, "but Ford was really scared." [39]

Elaborate preparations went into the Foundation's statement to the Reece committee, including an extensive security check of all personnel and grant recipients. "To the best of our knowledge," President Gaither assured the committee in a prepared statement during his testimony on July 16, 1954, "the Ford Foundation had no Communists in its employ, only loyal, responsible Americans." With regard to a grant made to someone subsequently cited by the McCarran committee, he testified that "obviously, if such charges had been known at the time the grant was made, they would have been carefully investigated." [40]

Clearly, neither the foundation's trustees or officers wished to appear uncooperative, much less hostile. What the 1956 annual report approvingly referred to as "a prudent awareness of public attitudes" undoubtedly influenced the foundation's response to the McCarthyistic tactics used by Reece and his staff. In adopting that strategy, as the foundation's Office of Reports later indicated, it was depending on public opinion being "not necessarily pro-foundations, but pro 'fair play.' " Judging by the editorial reaction to the hearings and to the committee's report, which was called "a crushing defeat for the committee," this proved to be a winning strategy.[41]

Nonetheless, prudence suggested a careful review of foundation programs, one that would assess a given program's potential not only for advancing human welfare but for avoiding adverse criticism. Accordingly, it can at least be argued, as Hutchins did at the time, that the Reece investigation had "a chilling effect" on whatever earlier willingness had existed among trustees to back unpopular undertakings. For example, the frequency with which the foundation's Behavioral Science Program came under attack during the investigation did little to endear it to trustees already dubious about its intellectual merits and probably contributed to their decision to terminate the program in 1956.[42]

Criticism directed at the Ford Foundation's international programs had also to be taken seriously. It was not enough to conclude that attacks on the Overseas Development Program, such as that from the *Chicago Tribune* for having "given away $10 billion to foreign countries," or, as per George Sokolsky, putting money earned in this country "into remote bottomless pits," could be dismissed as the embittered views of Republican isolationists who had lost the debate over foreign aid even within their own party.[43] It also required that future overseas projects be defended more explicitly in terms of their contribution to the cold war effort and their benefit to American institutions administering them.

Criticism of the Ford Foundation's support of the international studies enterprise might have given the foundation even more cause for concern. Certainly the Rockefeller Foundation's experience during the McCarran hearing on the Institute of Pacific Relations had done little to encourage philanthropic aggressiveness in East Asian studies. China scholars like Owen Lattimore and John K. Fairbank, whose opposition to American support of the Chiang Kai-shek regime was well known prior to the fall of that regime in 1949, had since the Communist takeover become favorite targets for congressional investigations. Senator McCarthy had called Lattimore "a top Russian espionage agent" and the McCarran committee had called for his indictment for perjury. During the McCarran hearings, Fairbank had been cited by the ex-Communist Louis Budenz as having Communist ties.

Moreover, during the course of these investigations, the academic East Asian studies community split into two ideological camps. In one were the accused and those who were prepared to defend their scholarly integrity; in the other, scholars such as George McGovern and Kenneth Colegrove of Northwestern, George Taylor and Karl Wittfogel of the University of Washington, and David Rowe of Yale, who offered testimony at both the McCarran and Reece committee hearings that at least allowed the inference that some of their colleagues had by their public pronouncements materially abetted the Communist cause in China.[44]

Yet the very ideological diversity within the East Asian studies community as revealed during the congressional hearings in the early 1950s could be used to defend continued foundation support for its scholarly activities. Indeed, at least in the case of Fairbank at Harvard, where university officials and colleagues supported his efforts to refute the charges leveled against him and he seemed prepared to forgo commenting on current policy questions with respect to East Asia, an argument could be made that support for Asian studies within the university would make the field less subject to the ideological currents that swirled around the more policy-oriented IPR when it provided the field with its principal source of identity and support. To be sure, such support would have to be evenly distributed between the Harvard "liberals" and Washington "conservatives," as was indeed the case at the Ford Foundation well into the 1960s.[45]

Whereas criticism directed at the Ford Foundation for its support of East Asian studies could only at best be contained, that directed at support of other components of the international studies enterprise could be returned in kind. Support of programs in Russian studies, such as those at Columbia and Harvard, as Philip Mosely and William Langer had no difficulty demonstrating in the early 1950s, were clearly in the national interest. Both merely had to list the military personnel in their programs and the military contracts supporting them to put to rest any charges that they were, as Langer put it, "fronts for Communist propaganda and activity."[46]

But it was support for South Asian studies that President Gaither used in his testimony before the Reece committee to hoist his critics on their own anti-Communist petards. Citing a charge by conservative columnist Paul Harvey that the Ford Foundation had squandered millions of dollars on such "exotic" projects as compiling an English-Telegu dictionary, Gaither noted that Telegu was spoken by some 30 million Indians. "It is true," he went on,

that the language has been neglected by us, but not by the Russians. Telegu-language publications from Moscow are distributed [in India] every day. There is no comparable English dictionary.[47]

There is considerable irony in Gaither's resorting to this ploy, quite aside from its being perhaps the most frequently quoted part of his entire testimony. Four years earlier, the study committee report that bears his name insisted that "national conduct based solely on the fear of Communism . . . is defensive and negative." Yet his response does suggest just how strong was the pull on any aspiring American enterprise in the early 1950s—philanthropic, academic, or whatever—to depict its purposes and that of prosecuting the Cold War as complementary, if not identical. In this instance, it may be argued, both the Ford Foundation and the academic international studies enterprise were products of the era. In any event, as long as the

Ford Foundation found it prudent to defend itself against charges from the ideological right of insufficient zeal in advancing the American cause in the Cold War, the funding prospects for academic international studies were pretty much assured.

THE BONANZA YEARS

The ITR Program clearly existed for the benefit of American universities; that's what it was for.

JOHN B. HOWARD, 1972[1]

The growth of American academic international studies after World War Two has been, on the most general level, attributed to the internationalist and interventionist terms in which American national interest then came to be defined. Such growth as the enterprise experienced, then, was what a Marxist might call an "epiphenomenon" of the Cold War. On a much more specific level, however, it has at least in considerable part been attributed to the sponsorship the enterprise received from the Ford Foundation's ITR Program. As already indicated, both these explanations must figure prominently in any comprehensive attempt to understand the postwar history of American academic international studies. Yet to limit a consideration of causal factors to either or both of these explanations would be to ignore several intermediate or "middle range" developments, without any of which it is unlikely that this hitherto struggling enterprise would have undergone two decades of growth in numbers, material prosperity, and institutional prominence unsurpassed in the history of American academic life.

This chapter examines four such developments. Each grew out of an assumption which, absent at the establishment of the International Training and Research Program in 1953, thereafter became operative and remained so for the life of the program. These assumptions were that: (a) the Ford Foundation had more to fear from capital accumulation than from capital depletion; (b) universities were singularly suited to the task of absorbing the foundation's surplus funds; (c) ITR was a particularly effective instrument for funneling such funds to the universities; and (d) ITR should heed the advice of leading international studies academics in allocating these funds. Each assumption encouraged a favorable disposition on the part of the Ford Foundation toward academic international studies; together they virtually mandated that the enterprise would enter into what one of its participant observers has called its "bonanza years."[2]

ॐ I

It was not until six years after the reorganization of the Ford Foundation in 1950 that its trustees fully realized the magnitude of the funds entrusted to them. The uncertainty resulted from the fact that Ford Motor Company stock, which constituted the foundation's endowment, had never been offered for sale. Market analysts agreed, however, that the assigned book value of $417 million for the foundation's three million shares of Class A (nonvoting) stock substantially understated its real value. If so, the grant levels for both 1951 and 1952, $22 million and $32 million respectively, fell well below that necessary if the trustees were to fulfill their stated intention to spend more than the foundation earned on a year-to-year basis. Such stinting levels also risked a judgment of noncompliance with federal tax laws prohibiting tax-free foundations from retaining "unreasonable accumulations of income." Even after doubling grant levels to over $50 million, as the trustees did in 1953 and 1954, they found themselves falling furthur behind in their struggle to match the foundation's income from its Ford stock, which in 1954 earned $195.6 million.

The already recognized need to spend more became imperative in 1955, when the Ford family accepted the trustees' plan to have the Ford Foundation gradually divest itself of Ford stock. As a preliminary step toward divestiture, the Foundation's 3 million shares of Class A stock were exchanged for 46 million shares of more marketable voting stock. Of these shares, some 10.2 million were sold on January 10, 1956, for $64.50 a share. Proceeds from this single transaction, then the largest in the history of the New York Stock Exchange, netted the Ford Foundation $642.6 million. More crucially, in establishing the market value of the foundation's remaining 36 million shares of Ford stock, the sale enabled the trustees to place a value on its fund: $2.75 billion.[3]

Even using the most conservative earnings projections, the trustees found themselves faced with the daunting prospect of having to dispense between $100 million and $150 million annually, just to offset anticipated income. The reaction of trustee John J. McCloy was shared by others on the board: "We had to reduce that fund. . . . It was too big." A similar conclusion was meanwhile being drawn by members of the foundation staff. "The IRS is breathing down our necks," one has since recalled the prevailing sentiment following on divestiture in 1955–56. "We've got to get rid of the money."[4]

And so the foundation did, or at least a big chunk of it. In just three months in late 1955 and 1956 the trustees authorized a series of special appropriations totaling $550 million. About $200 million went to assist 3,500 voluntary nonprofit hospitals, another $95 million to forty-five private medical schools. The remainder, some $260 million, was distributed among all 600 regionally accredited private colleges and universities in the United States for the sole purpose of raising faculty salaries. In effect, each of these institutions had its 1954–55 instructional budget matched by the Ford Foundation.[5]

Some foundation observers have since described those 1955–56 special grants to have been the most ill-advised in the history of private philanthropy. That they were hastily decided upon, reflected few qualitative standards, and had in many instances only the most transitory impact was later acknowledged by those who made them. One inside account has Henry

Ford II, as chairman of the trustees, insisting that the medical-school grants total an uneven number, "perhaps 91 million point something—so it will look like we have considered the matter closely."[6]

Yet, from a public relations perspective, these grants were an unqualified success. This was especially true of the faculty grants. "For once," the often critical Dwight Macdonald wrote of them in the *New Yorker*, "the Ford Foundation seemed to have done something that everybody agreed was constructive, sound, and forward-looking." On the off chance that these efforts had escaped the notice of the foundation's recent inquisitors, a booklet listing the colleges receiving grants—by state and voting district—went to all members of the Senate and the House of Representatives.[7]

Thereafter, the trustees looked far more favorably upon large grant proposals than upon small ones. What they really wanted from the staff, trustee Donald David reportedly urged after 1955, were "neat and costly packages" that would move along large sums of money without requiring large in-house staffs to administer them. That "it can take as much staff work to give a $3,500 Guggenheim Fellowship as to give $3,500,000 to a well-known university," became, even more than earlier at Ford or at the other large foundations, an operational maxim. Under this new dispensation, as one official recalled it, "the question was how could we convert [a] small retail and high-overhead operation into a large scale wholesale program, with hundreds of times the volume, with as little loss of sophistication as possible."[8]

Not surprisingly, already operational programs like ITR, no matter how modestly funded before, but with established links to the major universities, were able to respond more effectively to this call for "neat and costly packages" than were programs with institutionally scattered and less familiar clients. Indeed, as the level of annual grant authorizations moved over the $100 million mark in the late 1950s, from there to $200 million in the early 1960s, and then to over $300 million in the mid-1960s, the complaint registered about the 1956 faculty grants—that they "disappeared without a trace"—only further commended universities to the Ford Foundation as being uniquely able to absorb embarrassing surpluses and as a most accommodating ally in its struggle against capital inundation.

ঌ II

By 1960 almost exactly half of the Ford Foundation's expended largesse—$646 million of $1.3 billion—had gone to American universities. Over and above their spongelike qualities, universities became the foundation's favored beneficiary because Ford officials, like many other Americans in the 1950s and 1960s, became increasingly persuaded by the argument that universities deserved all the support they could get. This argument had both a retrospective and a prospective component. Retrospectively, it was argued that universities had made significant contributions to the national good, in training provided, research undertaken, service extended. Specific references to their recent efforts in winning World War Two sufficed to confirm this. Prospectively, it was argued that universities were currently so beset with critical problems that, unless they were effectively met, universities would not be able to make such contributions in the future. Put bluntly, unless "the crisis of the university" received priority attention, the university could not be counted on to help with the nation's future crises.

The argument that society suffers if the needs of American universities go unmet was hardly new in the 1950s. An early invocation of it had occurred in 1636 on behalf of the as yet unnamed Harvard College. Calling upon "friends of New England—to advance learning and perpetuate it to posterity," an anonymous promoter of the college argued that a failure to respond to this appeal would be "to leave an illiterate Ministry to the Churches, when our present ministers shall lie in the dust." 9 In the next third of a milennium, little changed except for the secularization of the specter.

If spokesmen for American universities in the 1950s broke

no new ground in depicting the problems facing their institutions as "a crisis" of societal importance, they did enjoy unprecedented success in doing so. Never before had the argument that universities both needed and deserved more outside support than they were receiving been so widely endorsed by Americans not professionally identified with higher education. Few did so more wholeheartedly than officials of the major foundations, and none of these more so than those of the Ford Foundation. Indeed, in characterizing "the impending crisis in American education" as "offering a large foundation its greatest current opportunity for service," as its 1954 annual report did, the foundation moved beyond the point of merely endorsing the "crisis" argument to arrogating it.[10]

Part of the effectiveness of the "crisis" argument turned on its plausibility. Considerable evidence did exist that American universities, particularly private ones, faced difficult times in the 1950s. The failure of Congress to provide direct federal support for higher education had been disappointing, especially to those universities that had expanded beyond their means to accommodate veterans attending under the GI Bill, in anticipation of the regularization of federal assistance. Moreover, as both the Social Science Research Council and the American Council of Learned Societies pointed out, the federal funding that was available went almost exclusively to support the physical and biological sciences, thereby threatening the relative standing of the social sciences and the humanities even within private universities with substantial endowments. Several private universities lacking such endowments, as well as several municipally owned institutions, survived the 1950s only by merging into state-supported systems.[11]

The most immediate concern of university administrators in the early 1950s was declining enrollments. As the last of the World War Two veterans graduated, their places could be only partially filled from the smaller cohort of college-age Americans born during the Depression. That fewer of these were eligible for veterans' benefits only further reduced their likelihood of going to college. After 1950, when nearly 500,000 bachelor's degrees were conferred nationally, the number dropped in each of the next five years, until, in 1956, it bottomed out at 375,000. It would not be until 1962 that a national graduating class of college seniors exceeded that of 1950. The drop in graduate enrollments was less sharp and less protracted, but the fact that the number of master's degrees awarded in 1951 (65,077) was not surpassed until 1958 indicates that the slack in undergraduate enrollments was not made up in graduate enrollments.[12]

However genuine a problem, particularly for private universities largely dependent upon tuition revenues to cover operating expenses, the enrollment slump was recognized to be temporary. Administrators coping with its implications in the mid-1950s could look ahead to the arrival on campus, beginning around 1960, of the much larger generation born in the 1940s, and with it to a return to filled classrooms. But if time promised to solve the enrollment problem, it seemed likely, warned some university observers as early as 1954, only to exacerbate an even more critical "problem": recruiting and retaining qualified faculty.

The key word in discussions of the faculty-supply issue from the early 1950s to the mid-1960s was "qualified." Ordinarily not the easiest condition to define, much less to quantify, "quality" in these discussions was generally defined as the National Education Association defined it in its first *Report on Teacher Supply and Demand in Colleges and Universities, 1954–1955:* faculty with PhDs were qualified; those without, were not. With such a no-nonsense definition as this it became simple, or so the NEA's reports asserted, to measure whether the quality of the American professoriate was improving or deteriorating, and at what rate. This could be done, the NEA pointed out, by comparing the percentage of continuing faculty in a given year possessing a PhD with the percentage of faculty hired that year similarly credentialed. In 1953–54, for example, the NEA calculated that 40.5 percent of all continuing faculty had a PhD, as against only 31.5 percent of the "new hires." In 1954, the percentage of new hires with PhDs dropped to 28.4. Subsequent NEA reports, published biennially through 1965, registered further declines in this percentage of new faculty with a PhD, and drew from this statistical observation the conclusion that the overall quality of the American professoriate was "deteriorating year by year." [13]

"To expect that by 1970 the proportion of college teachers holding the Ph.D. degree will have declined from the present 40 percent to 20 percent," a Ford-Foundation-sponsored conference of fifteen leading university authorities concluded in its report, *Graduate Schools, Today and Tomorrow,* "is not statistical hysteria but grass roots arithmetic." Although a few observers of American higher education during these years viewed the alarms skeptically, among them Harold Orlans, and at least one, Bernard Berelson, disputed the NEA findings, most accepted them at face value. References to the "cumulative deficit" in PhDs available for academic employment became commonplace and remained so through most of the 1960s. As late as 1967, PhDs prepared to accept academic positions were being described as "one of the nation's scarcest resources"; in 1968 a "shortage" of English PhDs was still being divined! [14]

It was not until 1965 that the labor economist Allan M. Cartter challenged the statistical base upon which the faculty-shortage argument rested. Even accepting the NEA's definition of quality instruction, that provided by a teacher with a PhD, Cartter showed that by adding teachers who received their PhDs subsequent to their initial academic appointment to those hired with degree in hand, the percentage of doctorate-holding teachers had not been declining but increasing. In 1950–51, according to his calculations, 36.6 percent of the American professoriate held a PhD; in 1963, the percentage had increased to 44.5. Cartter went on from there to suggest that in some fields, particularly in the humanities, the supply of available PhDs had already exceeded academic demand.

But as Cartter later remarked, the hardiness of the faculty-shortage and deteriorating-quality arguments had less to do with their statistical elegance than with their promotional utility. When Cartter first approached the American Council of

Education's Commission on Plans and Objectives for Higher Education in 1964 with a proposal to study whether American colleges and universities had actually experienced a deterioration in faculty quality, he came away empty-handed. "Everyone knew there was a crisis that would continue another 20 years," he later recalled as being the sentiments of university presidents on the commission; "let's study something we can do something about."[15]

In endorsing the argument that a persistent and growing shortage of qualified college teachers existed in the United States, as it did in its 1954 annual report, and in publicizing it in its reports for a decade thereafter, the Ford Foundation additionally took upon itself the task of accounting for this situation. The problem, as the 1955 report assessed it in announcing the $260 million in faculty-salary grants, was primarily one of money, or, more precisely, the lack thereof. Academic life in the United States, the report declared flatly, had become "intolerably unrewarding financially." An accompanying bar graph showed the 43 percent increase in purchasing power that factory workers had enjoyed between 1939 and 1954, comparing it to a decline of 24 percent for college professors.[16]

Prominent among the organizations applauding the decision of the Ford trustees "to do everything they can to emphasize the cardinal importance of the college teacher in our society" was the American Association of University Professors. The salary data cited by the Ford trustees when announcing the faculty grants in 1955 had been compiled by the Association's Committee Z, which annually updated these data thereafter. These grants notwithstanding, the Committee's report for 1955–56 concluded that "the profession has retrogressed so much in economic status over the past sixteen years that, as things stand, its capacity to maintain and renew itself may be gravely weakened."[17]

Even accepting the argument that American higher education in the 1950s was in crisis, it could hardly be described as having escaped public notice. The plight of the universities and their ill-paid faculty received extended and sympathetic cov-

erage in the annual reports of the major foundations, in foun-
dation-supported studies, and in surveys issued by the NEA,
the AAUP, and the American Council on Education. More
widely circulated publications like *Time, Newsweek, Saturday
Review,* and the *New York Times Magazine* also took up the
academy's cause. So, too, did a President's Committee on Education Beyond the High School, convened by President Eisenhower in the spring of 1956. In its final report, issued in
July 1957, the committee warned of "the mounting shortage
of "excellent teachers," before going on to recommend that
faculty salaries be doubled within ten years.[18]

Three months later the Russians launched their Sputnik. What
was already a vigorous lobbying effort on behalf of universities soon acquired the character of a national crusade.
Congressional proponents of federal aid to higher education,
until then stymied by White House opposition, in 1958 secured passage of the first comprehensive federal aid legislation,
the National Defense Education Act. A decade of ever larger
and more comprehensive appropriations followed in its wake.
By 1966 annual federal assistance for American colleges and
universities exceeded $2.6 billion, six times what it had been
in the mid-1950s.

By the early 1960s it required considerable ingenuity to
characterize universities as among America's needier institutions. Increased income from foundations and individual donors, alumni giving, return on endowment, and state as well
as federal assistance combined to provide American higher education with the firmest financial base in its history. From 1954
to 1966 the income of American colleges and universities grew
at twice the rate of the gross national product. Enrollment
projections, which into the early 1960s still pointed indefinitely upward, gave further credence to the seldom acknowledged but palpable reality that higher education had become
America's leading growth industry.[19]

Likewise, the case for academics permanently consigned to
lives of genteel poverty had become increasingly difficult to
support. In 1954 and for the next twelve successive years, in-

creases in faculty salaries nationwide exceeded those of the American workforce overall. The loss of purchasing power that academics sustained in the 1940s and early 1950s was recouped by 1958; thereafter they annually registered impressive improvements in their economic standing. In its report for 1961–62, the AAUP's Committee Z actually acknowledged grounds for "some optimism that higher education was at last getting the serious attention befitting its great role and multiplying tasks in our society." The doubling of faculty salaries within a decade, called for in 1957, had by 1965 already been achieved at nearly all public institutions and most of the leading private universities; everywhere else it was within easy reach. Though they were perhaps reluctant to acknowledge it, American academics had entered the comfortable middle class.[20]

More than a closing of the economic gap between their salaries and those of other professionals distinguished the early 1960s as the "bonanza years" for American academics. Increased prestige also came to be attached to their jobs. To be sure, college professors had enjoyed high prestige since the 1920s, when sociologists first began compiling occupational-prestige rankings. Yet through the 1930s the image of the academic as engagingly ineffective in "real world" matters held sway. Indeed, part of the professor's appeal turned on his image as one "who does not lust after power . . . the glories of the world seem little and remote to him."[21]

If the war marked the demise of the academic-as-Mr.-Chips, it introduced Americans to the academic as man-of-affairs. In 1947 college professors ranked eighth among one hundred occupations, just below "mayor of a big city" and "diplomat," but well above "member of a board of directors of a large corporation" and "lawyer." In 1963 college professors again ranked eighth, tied with United States congressmen, while both diplomats and mayors dropped below them. The only two occupations that moved ahead of them in the intervening fifteen years—"nuclear physicist" and "scientist"—were both partially academic in character.[22]

Though a less quantifiable phenomenon, the conspicuous

place academics enjoyed in the Kennedy and then in the Johnson administrations undoubtedly contributed to a growing
awareness among college students and their parents that the
life of a professor need be neither impoverished nor cloistered.
The notion of a professor comfortable in the corridors of
power, even actually interested in its exercise, was still new in
the early 1960s, not yet, as it would be later, implicating. Surely
Arthur Schlesinger, Jr., intended it as a compliment when, in
his account of his faculty colleague and dean *cum* Kennedy security adviser McGeorge Bundy, he wrote that he had seen
Bundy "learn how to dominate the faculty of Harvard University, a throng of intelligent and temperamental men; after
that training, one could hardly doubt his capacity to deal with
Washington bureaucrats." [23]

Perhaps the most telling indicator of the rising fortunes of
the American academic profession in this period was the
clamoring of undergraduates to join it. A national survey of
35,000 college seniors in 1961 found nearly half were seriously
considering careers in teaching or research. Of those who were
not, two-thirds expressed doubts about their having "the necessary ability," but only 6 percent rejected academic life because there "was not enough money" in it. The survey also
found that the seniors most favorably disposed toward academic careers were those with the best academic records from
the most academically demanding institutions. These were
precisely the seniors who, beginning in the mid-1950s and in
accelerating numbers for a decade thereafter, proceeded directly to graduate school, secured their PhDs, and joined the
swelling ranks of the American professoriate. [24]

Quite suddenly, in the space of a decade, the American academic community had not only more than doubled in size—
from less than 300,000 in 1955 to 600,000 in 1965—but it had
also become the repository of a much larger share of the nation's identifiable intellectual resources than ever before. A development of these dimensions naturally prompted speculation
as to its long-term implications for American society. Among
the more provocative extrapolations was one offered by the

then Columbia sociologist Daniel Bell. "Is it *hubris,*" he asked in 1966,

to say that if one were to look back at the present from the year 2000 . . . one would discern in the second half of the twentieth century the transformation of the university into a primary institution of the emerging post-industrial society, just as the business firm had been the most important institution in the previous century and a half?[25]

"Hubris" or not, others shared Bell's view that universities were about to displace not only business firms but even government as the driving force in American life. Nor were those who believed it found exclusively in the academic community, where such speculation could perhaps be discounted as wishful thinking. Conspicuous among those outside the university intrigued by the prospect that a transfer of power from corporate to academic America was already under way—and in an almost unique position to help accelerate the transfer— were those charged with dispensing the accumulated fortunes of the great industrial enterprisers.

ê III

The "philanthropoid," Dwight Macdonald observed in giving the term currency in 1955, "has a weakness for cerebration." This he attributed to the foundations' recruiting their personnel from the universities rather than from the business or professional communities. Although not initially the case at Ford in the early reorganization years, when those from government outnumbered those from campuses, it soon became so. By the early 1960s, staffing the foundation had become, according to one close observer, "where you hire this nice young fellow and he's got his PhD from someplace and it's in sociology so you stick him in a little office and he processes grants." Program officers without PhDs in programs like ITR that dealt with universities were unusual enough to be identified as such in internal memoranda. Similarly, it was a rare staff member who did not have a personal tie with one of the major universities, most often Chicago, Harvard, Yale, or Columbia, or was not giving some thought to moving back into the university world after a tour with the foundation. Many did just that, to be promptly replaced by a restive assistant professor or newly minted PhD.[26]

Some of the deference with which foundation officers treated senior academic emissaries from the leading universities can be attributed to a realistic perception of the grantor-grantee relationship. As one Ford official put the case for modesty: "It's not our money and we don't do the work." Yet some of it may have reflected a prolongation—on both sides—of an earlier pattern of interaction based on their earlier roles as mentor and student. Thus the professor was allowed to carry himself head high and hand out, while the student, now foundation official, engaged in some of the footshuffling expected in his earlier lowly station. Some hostility may also have occasionally operated beneath the surface in these dealings, but not likely the kind that stems from the clash of different occupational values. In explaining the affinity between his colleagues and their academic clients in the early 1960s, a Ford official pointed to the similarities between the university and foundation worlds, not least of which was that they were both "relatively corruption-free." "We have always," he said of the universities, "lived closer to that world, at least we did before we went into the streets."[27]

The predilection of their staff for the universities did not escape the notice of trustees, particularly those from the corporate world. "They," by which banker-trustee John J. McCloy meant foundation staffers, when he was recalling the 1955 deliberations about reducing the foundation's endowment fund, "would have reduced it by giving it to the purely academic world, which would not have made as good use of it." Henry Ford II, during the later years of his tenure as chairman of the trustees and still later as an increasingly disaffected trustee, harbored similar views, or so his 1978 resignation letter indicated. In any event, neither he nor McCloy would be likely to dispute that Dwight Macdonald's assessment of the overall performance of America's large foundations applied with special force to their own:

They have proved more responsive to the values of the professionals who run them and of the academic concerns on whose borders they operate than to those of the rich men who founded them.[28]

Even among Ford officials who reject the argument that in the late 1950s and early 1960s they had in any way become the willing captive of the universities, there is considerable agreement that during the presidency of Henry T. Heald the ties between the foundation and the universities became stronger and more numerous than ever before—or since. Unlike his predecessors Hoffman and Gaither (the latter resigned in 1956 because of failing health), Heald came to the presidency directly from the university world. At the time of his election he was chancellor of New York University, a position he had held since 1952; during the fourteen years before that he had been president of the Armour (now the Illinois) Institute of Technology. As president of the Ford Foundation, Heald displayed little patience with several of the businessmen-trustees he inherited; they, in turn, resented his lecturing them. Trustee discontent surfaced in 1962 with the publication of a trustee-sponsored report recommending that the president's authority be restricted. His resignation followed three years later, but not before the Heald era had secured its place in the history of American philanthropy as the years in which the Ford Foundation established itself as American higher education's underwriter of first resort.[29]

"Basically," an associate has characterized Heald's philanthropic strategy, "he felt that the university was the center of things, that the kinds of change that [the foundation was] capable of effecting in society could and would be done through the university." In programmatic terms, as another foundation official put it, this meant that "education and big money grants to established educational institutions were *the* thing. If you weren't in that picture, you really weren't in the center."[30]

At its core, then, the relationship between the university official seeking support and the program officer charged with dispensing it was professionally symbiotic. Both benefited from increased levels of funding, in that the university official was judged by the funds received, the program officer by those dispensed. As Heald's more financially constrained successor, McGeorge Bundy, remarked ruefully of his predecessor's era, "it is relatively easy to strike bargains with our friends when their awakening interests intersect with ours."[31] None of the Ford Foundation's many programs more successfully tested the limits of this happy premise than did ITR.

ໄ IV

The actual administration of a still new and ambitious foundation program like ITR in the late 1950s largely turned on developing defensible recommendations for making new grants. Although as John Howard, its director, later stated, "the ITR Program clearly existed for the benefit of American universities; that's what it was for," it had not begun with nearly so clear a mandate. Early grants went to the American agencies promoting student exchanges, such as the American Friends Service Committee and the Institute of International Education, as well as to support programs sponsored by the 4-H Club Foundation, the YMCA, and the North Central Association for Secondary Schools. ITR also helped fund such professional organizations as the International Federation of Business and Professional Women and the International Press Institute and such nonacademic publishing ventures as those of the Institute of Current World Affairs.

Some of this early inclusiveness was likely intended to allay misgivings within the foundation about the propriety of meeting a sizable share of its international responsibilities by funding American academics. William McPeak, one of the authors of the Gaither report and in the mid-1950s a Ford Foundation vice president, made clear to Howard early on that he thought that ITR support of academic research "was a waste of time and money and everything else." Even those favoring support of academic research as a legitimate means by which the Ford Foundation could achieve some of its international goals insisted that the research not become an end in itself. Its ultimate objective, Vice President Don K. Price wrote in 1954, was "to put such knowledge more effectively at the disposal of those who are responsible, in government and in private life, for representing the United States in international affairs."[32]

As ITR grew, however, its nonacademic clients became fewer, their grants proportionally smaller. In part the increasingly exclusive identification of ITR with its academic clientele was a byproduct of a clearer demarcation of responsibilities among the foundation's three international programs. Some early nonacademic ITR grantees, particularly those whose efforts were directed at West European audiences, were assumed by the International Affairs Program. Others, involved in the technical training of foreign nationals, were picked up by the Overseas Development Program. But still others, most conspicuously clients identified with the aims of educating the American public about international affairs and encouraging "people-to-people" contacts, were simply dropped.

In divesting itself of its nonacademic clients, ITR could depend on the backing of President Heald, whose opposition to what he called "do-good" efforts was well known. Exchange projects such as those sponsored by IIE and AFSC which, as an ITR staffer who identified with them said, were characterized as "trying to encourage connections—human connections," Heald dismissed either as "rather 'softer' than the type we ought to be concerned with," or, more emphatically, as "women's club stuff." Indeed, his contempt for such efforts was perhaps exceeded only by that some of ITR's academic clients felt for efforts in public education that in the 1960s acquired the label of "outreach."[33]

By the late 1950s the academicization of ITR had become a measurable reality. Of the sixty-nine grants made by the program in 1958, only nine went to American organizations other than universities and scholarly associations serving the academic community. Several universities, among them Chicago,

Columbia, Cornell, and Harvard, received several grants, each involving a different world area or international topic. Of ITR's total expenditure in 1958 of $5.6 million, over $4.5 million—80 percent—went to support projects in academic international studies. Back in the early 1950s Dwight Macdonald, upon reading through Robert Redfield's proposal for his Comparative Study of Cultures project, which received a $75,000 Ford grant, remarked that its "budget reads like an academic WPA." One wonders what his reaction would have been to the subsequent proliferation of such projects, just one of which, a comparative study of labor movements, eventually consumed $850,000 in Ford grants (plus another $200,000 from Carnegie) in employing the services of some ninety-six academics over twenty years (1954–1973) to sponsor ten conferences, present fifty papers, and publish forty books.[34]

Yet the growing success ITR experienced in eliciting fundable project proposals from leading academics became itself by the late 1950s a matter of serious concern among those within the program. ITR, as Howard was perhaps the first to realize, had become almost too successful. He knew full well that he could not come to the trustees year after year with a longer and longer list of international studies projects, all of which merited funding. Not to reduce the number of grant proposals submitted to the trustees was to risk their growing bored with the program altogether, something Howard was determined to avoid. Yet to have his small staff not only administer and monitor this ever growing number of projects but to pass judgment on the relative merits of new proposals, especially when several came from the same university, was equally undesirable and potentially no less fatal.

In part to avoid, or at least to indefinitely defer, the fate of other Ford programs "of a certain age" (the Behavioral Sciences Program being a case in point), Howard decided to change ITR's strategy from one of funding relatively short-term individual projects that ITR judged to have merit to one of providing long-term funding to selected universities, each of which would then take it upon itself to decide which among its many international studies proposals and ongoing projects deserved support. That such a change would likely involve larger sums being made available to the selected universities than previously, while effectively transferring the responsibility for allocating those sums to international studies academics at these universities, was lost on neither ITR nor the academic international studies community.[35]

Before ITR could possibly have responsibly recommended to Heald and the Ford trustees a move to long-term university-wide grants, as it did in 1959, it had to have first sorted out which universities it was prepared to recommend for such grants. Several years' experience negotiating and monitoring project grants at more than twenty different universities went into ITR's preparation; so too did not a little rethinking of its initial funding inclinations.

The first grant proposals ITR received had almost necessarily been considered on a case-by-case basis, with the principal criterion being the scholarly standing of the personnel involved. The grants to Robert Redfield at Chicago for his comparative study of cultures, to Melville Herskovits at Northwestern for African studies, and to W. Norman Brown at Pennsylvania for South Asian studies are early examples. But more general considerations also appear to have influenced whether a given project was provided or denied support by ITR. Two early favorable decisions, on proposals from the University of Southern California for Japanese studies in 1953 and from Boston University for African studies a year later, illustrate three such considerations—and their subsequent modification.[36]

First, ITR, like most Ford programs dealing with higher education, favored private universities as against public. Public universities, the reasoning went, were a fair charge on the state legislatures and taxpayers who directed their affairs, while private universities had legitimate claims on the largesse of private philanthropy. This bias was never absolute, as indicated by the substantial support both Berkeley and UCLA received, but it did influence ITR funding throughout its history. The seven largest beneficiaries of ITR—Harvard, Columbia, Chicago, Cornell, Stanford, MIT, and Yale—were all private universities. Wisconsin and Michigan spokesmen had a point in the late 1960s when they complained that international studies programs at small private universities, such as Syracuse and Duke, had been far more generously provided for by ITR than had their own arguably more distinguished programs.[37]

A second funding consideration turned on whether ITR ought to favor the "have-not" universities as against the "haves." "In the early days it wasn't popular to make a grant to Harvard," Howard later recalled, "just because there was so much Harvard." President Heald favored this view, much preferring "to support NYU than Harvard any day." Yet in practice it proved difficult for ITR staff to turn down well-conceived proposals from Chicago, Columbia, or Harvard, while funding those from the University of Southern California and Boston University, particularly after some early ITR grants to the latter sort of universities, without either a tradition in international studies or an endowment sufficient to sustain that tradition, "did not work out." As ITR staff found it necessary to seek advice on the comparative merit of grant proposals, they increasingly turned for it to those directing programs at the leading universities. Not surprisingly, they recommended that ITR put its money on already established programs or on new programs at universities with proven track records in international studies. As Howard later characterized the rationale for ITR's funding the "haves": "You can't be in a field like foreign area training without making some grants to Harvard." Some $63.2 million, about one-third of all of ITR's direct grants to universities, went to Harvard, Chicago, and Columbia.[38]

A third funding consideration turned on deciding which world areas were most in need of study and thereby most deserving of the foundation's support. ITR's initial inclination was to regard the Middle East, South Asia, and Africa as the most neglected world areas in terms of American scholarly attention, and East Asia and Latin America the most thoroughly studied. Russia and East Europe fell somewhere in between, neither so neglected as to require special emphasis nor so closely attended as to be considered, as some in ITR in the early 1950s regarded East Asian studies, "already taken care of."

But here, too, in practice it proved difficult to discriminate against world areas where the leading international studies academics were concentrated, in order to favor areas that had yet to acquire their academically prestigious spokesmen. What had been decided with respect to Harvard and Columbia held equally well with respect to East Asia and Russia—those identified with these institutions and world areas were too central to the entire international studies enterprise to be slighted by a foundation program increasingly committed to underwriting that enterprise.[39]

The case that those in Russian and East Asian studies made on behalf of funding for their fields was not that they were more neglected than others, but that if the Ford Foundation more generously funded other fields than they did Russian and East Asian studies, they soon would be. Indeed, so attractive was this line of reasoning that academics studying Western Europe laid claim to it in the early 1960s, by arguing that ITR funding of scholarly work on other world areas had resulted in neglect of theirs. Eventually, some $10 million of ITR funds went into the support of "Western European studies."[40]

Yet surely both ITR officials and the enterprising academics with whom they worked in the late 1950s appreciated a funding strategy that used a relative scale of "neglect" based on how much support those studying a given world area had previously received from ITR. In subscribing to the biblical injunction that "the last shall be first," both ITR and its academic clients insured themselves against the possibility of ever running out of a "neglected" world area in need of scholarly attention and philanthropic favor.

Similarly, the specter of sufficiency could be indefinitely put off by subdividing world areas. To suggest, for example, that East Asian studies "was taken care of," and to point to work being done on China as evidence, was to strengthen the case for additional support of Japanese studies. To support proposals for additional studies of Japan was to invite proposals from those prepared to study Korea and Mongolia. Likewise, to approximate comprehensive disciplinary coverage in one world area was to point up the spottiness of such coverage elsewhere. To provide a South Asian program with language instruction in Hindi, Bengali, and Urdu only revealed the neglect of Tamil, Marathi, and Punjabi. In 1964 Uralic and Altaic were described as "the neglected area" in a review of the non-Western world in higher education, not because they were not taught extensively at several universities, but because at only one, Indiana, was there an independent Altaic department![41] In sum, the needs of an academic enterprise defined in relative terms were as insatiable as the purposes of a philanthropic program defined without reference to any fixed goal were unfulfillable. Just so.

৯ V

Persuaded by their own experiences early in the program of the advantages of concentrating support on universities with established reputations in international studies, while allowing the question of which areas to support to be decided by international studies academics in part on the basis of relative neglect, ITR officials in the late 1950s turned their efforts to creating the appropriate funding mechanism. What they came up with was the "institutional block grant." Unlike a project grant, typically for a relatively short-term and quite specifically targeted effort (e.g., to Cornell for a study of political life in Indonesia), of which a single university might have several, an institutional block grant would provide a selected university with a single, long-term, comprehensive grant to be distributed among its various international studies programs as it saw fit. This transfer of responsibility for the actual allocation of funds from the foundation to the university assumed that, if the university being considered for such a grant did not have a central administrative mechanism to establish funding priorities among the university's various international programs, it would promptly establish one.

As with most ideas germinated in a bureaucratic organization the size of the Ford Foundation, block grants to universities for international studies required selling. The principal responsibility for doing so fell to ITR's director, John Howard, with whom the idea most likely originated. By the late 1950s Howard had accumulated considerable experience defending ITR against critics like Vice President McPeak, who eventually conceded that ITR "was booming along," if only because of Howard's skill at promoting its cause. Similarly, when a 1956 organizational reshuffling shifted ITR from the jurisdiction of the vice president of international programs to that of education, Howard promptly made his new boss, Clarence Faust, who had had no previous involvement with either international studies or ITR, a loyal supporter of the program.[42]

The ultimate test of any program director's persuasiveness at that time was winning over an initially skeptical President Heald. In his dealings with subordinates, he could be and often was "very caustic, very rough." Moreover, he showed little interest in international matters generally, and even less in international studies, and he was hostile to making grants to precisely the kinds of universities ITR envisioned as likely block-grant recipients. Always balanced against these "deficiencies," however, was his abiding faith in the social efficacy of universities and his desire to improve their financial management.[43]

Howard also had going for his block-grant scheme the assurance that if it were adopted there would be far fewer project requests from ITR to clog the trustees' agenda. Indeed, it could be argued—and likely was—that such block grants represented the ultimate in "neat and costly packages" that trustee Donald K. David, now vice chairman of the board, had earlier called for, while—and also in keeping with the David philosophy—requiring a minimum of in-foundation administration. Finally, and perhaps most decisively, Howard could hold out the prospect that moving to block grants would oblige university presidents, theretofore able to avoid setting priorities among their several international studies programs which were simultaneously appealing to Ford for funding, to put in place mechanisms for doing so.

By early 1959 Howard had won Heald over. That spring officials at Harvard, Chicago, and Columbia were invited to submit tentative proposals as to what uses they would make of block grants if they were proffered. Harvard submitted its proposal in October, via a nine-man delegation that included professors John K. Fairbank, Edwin D. Reischauer, Merle Fainsod, and Abram Bergson. The occasion was highlighted by the then dean of Harvard College McGeorge Bundy tracing the history of international studies at Harvard back to 1800 before gathered trustees and officers. It was, as one of the audience later recalled, "a virtuoso performance." [44]

Three months prior to the Harvard visitation, in July 1959, a Committee on the University and World Affairs came into being. Although formally convened at the request of Secretary of State Christian Herter, the committee was Howard's brainchild and its membership was at his and Heald's direction. Beside J. L. Morrill, former president of the University of Minnesota, as chairman, the committee included two other university chancellors and Senator J. W. Fulbright, the Secretary of Health, Education, and Welfare, the presidents of both the Rockefeller Foundation and the Carnegie Corporation, and two corporate chief executives. Howard served as the committee's staff director and, it would appear, its guiding force. [45]

The Committee's report, *The University and World Affairs* (the Morrill Report), of which some 100,000 copies were distributed following publication in July 1961, called upon American universities to take a larger role in meeting the nation's responsibilities in world affairs than the "sporadic and unplanned" one they had taken heretofore. At several points the report made reference to the university's "unique combination of resources for training, research, and other forms of service to society," and to its "serv[ing] the high needs of society, as no other institution can, primarily through its teaching and research." Indeed, by its summary, the report, in congratulating the American public for its "just awakening to the fact that world affairs are not the concern of the diplomat and soldier alone," came very close to endorsing the notion that concern with world affairs might more properly be entrusted to the scholar alone.[46]

The Morrill Report contained several recommendations for making the universities a larger force in world affairs. One was for the creation of an organization through which universities would communicate their international studies needs to the various funding agencies. Out of this recommendation came Education and World Affairs, which, from its establishment in 1963 to its demise in 1966, utilized Ford Foundation funds to promote the cause of academic international studies. As such, EWA became the 1960s' successor to the SSRC's Committee on World Area Research that had helped launch the enterprise back in the late 1940s.[47]

The most specific recommendation contained in the report related to funding. Funding for international studies, it urged, whether from government agencies or foundations, should be long-term and institutional in character. To do so "treats the university as master in its own house," while providing "the individual scholar a degree of independence from the problems of fund-raising." In short, the Morrill Report endorsed precisely the funding mechanism Howard had been advocating within the Ford Foundation since early 1959—and for precisely the reasons that made it so attractive to university administrators and international studies academics.[48]

The announcement of three such institutional grants by the Ford Foundation actually anticipated the publication of the Morrill Report by several months. Proposals submitted by Harvard, Columbia, and California had gone to the trustees in early 1960, following negotiations with ITR staff. They resulted in long-term grants of $5.6 million for Harvard, $5.5 million for Columbia, and $4 million for California (to be divided between its Berkeley and Los Angeles campuses). The intent of these grants, the accompanying statement indicated, was "to help put non-Western studies on a permanent, competitive footing with other subject-matter fields and to develop other international programs at the graduate and professional level." Notably lacking from this statement were earlier assurances that such expenditures would have an important and beneficial impact on American society, much less on "The Establishing of Peace." Sufficient to the launching of this first series of institutional grants, which resulted in the expenditure of $41,250,000 in Ford funds, was the prospect that it would advance the cause of the international studies enterprise within the university.[49]

In 1961 seven more universities—Chicago, Indiana, Michigan, Pennsylvania, Princeton, University of Washington (Seattle), and Yale—received institutional grants from ITR totaling $19.2 million. A year later Cornell, Stanford, and Wisconsin joined the ranks of long-term grant recipients, with an additional outlay from Ford of $7 million. Thus, in three years and in only thirteen grants, ITR had spent over $41 million of Ford Foundation money on academic international studies; before shifting to block grants it had taken Howard and his staff of five associates twice that long to spend only half that much. Nor were they about to stop there. "Despite the recent developments that have taken place," an ITR staff memorandum indicated in late 1961, "because of the increased pressures and complexity of international events and increased awareness of the potential role of the universities and colleges, the gap in American competence cannot be said to have narrowed as yet."[50]

In 1962 the total appropriated expenditures attributable to ITR passed the $100 million mark. Fully as impressive as the sheer magnitude of this support were the varied forms it took. A 1961 staff report by ITR associate Doak Barnett on the results of a "two-year push" on China studies listed the following: block grants to several major universities with China programs; a grant to the Joint ACLS-SSRC Committee on Contemporary China, specifically for its Program on the

Chinese Economy; a grant to Cornell's language program in Taiwan and another to the Modern Language Association for its Chinese language efforts; and senior social science fellowships to provide non-Chinese academic specialists (e.g., in diplomatic history) with travel and research opportunities. Barnett also mentioned discussions under way with several "second rank" universities whose pending proposals for long-term grants made reference to introducing programs in Chinese studies. Finally, he cited the increase in foreign area fellowships available for study in Taiwan, noting that their numbers were "still below Russianists."[51]

To be sure, Chinese studies was something of a special case, Howard having quietly committed ITR to "salvaging" the field in the aftermath of the McCarran-McCarthy assaults on many of its leading scholars. Not all world areas were so well provided for. Prior to 1963, for example, Latin American studies received little ITR support. That year, however, a Foundation-underwritten survey showing that Latin American studies "lag behind" other foreign-area programs—in receipt of foundation funding—led to a special $1.5 million appropriation to expand research and training on Latin America. In providing for such "laggard" fields, ITR officials did not suggest that support for the more generously funded fields be correspondingly cut back. Such was the philanthropic economy of the early 1960s that all assumed that Paul would be paid not only without robbing Peter but with his approval.[52]

This happy situation obtained for universities as well as for specific world areas. In 1963, under the programmatic rubric of "enlarging the nation's resource base," ITR initiated another series of long-term grants, these to fourteen universities where international studies had yet to establish itself as a permanent fixture. A desire for geographical distribution and an institution's expressed interest in providing its ongoing overseas activities with a more scholarly complement, rather than any established reputation as a center for international studies, appear to have been the principal criteria ITR used in selecting the fourteen. UCLA, Northwestern, Pittsburgh, McGill,

Minnesota, Michigan State, and NYU were among those receiving grants in excess of $1 million, with smaller grants going to Duke, Syracuse, Denver, Washington University (St. Louis), Kansas, Illinois, and Oregon.[53]

Scarcely had this $16 million gesture to institutional egalitarianism been made, however, than ITR began a second round of negotiations with the universities that had received block grants in 1960 and 1961. The first results of these negotiations were announced in 1964: grants of $12.5 million, $10.9 million, and $7 million to Harvard, Columbia, and California (Berkeley and Los Angeles) respectively. In 1965 five more major international studies universities received their second institutional grants from ITR—Chicago ($8.5 million), MIT ($8 million), Yale ($6.3 million), Michigan ($4 million), and Indiana ($3 million). Grants to Cornell ($6 million), Stanford ($6 million), and Wisconsin ($1 million) followed shortly thereafter.[54]

In all, this second round of block grants transferred $71 million from the accounts of the Ford Foundation to those of eleven American universities. Almost exactly one-third of this, $24 million, went directly into the endowment of eight of these universities for purposes of establishing forty-five fully endowed and four partially endowed professorships in international studies. Even more than the buildings that Harvard, Chicago, and Columbia constructed with funds from their grants, these chairs provided the academic international studies enterprise with a permanent place in the life of those universities—and ample insurance against the day when ITR would be no longer.

Neither university nor ITR officials thought that day imminent. On the contrary, as the Ford trustees cheerfully noted in their annual report for 1964, "a year when the Federal government stretched public philanthropy to vast new proportions," the foundation seemed about to acquire Washington as a full partner in its efforts to meet the open-ended needs of the academic international studies enterprise. The principal means by which the government was supporting international studies, Title VI of NDEA for language and area centers, had grown from an annual appropriation of less than $500,000 in 1960 to $13,000,000 in 1965. Moreover, the backing of President Johnson and of the Democratic leadership in Congress for an International Education Act that was being considered in early 1966 gave promise of tens of millions more for international studies.[55]

Yet in the face of so much no one questioned the need for more. In testimony submitted to a congressional hearing on the international education bill in January 1966, international studies academics and foundation and government officials all urged its passage. George M. Beckmann, then professor of Japanese history at the University of Kansas, warned the legislators that

the demands upon the United States arising out of its involvement in world affairs show no signs of lessening in the decade ahead. If anything, a greater effort will be required to produce the personnel, knowledge, and understanding required for the tasks at hand and in prospect.[56]

Beckmann, who had been an ITR program associate from 1961 to 1964 before rejoining the academic ranks, acknowledged the support that foundations had provided to international studies since the 1930s. "In light of national need," he quickly added, they are "still doing too little." Thus, after fifteen years of ITR, during which the Ford Foundation expended over a quarter of a billion dollars on the academic international studies enterprise, there was little progress to report. If anything, Beckmann concluded, as "between the demands of American society for more well-trained personnel and new kinds of knowledge and the capacity of American higher education to supply them, . . . the gap is widening instead of narrowing."[57]

THE FRUITS OF PHILANTHROPY

The advantage of enclosure is greater for pasture than for corn.
ADAM SMITH, 1776[1]

The question this chapter examines—what differences, if any, did ITR make?—prompted provisional responses even during the lifetime of the program, though more and more categorical ones since its demise. At one extreme, it has been argued, the differences attributable to ITR have been crucial, even determinative. ITR support for Chinese studies, especially in the 1950s, when many of those engaged in such studies were ideologically suspect, has been so described. "No matter how demandingly history may knock on the door," John Fairbank has written recently of the Ford Foundation's investment in Chinese studies, "without funding nothing much happens. Let us give credit where credit is due." Only slightly less sweepingly positive was the assessment offered by the Columbia Russianist Philip E. Mosely, who in 1967 credited ITR with "a central, indispensable, but not determining role in the growth of international studies."[2]

At the other extreme, it has been argued that ITR made relatively little difference and that what it did do would have been done by others in its absence. Without Ford money, so this argument has it, other money would have been forthcoming and would have produced pretty much the same result.

Some ITR officials during the program's heyday promoted this self-effacing view by implying that ITR was simply a philanthropic idea whose time had come. To do so was to render positively the critically disposed view of foundation observers in the 1950s that foundations "have been doing no more than mirroring the times."[3]

I admit to finding this contrafactual line of reasoning intriguing, as I find refreshing the idea that the infusion of more than a quarter of a billion dollars into a single academic enterprise was without effect. Moreover, insofar as earlier chapters in this work have located the beginnings of American international studies a century—and those of its academic component several decades—prior to the establishment of ITR, they seem to support these efforts to assign ITR only a modest role in the history of the enterprise.

Yet to demonstrate that ITR was not present at the creation of American international studies or at the establishment of its first academic beachheads does not require adopting the view that ITR did not matter, or matter crucially, in the history of the enterprise. I am persuaded that ITR made a transforming difference, not only in the development of international studies during the 1950s and 1960s, but also since. Indeed, my principal disagreement with those who have stressed the importance of ITR is that they have too narrowly construed the range of the program's impact, while too uniformly characterizing its quality. Most available assessments limit themselves to a consideration of changes within academic international studies, and they are typically found to have been wholly beneficial. But what of ITR's impact on international studies as an intellectual enterprise? On universities as a whole? On American society still more generally? Here, too, this chapter argues that the impact has been palpable, while not in every case positive.

ಹಿ I

The most conspicuous fact about academic international studies during the ITR era was its growth. The production of international studies PhDs by the sixteen sample universities used in chapter 5 again provides a means of measurement. It was steady through the 1950s, when the annual growth was about 7 percent, and then accelerated in the 1960s, when it exceeded 9 percent. In 1951 the sample universities together awarded 181 international studies PhDs; in 1966 they awarded well over twice as many, 379. In the same fifteen-year span, the total estimated national production of international studies PhDs increased from around 225 in 1951 to 550 in 1966, or about 144 percent (table 8.1).

TABLE 8.1. International Studies PhDs Awarded by Sample Universities and National Estimates, 1951, 1960, and 1966

	Number Awarded by Sample Universities [a]	Estimated Number Awarded by All Universities
1951	181	225
1960	241	325
1966	379	550

Source: Derived from Association of Research Libraries, *Doctoral Dissertations Accepted by American Universities* (New York: H. H. Wilson, 1952); *American Doctoral Dissertations* (Ann Arbor, Mich.: University Microfilms, 1961, 1967).
[a] Sample universities are listed in table 5.1.

Growth alone did not set the ITR era apart. Academic international studies expanded even more rapidly in the late 1940s, during its "takeoff," and would continue to grow in the decade after ITR. But unlike the enterprise's growth in the years immediately after World War Two, which was regionally, disciplinarily, and institutionally concentrated, that of the ITR years was in all three ways dispersed. If one pictures the academic international studies enterprise in 1951 as a pyramid in which recent growth had occurred at its peak, the growth of the ITR years is most accurately seen as lateral, occurring at the base. Academic international studies grew both up and out between 1951 and 1966, but significantly more out than up.

Although the three most-studied world regions in 1966—Russia-East Europe, Latin America, and East Asia—were the same ones as in 1951, both their relative positions had been altered and their collective share of the enterprise's total PhD production had dropped from nearly two-thirds to just over half. After enjoying a surge in the 1950s, Russian studies thereafter fell off, so that it found itself in 1966 with about the same share of the enterprise as fifteen years earlier. East Asian studies experienced a relative decline in the 1950s but recouped lost ground thereafter. Latin American studies experienced an absolute decline in PhD production between 1951 and 1960,

TABLE 8.2. International Studies PhDs at Sample Universities, 1951, 1960, and 1966, by Area Focus

	1951		1960		1966	
	N	%	N	%	N	%
Russia and East Europe	31	17	50	21	71	19
Latin America	54	30	44	18	65	17
East Asia	29	16	31	13	60	16
South Asia	16	9	49	20	58	15
Middle East	24	13	28	12	40	11
International or other	17	9	16	7	36	9
Africa	3	2	14	6	31	8
Canada	7	4	9	4	18	5
Total	181	100	241	101	379	100

Sources: see table 8.1.
Note: 1960 percentages do not add up to 100 because of rounding.

and a precipitous relative decline from 30 percent of all international studies PhDs to 18 percent, but by 1966 its numbers had increased and its relative trajectory had bottomed out (table 8.2).

Correspondingly, the fastest growing areas of study during the ITR years, in both absolute and relative terms, were precisely those areas that had earlier figured least prominently in the enterprise's overall reconnaissance. During the 1950s South Asian studies tripled its annual production of PhDs, increasing in the process its share of the enterprise's total output from 9 percent in 1951 to 20 percent in 1960. Even more spectacular was the growth of African studies, which increased its annual

PhD production almost fivefold from 1951 to 1960 and more than doubled the number again by 1966.

Plotting growth rates is a more certain business than accounting for them. Still, some speculations as to cause seem in order. It is, for example, likely more than coincidental that the two fastest growing areas of study, South Asia and Africa, shared five characteristics that set them apart from the more slowly growing areas of study, particularly Russia and East Asia. First, both were specifically identified in the immediate postwar years as the hitherto *most* neglected areas within the American scholarly purview, but which, with European control ending in both areas, were no longer to be intellectually off limits. Second, both areas became the focus of extensive overseas development efforts, which increased American exposure to and curiosity about them. Third, the growth in intellectual interest in both areas more often took the form of political, economic, and anthropological studies than of historical and humanistic studies, which are more dependent upon extensive library resources and highly developed linguistic skills. From this third characteristic flows the fourth: lack of knowledge of even one of the principal native languages of either South Asia or Africa did not prevent one from becoming a recognized scholar of either world area. Fifth and finally, the study of both areas received early and continuous funding priority from ITR.

A similar growth-by-dispersion pattern brought about comparable shifts in the disciplinary composition of academic international studies during the ITR era. The most spectacular of these was the relative decline of history. In 1951, with fifty-four PhDs in international studies, history accounted for 30 percent of all those produced by the sample universities; in 1966, with seventy-seven, it accounted for only 20 percent. Meanwhile, the next two leading disciplines in 1951, political science and economics, managed to increase their collective share of the overall output only from 36 percent in 1951 to 39 percent in 1966, while anthropology's actually dropped slightly (table 8.3). History's relative decline as the principal discipline within the international studies enterprise during the ITR years, therefore, is attributable not to gains registered by its immediate neighbors in the social sciences, but to gains in the humanities, specifically in language and literature and the disciplines included here under the category "other humanities." Between 1951 and 1966 disciplines in the humanities increased their share of international studies PhDs produced in the sam-

TABLE 8.3. International Studies PhDs Awarded by the Sample Universities, 1951, 1960, and 1966, by Field and Discipline

	1951		1960		1966	
	N	*%*	*N*	*%*	*N*	*%*
Social sciences	*146*	*81*	*196*	*81*	*284*	*75*
History	54	30	54	22	77	20
Political science	30	17	51	21	73	19
Economics	35	19	41	17	75	20
Anthropology	23	13	33	14	47	12
Sociology	4	2	17	7	12	3
Humanities	*35*	*19*	*45*	*19*	*95*	*25*
Language and literature	28	15	35	15	71	19
Other humanities	7	4	10	4	24	6
Total	*181*	*100*	*241*	*100*	*379*	*100*

Sources: see table 8.1.

ple universities from 19 percent of the total to 25 percent, and in so doing reversed a pattern of declining interest in the humanities generally that had dated back to the early 1900s.

Here, too, even the most passing attempt to account for this pattern of disciplinary dispersion cannot ignore the likely influence of ITR. Without ever specifically setting quotas or establishing guidelines, ITR officials consistently communicated the view that international studies programs with broad disciplinary involvement were preferable to—i.e., more likely to be funded than—those which had only limited disciplinary involvement. Encouraging the making of joint appointments also helped increase disciplinary diversity. Moreover, such appointments, typically split with an area or regional program, were viewed by departments as an economical means of expanding, while avoiding the tensions that resulted from the alternative policy of expanding by doubling up on already covered specialties. The result was that, on campuses enjoying ITR funding as well as on those seeking it, for a department not to go into international studies was to invite the double charge of intellectual provincialism and entrepreneurial indolence. With few departments ready to confess to either, the dispersion of academic international studies proceeded apace.[4] And inasmuch as ITR's stated objectives included both extending the scope of international studies to embrace study of the hitherto least studied areas and enlisting the efforts of disciplines hitherto least involved in such studies, both the regional and the disciplinary dispersion that took place during the ITR era were intended consequences. One may go even further and suggest that ITR policies played an important role in bringing them about.

Ironically, however, the type of dispersion for which the statistical evidence is most compelling, institutional dispersion, is that for which the conscious contribution of ITR is most problematic. In the early 1950s, ITR seemed committed to a policy of extending support for international studies so as to extend the institutional boundaries of the enterprise beyond the handful of universities that had dominated it for half a century. But by the late 1950s, with the introduction of block grants, policy swung back in favor of "the Harvards." Subsequent grants made to fourteen "second-rank" universities in 1963–64, under the programmatic rubric "Enlarging the Resource Base," and inclusion of such relative newcomers to international studies as Indiana and MIT in the second round of block grants, only slightly qualified ITR's growing disposition to concentrate its support for international studies on the half-dozen universities that had the longest and most distinguished involvement in the enterprise. Ultimately just three such universities—Harvard, Columbia, and Chicago—received more than one-third of all ITR funds expended directly on university programs. Thus, rather than being attributable to policies consciously adopted and pursued by the Ford Foundation, the institutional dispersion of academic international studies during the ITR era occurred either irrespective of ITR policies or in the face of them.[5]

The fastest growing institutional sector of academic international studies in the 1950s consisted of universities that had only since World War Two begun producing PhDs of any kind in any significant number. Syracuse and UCLA are examples, as are the University of Washington, Michigan State Univer-

TABLE 8.4. International Studies PhDs at Sample Universities, 1951, 1960, and 1966, by Generational Clusters

	1951		1960		1966	
	N	%	N	%	N	%
Ancients	119	66	149	62	203	54
In-Betweens	54	30	65	27	122	32
Moderns	5	4	27	11	54	14
Total	181	100	241	100	379	100

Source: see table 8.1. For definitions of generations and composition of clusters, see table 5.1.

sity, and Indiana. Most of the international studies PhDs produced by these "moderns" in the 1950s were in Latin American, South Asian, and African studies, but not all; three of the first international studies PhDs produced by the University of Washington were in Russian history.

During the early 1960s the production of international studies PhDs increased fastest at universities of the "in-between" type, those which had been significant producers of PhDs before World War Two but not in international studies (see table 8.4). Among these, Berkeley, Michigan, and Stanford increased their production of international studies PhDs at rates well above those of the "ancients" or "moderns" overall. Still, among the former, Cornell, principally in Southeast Asian studies, and among the latter, UCLA, in Middle Eastern studies, recorded comparably sharp increases. Whereas in 1951 only five of the sixteen sample universities produced a dozen or more international studies PhDs annually, by 1966 thirteen were doing so.

Growth at the margins, institutional or otherwise, was hardly unique to the academic international studies enterprise; it was common to American higher education throughout the 1950s and 1960s. In point of fact, graduate work in international studies probably dispersed no more than did graduate work in the humanities and social sciences overall. In 1966, when the sample universities' share of the national production of all PhDs in the humanities and social sciences was 42 percent (down from 53 percent in 1951), the same universities—as reference to table 8.1 will show—continued to account for an estimated 69 percent (as against 80 percent in 1951) of all international studies PhDs produced. Clearly, the substantial investment in language-training facilities and library acquisitions needed to introduce certain kinds of international studies programs, most notably Russian and East Asian, placed real limits on the institutional dispersion of the entire enterprise.[6]

Yet the fact bears repeating that the international studies enterprise experienced substantial growth at universities that were not principal ITR beneficiaries, and at still others that received no direct ITR support at all. Moreover, if ITR funding policies did not directly mandate institutional dispersion, the specific cases of ITR support for international studies at UCLA, Michigan State, and Wisconsin all suggest that at some institutions even comparatively modest ITR support greatly advanced the enterprise's cause locally. Indeed, from the perspective of ambitious academic administrators in Los Angeles, East Lansing, and Madison in the early 1960s, the size of an ITR grant mattered less than the institutional company they found themselves in upon receiving one.

For UCLA and Michigan State, intent upon achieving parity with intrastate rivals Berkeley and Michigan, or for Wisconsin, determined to retrieve national standing, international studies became an important means for advancing their institutional ends. Not only was the perceived qualitative gap separating these universities from their competition smaller in international studies than in older academic enterprises, but in some parts of the enterprise the gap was nonexistent. Accordingly, whereas the University of Michigan's headstart in East Asian studies was not likely to be quickly overcome, African studies provided Michigan State with an opportunity to become, almost overnight, not only Michigan's preeminent institution but one of only a handful of institutions with national reputations in the field. The comparable effort UCLA put into African studies in the 1950s and Middle Eastern studies later can also be explained in part by the prospect both held out as means for outpacing rival Berkeley.

At Michigan State, regarded in some quarters during the mid-1960s as the archetypical "university on the make," international studies vied with football and cornering the market in National Merit scholars as generators of national attention. East Lansing officials, for example, made much of the fact that during the 1963–64 academic year more Michigan State faculty were abroad than those of any other university. Not to be outdone, in 1966 the Office of International Studies of the University of Wisconsin published a *Directory of Faculty with International Academic Qualifications,* listing more than 500 faculty members having even the most passing acquaintance with a foreign locale of interest in international studies.[7]

Not only aspiring universities but ambitious academics were attracted to international studies during the ITR era. "Thus the characteristic feature," one observer of the enterprise as it operated at Berkeley noted at the time,

was a procession of individual professors to foundation doors seeking support for curricular and research programs focussed on particular world regions. An aura of power began to cling to those who were successful in these efforts.

Still another close observer of the California academic scene, the sociologist Robert Nisbet, writing in the early 1970s about the lamentable changes that had overtaken the American university during the previous two decades, specifically included the "rising to mastery" of those who held the directorships of precisely the kinds of "fast-multiplying institutes, centers, and bureaus" that housed the international studies enterprise. Upon them he conferred the by no means honorific title, "new men of power."[8]

For some who directed international studies programs the next step to directing larger parts of their universities was short, natural, and, in some instances, calculated. The ITR requirement that block grants be administered by a centralized mechanism virtually mandated the creation of vice presidencies for international studies on every campus in receipt of such a grant, and it encouraged universities seeking grants to do likewise. Not surprisingly, entrepreneurially accomplished international studies academics were thought to be especially suited to filling these posts. Fred Harvey Harrington, who began his academic career at Wisconsin as a diplomatic and East Asian historian, and later represented Wisconsin in negotiations with ITR officials that produced two block grants, is an acknowledged case in point. "Quite clearly," he reminisced in 1979, "the Ford Foundation grant to strengthen our campus in foreign area studies was of great and lasting importance in university history. It also, for better or worse, helped make me president."[9]

ẽ⁓ II

Surely part of the glamor that came to be attached to international studies during the ITR years has to do not only with the fact that it grew rapidly but also with the fact that it grew more rapidly than did virtually any other aspect of American graduate education. It thus successively came to constitute a larger and larger part of the academic enterprise. In 1951 international studies PhDs accounted for 17 percent of the social science and humanities PhDs produced at the sample universities; by 1966, they accounted for 22 percent, which meant that since 1951 international studies' share had increased by nearly a third.

The rise of international studies to numerical prominence

during the ITR era is even more striking when the era is divided at 1960 and institutional instances are cited. At Columbia, between 1951 and 1960, the proportion of international studies PhDs among all social science and humanities PhDs went from 17 percent to 27 percent; at Cornell, from only 8 percent to a spectacular 38 percent; at Syracuse, which produced no international studies PhDs in the social sciences or humanities in 1951, five of sixteen such PhDs, or 31 percent, were awarded in international studies in 1961. Indeed, of the sixteen sample universities, only at Michigan did the growth

TABLE 8.5. International Studies PhDs at Sample Universities, 1951, 1960, and 1966, As a Proportion of All Social Science and Humanities PhDs, by Institution

	Percentage of Social Science and Humanities PhDs Awarded in International Studies		
	1951	*1960*	*1966*
Ancients	16	22	24
Yale	14	16	14
Cornell	8	30	30
Harvard	21	20	31
Columbia	17	27	22
Chicago	11	16	26
In-Betweens	21	21	20
Wisconsin	14	17	11
Berkeley	19	32	24
Michigan	27	21	24
Stanford	18	26	23
Pittsburgh	8	0	22
Texas	33	10	11
Moderns	14	15	20
Indiana	10	11	9
UCLA	17	19	25
Washington (Seattle)	43	19	15
Michigan State	0	7	20
Syracuse	0	31	19
All sample universities	17	20	22

Source: see table 8.1.

of international studies fail to match overall growth in the social sciences and humanities, and only at Texas did the absolute number of international studies PhDs produced decline. The sharply accelerated growth in the production of international studies PhDs between 1960 and 1966 kept the enterprise's rate of growth well above that of the humanities and social sciences overall. Over the entire period the most spectacular relative growth occurred at Michigan State and UCLA, with only slightly less impressive gains registered at Harvard and Chicago, where, as at Cornell, by 1966 more than a quarter of all the PhDs produced in the social sciences and humanities were in international studies. In 1951 only four sample universities produced 20 percent or more of their social science and humanities PhDs in international studies; in 1960 there were seven; in 1966, ten (see table 8.5).

The disproportionate growth of international studies during the ITR era was attended by comparable increases in the international studies component of virtually all the disciplines that contributed to the enterprise (table 8.6). The single exception was history, where international studies PhDs constituted 34 percent of the discipline's total production in 1951, but only 28 percent in 1960 and 1966. International studies' share of political science PhDs, on the other hand, went from 27 percent in 1951 to 41 percent in 1960 and 46 percent in 1966. By 1966, 30 percent of all social science PhDs produced by the sample universities were in international studies; fifteen years earlier it had been 23 percent. Even in language and literature, despite the simultaneous surge in English and American literary studies, international studies PhDs increased their share of the total production from 10 percent in 1951 to 13 percent in 1966.

In sum, during the ITR era leading American universities and many of the academic disciplines at their intellectual core became "internationalized." That they did so has almost universally been deemed a favorable outcome of the Ford Foundation's efforts—calls for the "provincialization" of American universities are rarely heard—and one for which foundation officials have since taken some credit. ITR officials at the time,

TABLE 8.6. International Studies PhDs at Sample Universities, 1951, 1960, and 1966, As a Proportion of All Social Science and Humanities PhDs, by Field and Discipline

	Percentage of Social Science and Humanities PhDs Awarded in International Studies		
	1951	1960	1966
Social sciences	23	27	30
History	34	28	28
Political science	27	41	46
Economics	16	17	23
Anthropology	43	62	66
Sociology	4	17	10
Humanities	8	10	12
Language and literature	10	12	13
Other humanities	5	6	10
All disciplines	17	20	22

Source: see table 8.1.
Note: Numbers of international studies PhDs in each discipline are shown in table 8.3.

however, did not, and with good reason. "Internationalization," as the phrase came to be used in the 1960s with respect to American universities, was not a process for which ITR staff had ever devised a means of measurement, primarily because it had not been an initial objective of the program. Consequently, they were in no position to gauge the success of the program in terms of the degree of "internationalization" effected, short of declaring the process complete and the university totally internationalized. Instead, they implied that the process had yet a good way to go before that would occur.

This, of course, was as the academic international studies enterprise would have it. No one in the enterprise saw much purpose in identifying the point at which a given university or discipline could be said to be sufficiently internationalized. To do so was to invite curtailment of support. Thus, the fact that by the mid-1960s well over half (275 of 500) of the University of Chicago's graduate students in history and political science were in international studies, or that four out of every ten members of the faculties of political science and philosophy at Columbia were affiliated with one of the university's seven regional institutes, only brought forth from both universities still more elaborate proposals to make them still more "internationalized." The beauty of "internationalization," as its promoters in both the Ford Foundation and the academic community must have appreciated, was in its admitting to almost infinite regression.

&» III

In making the internationalization of American universities their common objective, albeit belatedly and even after the fact, Ford officials and international studies academics fixed on a goal for ITR that was both operationally elusive and retrospectively commendable. But they also, likely without intending to, did something else. In focusing attention on the internationalization of American universities as ITR's principal accomplishment, attention was deflected away from a parallel if more problematic process that also marked the ITR era: the academic enclosure of American international studies. With virtually all the growth and dispersion of international studies during those years occurring within universities, the entire intellectual enterprise came to be regarded as, and to be, synonymous with its academic component. Of this development, arguably as significant in the history of American intellectual life as the internationalization of American universities, and no less plausibly attributable to ITR, some consideration is in order, not least because it has been virtually ignored by foundation officials and international studies academics alike.

Before proceeding to this consideration, three prefatory qualifications should be made explicit, though they have been implied earlier. First, academic enclosure is not a process peculiar to international studies or to the ITR era; it is both a more general and a less chronologically restricted phenomenon of American intellectual life. Second, just as international studies was not the first American intellectual enterprise to undergo academic enclosure, the enclosure it has undergone does not necessarily exceed that of all other enterprises. Classical and philosophical studies, for example, may be more fully enclosed within the universities than international studies, and they certainly were enclosed much earlier. Third, as compared with the academic leadership that brought about the enclosure of, for example, the social sciences at the turn of the century, international studies academics during the ITR era were probably less consciously intent upon excluding nonacademics from their enterprise. It was not that international studies academics (still less ITR officials) set out to make international studies a wholly academic enterprise, but rather in their zeal to advance international studies within the university, they consistently neglected the needs of the enterprise outside the university. Nonetheless, however belated, incomplete, and even inadvertent, the academic enclosure of American international studies during the ITR era was real enough. Accordingly, of all the outcomes of the intervention of the Ford Foundation into the life of this intellectual enterprise, its enclosure may well have been the least intentional, yet the most consequential.

This brings us to the second level of the argument. Not only was the academic enclosure of American international studies an unintended consequence of the Ford Foundation's intervention into the life of the enterprise, but its enclosure also contradicted two of the explicit purposes prompting the intervention in the first place. These were, as stated in successive Ford Foundation annual reports in 1952 and 1953, the following: to increase "the numbers of Americans trained for service in government, education, and business . . . in relation to foreign affairs"; and "to broaden the base of public understanding of international problems."

The vast increase in the academic international studies enterprise need not in itself have been inconsistent with ITR's purposes. It could be rendered consistent with them, however, only if its expansion resulted in the enterprise providing proportionally larger numbers of Americans with training in international studies for careers outside the university, while it permitted the enterprise to perform more effectively in its assigned role as public educator. In point of fact, expansion was attended by neither of these results. Rather than train proportionally more students for outside careers, the academic international studies enterprise retained more and more of its best students to serve its own expansionary needs, thereby depriving occupations outside the university of their training. Serving these same internal needs of the enterprise similarly took increasing precedence over serving those of the as yet to be enlightened American public.

Perhaps as striking a difference between the situation of international studies academics during the ITR era and that of their prewar counterparts as the increased size and enhanced institutional standing of their enterprise was the much greater success they enjoyed in placing their PhDs in academic positions. As was pointed out in chapter 4, among the international studies PhDs produced in 1934 by Berkeley, Chicago, Columbia, Harvard, Wisconsin, and Yale, only 38 percent subsequently obtained permanent academic employment; in 1940 the proportion was still only 41 percent. But beginning around the late 1940s, the preponderance of nonacademic careers was overcome, and by the early 1950s it had been reversed (table 8.7). Whereas in the 1930s about three of every five international studies PhDs permanently left the university upon receiving their degree, in the 1950s more than three of every five stayed on to take up academic careers. By the early 1960s upwards of 70 percent of the international studies PhDs at several of the six universities examined proceeded directly to academic positions, if they had not done so earlier. At the University of Chicago, the proportions frequently approached 80 percent, for example among PhDs in South Asian studies.[10]

To be sure, the incidence of subsequent academic careers among international studies PhDs varied according to their regional specialty and discipline. East Asianists, for example, were somewhat less likely to go into academic life than South Asianists, and a good bit less likely than East Europeanists.

Similarly, economists in international studies more often found employment outside the university than did historians or those in language and literature. These internal differences aside, it appears likely that during the ITR era international studies PhDs were at least as likely to pursue academic careers as PhDs in the same disciplines not in international studies. In both economics and language and literature, respectively the least and most academically enclosed disciplines, PhDs in international

TABLE 8.7. Proportion of International Studies PhD Recipients at Six Universities Going On to Academic Careers, 1934–1966

	Number Receiving International Studies PhD	Number Going On to Academic Career	Percentage
1934	42	16	38
1940	49	20	41
1951	136	78	57
1960	165	109	66
1966	238	153	64

Sources: number of PhD recipients, see table 8.1; number going on to academic career determined by examination of disciplinary and area association directories and alumni directories as available; *Directory of American Scholars*, 3d–7th ed. (New York: R. R. Bowker, 1957–1978); *American Men and Women of Science (Social and Behavioral Sciences)*, 13th ed. (New York: R. R. Bowker, 1976); and *National Faculty Directory* (Detroit: Gale Research, 1970). Determination of career made ten years after receipt of PhD (fifteen in the case of those receiving degree in 1934).

Note: The six universities included in this table are University of California at Berkeley, University of Chicago, Columbia, Harvard, University of Wisconsin, and Yale.

studies appear to have been less likely to stray from the occupational confines of the university than were their disciplinary peers not in international studies. Scattered statistical evidence suggests that in the early 1960s, despite the sharply increased annual production of international studies PhDs, academic demand exceeded supply. Reports from the field suggest as much. "The demand for qualified scholars in universities has been growing apace," the director of the Russian Research Center at Harvard reported in 1965. "Recently, in some fields it has been difficult to make suitable recommendations in response to inquiries from other universities."[11]

The existence of an academic "seller's market" for international studies PhDs was not likely to be lost on graduate students deciding on their areas of specialization. It seems also to have been noticed by large numbers of students enrolled in MA programs in international affairs and regional studies at Harvard, Columbia, and elsewhere, many of whom in the early 1960s switched over to PhD programs in international studies—and to the prospect of an academic career—rather than persist in their original nonacademic career intentions. The fact that fellowship support—principally Ford foreign area fellowships—was readily available to those who did so made the switch that much easier. More than a few others, already embarked on careers in business or government, found ample fellowship support for graduate studies and good academic employment prospects following upon receipt of a PhD sufficient enticement to leave their jobs, resume graduate training, and seek permanent residence within the academic international studies enterprise.[12]

If one were to press the argument that some aspects of the ITR program, while admirably serving the self-perceived needs of the academic international studies community, directly contradicted the program's larger and nonacademic purposes, a case in point might well be found in the history of the program's first and most durable grantee, the Foreign Area Fellowship Program. In 1952, when the Ford Foundation took over funding for the program from its original sponsor, the Carnegie Corporation, FAFP was not considered a graduate fellowship program, still less a program designed for aspiring international studies academics. Its stated purpose, like that of ITR generally, was the preparation of Americans "for careers in relation to foreign affairs." Appropriately enough, then, of the 103 recipients of foreign area fellowships in 1953, the first year the program was under ITR auspices, fewer than half subsequently became academics.[13]

The 1956 annual report reaffirmed the trustees' conviction that FAFP was "aimed not at producing a corps of narrow specialists but at giving economists, historians, lawyers and persons in the other social sciences, humanities, and professions an understanding of these other areas of the world." Yet by then the process by which these fellowships came to be perceived as primarily for graduate students planning on academic careers was already well advanced. Quite likely the composition of the selection committees, predominantly academic, favored such applicants over those of would-be businessmen or lawyers, although there exists testimony to the contrary. Self-screening was probably also a factor, in accordance with the principle invoked by Max Weber to explain the preponderance of lawyers over businessmen in elective office, "dispensability." Whatever the reasons, by 1962, despite nearly a doubling of the number of fellowships that had been awarded in 1953—from 103 to 201—the number awarded to recipients who subsequently went into government, the professions, or business dropped from twenty-five to just eight. Of those receiving a foreign area fellowship in 1962 whose subsequent careers are known, 90 percent became academics. [14]

The transformation of FAFP from a program promoting "careers in international affairs" to one providing research and travel opportunities for prospective international studies academics did not pass unnoted by ITR officials. "FAFP," an intraprogram memorandum concluded flatly in 1961, "has not been a successful vehicle for attracting persons from the non-academic fields." But instead of terminating the program, ITR transferred its administration to a joint committee of the American Council of Learned Societies and the Social Science Research Council, where it continued to receive Ford support. The effect of this transfer, as an administrator of the program during both its ITR and ACLS-SSRC phases has since concluded, was to "integrate it more closely into the academic community." There it continued for another decade to provide fellowship support to persons who, according to the same source, "have for the most part gone into teaching and research." [15]

Once in their first teaching positions, new international studies PhDs in the ITR era moved up rapidly. A survey of some 4,400 international studies academics conducted by Richard D. Lambert in 1969 allows the inference that they scaled the academic ladder faster than did their peers not in international studies. Compared with faculty members generally, they more often received their initial appointment at the assistant professor level, and while there they were paid more and taught less.[16]

It might also be noted that international studies academics during the ITR era were only about half as likely to be women (10 percent as opposed to 20 percent) as were academics generally. This may be in part attributable to the connection between earlier military service and international studies careers. It may also reflect the exclusionary tendencies which scholars like Patricia A. Graham have discerned operating throughout most of the history of American academic life, particularly among academic enterprises trying to establish their legitimacy.[17]

Some of these differences reflect, and in part result from, another that set international studies academics apart: they were far more likely to be employed by large PhD-granting universities than by small colleges. This was the case with nearly three-quarters of Lambert's international studies academics. Not surprisingly, then, they secured fellowship support more frequently than did nontenured academics generally, much of it from sources like the Ford Foundation and the Fulbright-Hays program, which favored international studies applicants. Finally, in view of these cumulative advantages, it follows that international studies academics received tenure earlier and more often than did academics generally. If, as Princeton's Leonard Binder recalls the situation in Middle Eastern studies during the ITR era, "it was awfully easy to become an area specialist and to get a job," it appears to have been equally easy in other parts of international studies. Nor was it difficult, with the enterprise expanding, to go on from there to tenure. Among the hundreds of international studies PhDs who did so in the salad years of late 1950s and early 1960s, Chicago's South Asian anthropologist Ralph Nicholas surely was not the only one who all the while "felt I was nursing on the Ford Foundation."[18]

ළ IV

The availability of ample, long-term, and relatively unre-
stricted outside funding during the ITR years permitted a vast
increase in the numbers of academic positions in international
studies and assured a growing supply of fellowship-laden PhDs
to fill them. It also reduced the dependence of the enterprise
upon sources of support other than the Ford Foundation. The
principal benefactors of the enterprise in the 1930s and 1940s,
the Rockefeller Foundation and the Carnegie Corporation, both
quickly cut back their support of academic international studies upon the appearance of ITR, having concluded that they
might more effectively direct their philanthropic energies elsewhere. By the mid-1960s, both the Rockefeller-sponsored
Russian Institute at Columbia and the Carnegie-sponsored
Russian Research Center at Harvard derived the bulk of their
operating expenses from Ford.

In addition to letting earlier benefactors off the hook, the
availability of Ford money exempted international studies academics from the need to cultivate other would-be—and once-
were—sustaining audiences. The most proximate of these was
undergraduates. International studies had always been viewed
as an expensive academic activity, primarily because of the
language instruction requirements and the limited appeal of its
seemingly esoteric concerns. Nonetheless, as Bolton's efforts
at Berkeley between the wars attested, international studies academics before ITR appreciated the value of encouraging large
undergraduate classes whenever possible. Likewise, the introduction of Oriental Civilization survey courses at Chicago and
Columbia in the 1930s, as well as the famous "Rice Paddies"
course on East Asia developed by Professors Fairbank and
Reischauer at Harvard, all reflect a willingness of the prewar
enterprise to support itself at least in part in the coin of the
academic realm—enrollments.

During the ITR era, such lecture courses designed to attract
large numbers of undergraduates lost much of their earlier
economic rationale. They became neglected, were passed from

one junior faculty member to another, often became in the process too specialized for most undergraduates, or, as at Columbia, were dropped altogether. "Too many other commitments" became the increasingly standard response of senior Chicago professors asked to teach such a course. Meanwhile, the "merely" curious undergraduate or the kinds of free spirits the East Asianist William Theodore de Bary recalled taking Chinese at Columbia in the late 1930s—earnest missionaries, journalists, political activists like Paul Robeson between concert tours, professors of English who took up Oriental languages as a hobby, society matrons—were displaced by earnest Chinese-scholars-in-the-making. The intensive regimen for language instruction, developed during World War Two but institutionalized thereafter, intimidated all but the most professionally committed, leaving no place in the curriculum for the amateur who wished to dabble in Chinese or Japanese. Yet few connected with the academic international studies enterprise during the ITR era, Chicago's Milton Singer and Indiana's Robert Byrnes being conspicuous exceptions, publicly shared de Bary's view that these changes were not all pure gain.[19]

International studies academics neglected undergraduates during the ITR era in part because the Ford Foundation did not insist otherwise. Some ITR money—about $7 million— did go directly for support of international studies at the undergraduate level, but not until well on in the history of the program. Similarly, graduate centers like Chicago, Columbia, and Harvard were encouraged to, and did, share their international studies facilities with faculty from neighboring colleges. Yet the fate of a training program for liberal arts college teachers launched by Harvard's East Asian Research Center in 1958, with ITR support, illustrates the operative priorities. After functioning for two years, the program was terminated, following the decision of the center's directors that "we should not divert limited funds from research training and actual research to teacher training, however strategic and well selected the teachers might be." The Ford Foundation concurred, even to accepting Harvard's derisory assessment of the aborted program as "essentially a national service." [20]

These and other equally transitory efforts, such as the University of Chicago Southern Asian studies program's "Flying Carpet" series of faculty lectures at Swarthmore, Haverford, and Bryn Mawr in 1963, did little to arrest what Clark Kerr and other observers of American higher education characterized as the general deprecation—and resultant deterioration— of undergraduate teaching. Some ITR-funded arrangements, such as an international studies program buying upwards of half its affiliated members' teaching time, so that they could devote more time to research and writing, likely contributed to it. "On the whole," as a Harvard international studies academic explained his colleagues' predilections to a sympathetic ITR staffer in 1963, "we seem to go in for the development of manuscripts and trying to publish them rather than holding meetings and discussions. We feel the time for talk has passed." [21]

The argument here is not that international studies academics bear a disproportionate responsibility for the neglect of undergraduates during the ITR era, even at those universities where ITR funds were concentrated and the neglect most pronounced. Nor is it that they were alone in being given over to what in retrospect seems to have been an excessive preoccupation with training their academic successors, or, as one of the more prolific among them put it, "to reproduce their kind until death or retirement prevents them from doing so." Both were general tendencies throughout academic life rather than distinctive features of any single enterprise. Yet insofar as international studies contributed to both those tendencies, there is considerable irony in their having done so, given the high hopes many academic reformers originally had for the enterprise's potential as a catalyst for curricular innovation. International studies were supposed to help meet not only the national challenge of intellectual parochialism but also, given its interdisciplinary nature, "the challenge of departmental parochialism" that some saw besetting American higher education.

As late as 1966, the Yale Latin Americanist Richard M. Morse argued that "the only conceivable justification for smuggling [international studies] into the standard curriculum . . . is that they serve as a Trojan horse for academic reform."[22]

Whatever the promise of international studies as a disturber of the academic status quo, it failed to materialize. Even at universities where regional programs acquired full departmental status, South Asian studies at Chicago and East Asian languages and culture at Columbia being examples, faculty members were careful to maintain their disciplinary base as well. Similarly, graduate students in international studies might take fellowship support from an area center, but they took their degrees in a specific discipline. "In the end one had to agree," concluded one academic who earlier felt some of its mystique, "area study was not a new discipline of organized principles. It was only an activity, something one did."[23]

What then of area centers? In the main they provided affiliated faculty and graduate students with a second home, one throughout the ITR era better appointed than the departmental home, and at more effective remove from the daily distractions of university life, not least those related to classroom teaching. Rather than as hotbeds of curricular insurgency, area centers by the early 1960s had come to be regarded almost everywhere among faculty concerned with the teaching of undergraduates as hostile bastions of academic entrepreneurship. Occasional utterances from within, such as reported to have come from a Michigan State international studies administrator in 1965, that "classroom teaching is a tame business," only confirmed the widely held view that curricular reform was hardly one of the international studies enterprise's pressing priorities.[24]

Nor, perhaps, should one have ever expected otherwise. Invoking Alvin Gouldner's useful distinction between academic "locals," those whose careers center on their employing institution and its teaching function, and academic "cosmopolitans," those whose careers are focused on their disciplinary (and in this case, area) activities and their research, few international studies academics during the ITR era left much doubt that they numbered among the latter. Their was a quite distinct enterprise, growing parallel to rather than converging upon other academic enterprises, and leaving those who labored within it, as one who did described them, "members of a cult, set apart. They felt both separate and more than equal."[25]

V

The establishment of area centers separate from and at some remove from departments likely contributed to the "resplendent isolation" that came to characterize international studies academics within the academic community during the ITR years. But so did the creation of their own professional associations, with their own journals, annual conventions, and office-holding hierarchies. Except for the American Association for the Advancement of Slavic Studies, founded in 1948, all five of the principal area associations—the others being the Association for Asian Studies (1957), the African Studies Association (1957), the Latin American Studies Association (1966), and the Middle East Studies Association (1966)—were founded during the ITR era and with ITR financial assistance.[26]

In view of the fact that American international studies had survived for more than a century after its organizational founding in the 1840s with the help of only one association, the American Oriental Society, the proliferation of such associations is itself indicative of the explosive growth experienced by international studies during the ITR era. At no time during its first hundred years of existence did the AOS have more than 500 members. The Association of Asian Studies had at its founding about 1,000 members; by 1965, it had over 2,000, making it one of the largest scholarly associations in the country. In 1966, when the AOS had approximately 800 members, the combined membership of the AAS, AAASS, ASA, LASA, and MESA approached 8,000. Although most of their members were also members of the various disciplinary associations—the American Historical or American Political Science Associations, and so forth—the two sets of professional associations had virtually no institutional connection of any kind between them.[27]

Nor could the institutional bifurcation, like that between the AOS and the newly formed disciplinary associations in the late nineteenth century, be attributed to any lack of professionalism on the part of the organizational representatives of international studies. Indeed, the largest among them, the AAS, was 90 percent academic. Similar proportions obtained in LASA and MESA; the latter at its founding seriously considered limiting membership to persons with PhDs in Middle Eastern studies. By the mid-1960s area associations were at least as dominated by academics as were the American Historical and Modern Language Associations, and more so than the American Economic and the American Political Science Associations. Again, in contrast with these organizations during their first decades, area associations do not seem to have systematically sought to exclude nonacademics from their organizational affairs, although individual members occasionally urged such a policy. But so long as the interests of nonacademics went unserved by these organizations, the outcome was much the same. No less than the disciplinary associations of the 1880s and 1890s, the area associations of the 1950s and 1960s became effective instruments of academic enclosure.

The almost wholly academic character of these associations revealed itself in the discord that intruded upon their activities in the mid 1960s, discord that put the survival of at least two—the Association of Asian Studies and the African Studies Association—temporarily in doubt. Although the specific grievances and specific occasions that sparked the respective disputes differed, the leadership of both the AAS and the ASA, into the mid-1960s drawn almost exclusively from the major institutional centers for Asian and African studies, underwent a "grass-roots" challenge from members not identified with these major centers. But both disputes, from the outset, were between academics; neither the place of nonacademics in association affairs nor the exclusively academic character of association leadership was at issue, at least initially. Again, the contrast between these organizational battles and those which occurred within the American Oriental Society in the early 1890s could hardly be sharper.[28]

Eventually, these disputes did become entangled with larger issues that transcended intraprofessional concerns. Within the AAS, for example, dissidents called upon the association leadership to speak out on public issues, particularly on that of American military involvement in Vietnam. When that leadership insisted upon adhering to the association's nonpolitical traditions, a group of graduate student members, with the tacit support of a few of their more politically engaged elders, chose the occasion of the 1968 AAS convention to form a Committee of Concerned Asian Scholars, which explicitly repudiated the AAS policy of political noninvolvement. However dramatic an expression on behalf of scholarly activism in public affairs, the Committee of Concerned Asian Scholars likely did not reflect the views of most American Asian scholars, even less those of the academic international studies enterprise generally. In response to a questionnaire submitted to the AAS membership in 1968, a majority supported the leadership's position opposing association statements on political issues. Moreover, among the many activities in which the association might wish to become engaged, the membership gave lowest priority to "public information and public educational activities." So much for fostering an enlightened citizenry.[29]

೪> VI

It is probably impossible to determine whether the nonacademic component of American international studies experienced an absolute numerical decline during the ITR era. Even if it could be determined that a decline had occurred, the role that either international studies academics or ITR played in its decline would remain problematic. Yet it can with some assurance be stated that international studies outside the university did not experience the exponential growth it did within the university, and that the relative standing of nonacademic international studies within the intellectual enterprise declined accordingly. Furthermore, it appears that international studies academics viewed this decline with considerable equanimity, if not approval. Finally, there is little evidence to suggest that they undertook any concerted effort to counteract it.

In its early years, ITR had tried to foster an interest in international studies within the professions. Graduate programs in agriculture, business, education, public administration, and law all received grants. Moreover, John Howard, its director, was himself personally interested in developing an international legal studies program, which, despite growing opposition from President Heald, received $15 million to help make international studies an integral part of legal education. Yet except at a few law schools—notably Harvard and Columbia, where a strong tradition in international law could be built upon—the program was not particularly successful. "Professional schools," a Ford Foundation report concluded in 1967, "were, and on the whole still are, largely oriented to domestic concerns."[30]

This same orientation seems to have carried over into the professions as well. To the extent that it did, international studies academics did little to alter the situation. Less dependent upon them for either financial support or recruits, they saw less need to cultivate contacts in the business and religious community than had their interwar predecessors. On the contrary, scholarly accounts emanating from the academic international studies community during the ITR era on the missionary movement or American corporate penetration of distant parts, whatever their intellectual merit, at times seemed calculated to sever whatever contacts remained.

In any event, the thought of an international studies academic with ideological ties to the missions, such as Yale's Latourette had, or a financial relationship with a business tycoon, of the sort Chicago's Samuel Harper had with Charles R. Crane, or even familial links with families of great wealth and some influence, as per Harvard's Archibald Cary Coolidge, had by the 1960s come to be viewed in some quarters within the enterprise as very nearly constituting a professional conflict of interest. Indeed, according to a close student of its recent history, no less venerable a meeting ground for international studies academics and "the Business Establishment" than the Council on Foreign Relations went into eclipse during the 1960s in part because of competition from the universities. One might go even further and suggest that the 1968 struggle over the editorship of the council's journal, *Foreign Affairs,* was in part a struggle over whether it too ought to be brought more completely under academic auspices.[31]

The fact that senior international studies academics enjoyed growing success during the ITR era in finding jobs for their PhDs within the university meant they had less occasion to look for them outside. This likely led them to neglect opportunities to establish the kinds of contacts that might produce leads on nonacademic jobs. But so too did the enhancement of the status attached to that of academic placement as opposed to other kinds. In a period when a professor's most talented PhDs had a choice among academic positions, and all who were more than mediocre could find a teaching job someplace, it became hard not to view the third or so who did not go into academic life as the bottom of the barrel. To the extent that they were so viewed, by their mentors and by themselves, whatever previous mutual respect existed between the academic and nonacademic sectors of international studies was replaced by, on the one side, patronizing derision, and on the other, not a little resentment.

Just as academic international studies became during the ITR era less dependent upon outside financial sources (other than ITR) and on outside employment for its PhDs, so it became less dependent upon outside audiences to consume at least a part of its intellectual fare. To be sure, for early international studies academics, like Yale's William Dwight Whitney and Chicago's James Henry Breasted, it was financial need that obliged them to address some of their writing to popular audiences. Nor did either do so without begruding the time lost to, as Whitney had put it, "doing something important." Nonetheless, down through World War Two, popularization was not viewed as an inappropriate activity within the international studies enterprise. Most of Archibald Cary Coolidge's writings, it may be recalled, began as lectures to nonacademic audiences and first saw print in nonacademic publications. Similarly, Herbert Eugene Bolton seldom let pass an opportunity to appear in the local California press, where he gave full play to his passion for his adopted state's history. Kenneth Scott Latourette remained throughout his career a regular contributor to the missionary press. Less of this kind of writing for popular audiences was done by international studies academics during the ITR era, and much of that which was done did those who did it precious little professional good.

Clearly, the deprecation of popularization as an appropriate activity was not peculiar to the academics in international studies during the ITR era. Internal pressures against approaching even intellectually sophisticated but nonprofessional audiences operated in most academic enterprises, even among those, such as sociology and history, which had substantial "educated laities." But no less than in sociology and history, for an academic in international studies to acquire a reputation as someone who wrote for other than "the profession" was to risk being thought insufficiently serious. There, too, "mere journalism" and "middlebrow punditry" came to be frowned upon. Accordingly, aspiring international studies junior faculty gained greater stature—and more likely access to tenure—for publishing articles in either their area or their disciplinary journals, which were refereed and read almost exclusively by fellow academics working in the same area or discipline, rather than articles or books designed for larger and less specialized audiences. In a survey conducted in 1971 by James N. Rosenau, 95 percent of his "elite" sample of international studies academics indicated that they devoted between none and 10 percent of their time "in journalism or writing for nonacademic audiences." Rosenau's study also indicated that there existed virtually no overlap between the journals these international studies academics did write for and those regularly read by the Department of State officials included in the survey.[32]

"Intellectual institutions," Edward Shils observed of the life of high culture in the United States early in the ITR era,

> are beginning to supply their own and each other's audiences, while the larger public which is not concentrating on intellectual things becomes the audience for intellectually mediocre culture and diversion and commercial advantage.

The academic enclosure of American international studies is a striking specific instance of what Shils describes in general terms. So, too, then, are the long-term consequences of the enterprise's enclosure subject to his summary judgment—that it "was not for the cultural good of its own society."[33]

﷼ VII

There was, however, one nonacademic audience which international studies academics had earlier cultivated and during the ITR era still cultivated: government officials charged with the formulation of American foreign policy. Particularly for those interested in contemporary affairs, government policy making, as one international studies academic has put it, "is the light bulb to which the moth is always returning."[34] The interest of policy makers constituted a form of validation as to the importance of one's academic research, while it also provided an opportunity to put one's theories to a practical test.

As indicated earlier, ties between international studies academics and foreign policy makers date back to the 1890s. Harvard's Archibald Cary Coolidge, Wisconsin's Paul Reinsch, Chicago's Samuel Harper, and, between the wars, Quincy Wright were all frequent visitors to the State Department. Whatever the actual impact of their visits, the fact that they made them established them back on campus as estimable "men of affairs."

Following World War Two, the services of more and more international studies academics were called upon, not only by State, but by the Department of Defense, the CIA, and later the National Security Council and the various agencies responsible for administering international aid. During the Kennedy administration especially, one of their number has since recalled, academics, many if not most of whom were at least peripherally identified with international studies, "proliferated throughout the White House and embassies abroad." Much the same thing occurred during the Johnson administration, which, in 1967, convened a China Advisory Panel that included in its membership Columbia's A. Doak Barnett, Michigan's Alex Eckstein, Harvard's John Fairbank, MIT's Lucian Pye, Berkeley's Robert Scalapino, and Washington's George Taylor, all prominent academic East Asianists and frequent beneficiaries of ITR support.[35]

On a more modest level, still other international studies academics participated in government-sponsored projects overseas, not all of which worked out. One that did not, Project Camelot, an Army-sponsored project designed to test various counterinsurgency strategies, begun in 1964 and terminated in 1965 following its exposure in Chile, employed the services of several international studies academics and planned to utilize those of dozens more. Another, a CIA-sponsored project in Vietnam ostensibly dealing with public administration reform, which lasted from 1957 to 1962, seems during that time to have involved a sizable portion of the Michigan State University international studies faculty. Nonetheless, at congressional hearings held in 1965 and 1966, international studies academics like MIT's Ithiel de Sola Pool called upon the federal government to make far more use of academic research, describing the extent to which it currently did "deplorable."[36]

Yet for all this evidence of persistent attentiveness on the part of international studies academics to the needs of foreign policy makers, other indicators suggest that during the ITR era the relationship between academic and policy maker changed. When Stanley K. Hornbeck went to the State Department in the early 1920s, he resigned his professorship at Wisconsin, informed Harvard he would not entertain an offer of a professorship there, and proceeded to cut his ties with the university world. Not so his successors. During the ITR era, academics typically took leave from their universities, and most of them fully intended to return. In effect, they remained academics, even while serving in the government bureaucracy, concerned with their university careers, their professional relationships, their publishing records.

Some students of government, among them Richard Neustadt, applauded Washington's use of these academic "inners and outers," seeing them as a functional equivalent of England's senior civil service. But the subsequent judgment of others, like that of the career bureaucrats themselves, has tended to affirm Robert K. Merton's paraphrastic dictum that "the honeymoon of intellectuals and policy makers is often nasty, brutish, and short." In any event, perhaps the closest one can come to the prevailing view of the academic international studies enterprise during the ITR era about the importance of Washington as an audience was supplied by one of its members when trying to account for the absence of academic luminaries involved in Project Camelot: "government work, while well paid, remains professionally marginal."[37]

Unlike those who devoted themselves to undergraduate teaching and curricular politics, or those who gave themselves over to popularization or punditry, international studies academics who became familar faces in Washington likely did so at no loss of professional status, particularly if they kept up academic connections while there. Yet in agreeing to serve the government they did forgo other academic roles, notably teaching. More to present purposes, by accepting the rules of confidentiality that defined most consultative arrangements, an international studies academic also to some degree forfeited his rights as an interested citizen and informed educator to try to influence public opinion on an issue bearing on his particular expertise. Having accepted access to at least the outer corridors of power, it ill became him thereafter to take to the streets, much less the barricades.[38]

Few did, or so it would appear from the scant participation of leading international studies academics in either the "stop the bombing" petition campaign begun in the *New York Times* in February 1965 or the "teach-ins" later that spring. However these efforts are viewed in retrospect, they were at the time considered by many Americans to be legitimate and serious attempts to stimulate a public debate on an important question of American foreign policy: the efficacy of American military involvement in Vietnam. As such, they constituted the two most spectacular attempts of the ITR era at educating the American public about issues involving a distant part of the world. Finally, the fact that both efforts were faculty-initiated—the petitions began circulating among academics in the Boston area and the idea of a "teach-in" seems to have originated among anthropologists at Michigan—has since led such close observers of the academic and national scene as Seymour Martin Lipset and John Kenneth Galbraith to conclude that academics played a major role in the antiwar movement of the late 1960s. "It was the universities," Galbraith wrote in 1971, "not the trade unions, nor the free-lance intellectuals, nor the press, nor the businessmen . . . which led the opposition to the Vietnam war."[39]

For all these reasons, then, the role played by leading international studies academics in these efforts provides, if not a test case, at least an important clue to the enterprise's commitment to public education. Early assessments of the petition campaign, for the most part by supporters of the war such as Irving Kristol, Meg Greenfield, and William F. Buckley, while acknowledging the prominence of signatories from leading universities, argued that the typical signatory was a junior faculty member or graduate student in a discipline that gave him or her no claim to relevant expertise or prior opportunities to publish on the subjects at issue. Similar assessments were offered of those organizing the "teach-ins." Of the majority of the sponsors of "national teach-ins" in Washington in May 1965, Meg Greenfield wrote dismissively in the *Reporter:* "completely unknown juniors."[40]

Widely accepted at the time, even among antiwar academic activists like Noam Chomsky and Marshall Windmiller, this image of the typical antiwar signatory and teach-in sponsor subsequently came under scholarly assault. In a paper first presented at the 1968 convention of the American Political Science Association, subsequently published in *Science,* and still later elaborated upon in *Minerva,* Everett C. Ladd, Jr., reported findings purporting to show that signatories came disproportionately from (1) the rank of full professor, (2) the social sciences generally, and specifically the "most relevant" of these, political science, and (3) the most professionally active sectors of their disciplines. Ladd stressed the tentativeness of his findings and called for further research on the subject. His own caution notwithstanding, others have since regularly cited Ladd as proving conclusively that the leading academic authorities—and by inference the leading international studies academics—led the movement against the Vietnam War.[41]

My own analysis of these petitioners differs from Ladd's, in part for technical reasons elaborated elsewhere, while concurring with those who earlier found a negative correlation between participation in the petition campaign or sponsorship of a teach-in and, as Max Lerner phrased it, "closeness to the subject matter." International studies academics, particularly on campuses most heavily involved with the petition campaign and the teach-ins, were conspicuous by their avoidance of both.[42]

At Columbia, where 40 percent (78 of 193) of all academics in the social sciences signed at least one of eight petitions examined, only 26 percent (14 of 54) of social scientists affiliated with Columbia's School of International Affairs did so. At the University of Chicago, the thirty-six-member Committee on South Asian Studies, the seventeen-member Committee on the Comparative Study of New Nations, and the nineteen-member Committee on International Relations were all repositories of expertise in subjects with which the petitions dealt. Yet their combined membership produced only one signatory. The University of Michigan program in Far Eastern studies had thirty-nine members in 1966–67, and only one of them signed an examined petition; its program in international and conflict studies had nine members, two of whom were signatories; its Center for South and Southeast Asian Studies, with twenty-four members, had no signatories. None of the twenty-five members of the Hoover Institution on War, Revolution and Peace at Stanford signed any of the petitions examined, nor did any of the nine members of the executive committee of the Center for International Affairs at Harvard.[43]

Other evidence points to the same conclusion. Of the 101 academics cited in the Rosenau 1971 poll of "the most distinguished and productive scholars" who were working in the specialties of international politics, international law, international organizations, and comparative politics, 30 were located at the five universities just cited. Of these, only 2 signed one of the examined petitions.[44]

The argument here, it should be stressed, is not that most leading international studies academics supported the Vietnam War, although many did. It is, rather, that the decision of an international studies academic to sign or not to sign a public statement on the war involved more than a personal judgment on the war. It also involved the professional implications of engaging on either side of a public debate on issues about which he lay claim to expertise. Thus, the disinclination of most international studies academics to engage in either the petition campaign or the teach-ins arguably turned less on their view of the war than on their view of themselves.

In point of fact, some leading international studies academics did participate in the first teach-ins, and several of them defended the Johnson administration's case at the "national" teach-in held in Washington. Many who did participate, however—among them Wesley R. Fishel of Michigan State, George E. Taylor of Washington, and Lucian Pye of MIT—thereafter publicly despaired of trying to speak on "enormously complex issues" in the face of the "name-calling, distortion, emotion-alism, and gross oversimplification" of their presumably less informed and more exercised colleagues. Those protesting the administration's policy in Vietnam, Fishel and his like-minded Asian scholars concluded, were "in our view guilty of non-academic behavior."[45]

Five months earlier, the East Asianist Robert Scalapino had urged his Berkeley colleagues to boycott a planned teach-in in which they were invited to participate, characterizing the event as "symbolic of the new anti-intellectualism that is gaining strength today. . . . This travesty should be repudiated by all true scholars irrespective of their views on Vietnam." Whether one regards this response as virtually mandated by the circum-stances or an act of intellectual abdication, the implication was much the same: the job of educating the American public as to the "realities" of American foreign policies in Asia was either seized by or fell by default to Harvard biologists, Stanford ge-neticists, Columbia professors of English, and MIT professors of linguistics.[46]

This chapter closes as it began, with questions. If the quality of the public debate over Vietnam in the 1960s is compared with that of the foreign policy debates of the late 1930s, is there any evidence that during the intervening quarter-century Americans had become more sophisticated in their under-standing of international affairs? If one finds little, what then of the more than a quarter of a billion dollars the Ford Foun-dation invested through ITR to enhance and elevate their un-derstanding? And might one go further than allow that this largesse failed to accomplish one of its stated objectives and suggest that the manner by which the largesse was expended actually, if inadvertently, subverted that objective? Specifi-cally, could not one argue that in underwriting the academic enclosure of American international studies, the Ford Founda-tion contributed to the depletion in other parts of American society of just those individuals most likely to provide it with an understanding of international affairs? Still more specifically, in rewarding international studies academics who jettisoned their traditional roles as undergraduate teachers and public educators for those of scholar and expert-adviser, did not the Ford Foundation contribute directly to the impoverishment of the public debate about America's international responsibilities, both as conducted within the university and without? To the extent that any of these last questions call forth affirmative answers, the consequences implied must also be numbered among the fruits of philanthropy.

EPILOGUE: THE AFTERNOON OF ENTERPRISE

We must not expect such growth to continue, and we must not waste time and energy in seeking too many palliatives for an incurable process. . . . It would seem much more useful to employ our efforts in anticipating the requirements of the new situation in which science has become, in some way, a saturated activity of mankind.

DEREK J. DE SOLLA PRICE, 1975[1]

The last two chapters have stressed the problematical, even inferentially negative, consequences of the intervention of the Ford Foundation into the life of American international studies. The resultant interpretation, after Adam Smith, has been primarily from the perspective of the disadvantaged "corn" rather than the advantaged "pasture." To have assumed the latter's perspective would have called for a more comprehensive tallying of the products of the enterprise, not only the numbers of specialists trained, areas and disciplines involved, and institutional participation, but courses offered, students enrolled, conferences mounted, books and articles published and cited. Such a tallying needs doing and not only for the enterprise's self-gratification. It will also be an essential element in any definitive attempt by the Ford Foundation to assess the consequences of its investment in international studies.

For the present and near future, however, something less than the last word and final tallying is all that can be reasonably attempted. Accordingly, my purposes in this concluding chapter remain those of an outsider advancing an interpretation of the history of American international studies that departs from and moves beyond the current one. Because that current interpretation is almost entirely lacking in self-criticism, a contrary one risks being overly critical. The knowledge, however, that neither the enterprise nor the Ford Foundation lacks those prepared to defend their partnership would seem to make such a risk acceptable. Indeed, to the extent that historical truth is approximated through a dialectical process of ever-tightening opposing interpretations, it may be necessary.

There is a more practical reason for taking issue with those who argue that the only unfortunate aspect of the partnership between academic international studies and the Ford Foundation is that it was dissolved in 1966. At that point, according to this argument, the international studies enterprise entered into a period of "crisis" from which it has not emerged. To so argue is at least implicitly to hold out hope for a renewal of that partnership, either, as during the ITR era, with the Ford Foundation again the principal backer of the enterprise or with the federal government succeeding to that role. So long as this hope lingers a retrospectively critical assessment of the ITR era is not likely to emanate from within the academic international studies enterprise. Nor is one from without likely to be welcomed. On the contrary, the promotional imperatives of the enterprise requires identifying the ITR era as the "golden age" of American international studies, if only to dramatize the problems in its aftermath.

The danger in positing a "golden age" in the history of any human enterprise is not limited to the likely violence it does to the historical actualities; it can also divert attention from the situation at hand by holding out the prospect of a return to that age when, supposedly, unlimited financial resources underwrote continuous growth which straightened every path and smoothed every road. Until the effort to recapture an unrealistic version of the past is abandoned, a serious effort to confront the present and plan for the future cannot be undertaken. Even if the ITR era was all that its restorationists remember it being, the elements that brought it into being are no longer present. Indeed, of those elements—political, ideological, economic, demographic, and philanthropic—that ushered in the ITR era in the 1950s, none is less likely to reappear in the 1980s than the philanthropic.

I

The decision to terminate ITR in 1966 could hardly have been more abrupt. That it followed hard on the appointment of McGeorge Bundy as president of the Ford Foundation only made it more unexpected. It had been Bundy, after all, who as dean of Harvard College in 1958, gave "a virtuoso performance" before the foundation's trustees chronicling Harvard's historic role in international studies, who later helped negotiate Harvard's first ITR block grant, and who later still, as National Security Adviser to both Presidents Kennedy and Johnson, presumably placed at least as high a value on the care and feeding of international studies academics as his predecessor. The view within ITR at the time of his appointment as Ford's president was, its director later recalled ruefully, "Bundy would take care of the Program. And then, *whammo!*" [2]

Easier to read with hindsight, a few signs did appear around the time of Bundy's appointment that the days of ITR might be numbered. John Howard's decision to leave the Foundation to become head of the new—and Ford-backed—International Legal Center in early 1966 was one. Another was the rumor, during the six months between Heald's resignation in June 1965 and Bundy's installation in January 1966, that W. McNeil Lowry, the foundation's acting chief executive officer, was of the opinion that the foundation should "cut ITR: the federal government's in the wings." [3]

Lowry's reference was to the anticipated infusion of federal funds into international studies—upwards of $100 million over five years—upon the funding of the recently signed Interna-

tional Education Act. Not until 1967 did the principal promoters of this legislation, among them then Secretary of
Health, Education, and Welfare John W. Gardner and Columbia philosopher and then Assistant Secretary of State Charles
Frankel, despair of IEA ever being funded. Thus the Ford
Foundation's decision to terminate ITR could have been
prompted by the trustees' mistaken assumption as to the imminence of a federal takeover of their responsibilities. Yet there
are also several reasons to think that Bundy would have urged
the trustees, as he put it in his first report as president, "to
take our men and our money and move to the next table"
even had he not been convinced that federal support was
"bound to come."[4]

First, it might well have been anticipated that an incoming
president would want to set his own philanthropic agenda.
Bundy's reputation for strong-mindedness made the odds of
his sticking with an inherited agenda particularly long. Moving "to the next table" commended itself simply in that it represented change. "If [a foundation] commits itself forever to
the same things done in the same ways," he wrote in 1968, "it
soon ceases to be an agent of change and becomes no more
than a buttress of the status quo."[5] The fact that Bundy very
much had other tables in mind—the advancement of Negro
rights and the problems confronting urban America chief
among them—only made his conclusion that the international
studies enterprise had become "a fair charge on others" all the
more plausible.

Bundy's experience as National Security Adviser may also
have left him disaffected with academics generally, if not international studies academics specifically. During the Kennedy
years, he later recalled not without some bitterness, "because
a Harvard man was President, and a lot of professors were
down there with him, academics—especially but not only those
residing in Cambridge—began to assume that the university
was running the country." It fell to Bundy, as one of the more
conspicuous administration academics, to point out that the
ends of government and of the university "are two different

things, and it is deeply dangerous to confuse them." Still later, under Johnson, Bundy defended the administration's Vietnam policies against growing criticism, much of it from academics, a role hardly conducive to mutual admiration.[6]

Whatever his reasons for doing so, few possessed Bundy's credentials as incoming president of the Ford Foundation to pronounce upon the capacity of the academic international studies enterprise to survive the termination of ITR. "Together with others," he wrote in 1967 of the Ford Foundation's role in that enterprise,

we have wrought a revolution: the study of Africa, Asia, the Middle East, and Latin America—above all the study of Russia and China—has become a necessary, built-in element of the American academic establishment. Intellectual fashions being what they are, these studies will have good times and bad. But they are here to stay.[7]

As it turned out, not even Bundy could get away that neatly. Announcement of ITR's termination prompted worried calls to the foundation from university presidents, most of whom had yet to shift more than a small portion of their international studies programs from dependence upon the "soft money" support provided by ITR to their regular operating budgets. In response, the foundation's International Division, which had assumed the administrative responsibilities of the defunct ITR, began discussions with these universities about the problems they faced once ITR monies were fully expended. Out of these discussions came a special grant proposal, submitted to and accepted by the foundation trustees in early 1969, for transitional support of international studies in American universities. The grant, for $9 million, was distributed among twenty-six ITR-beneficiary universities in amounts ranging from $900,000 (Harvard) to $60,000 (Pittsburgh). The funds went almost exclusively to support faculty research, rather than to graduate fellowships or programs of instruction. Undergraduate programs in international studies and those addressing nonacademic audiences were specifically excluded.[8]

During the 1970s the International Division of the Ford

Foundation continued to provide some support for academic international studies, primarily through grants to the Social Science Research Council for support of the joint international committees of SSRC and the American Council of Learned Societies and to the ACLS for support of the International Research and Exchanges Board (IREX), which supports exchanges and intellectual cooperation with the Soviet Union and Eastern Europe in the social sciences and humanities.[9]

Neither the transitional grant program nor the subsequent support of the international activities of the SSRC and ACLS implied a resumption by the Ford Foundation of its earlier role as the principal underwriter of the academic international studies enterprise. By the early 1970s the foundation's sharply eroded capital base prompted substantial cutbacks in overall expenditure levels and made any such revival of ITR financially inconceivable. But an earlier and clearer indication that nothing of the sort had ever been considered was the willingness of Howard's successor, Francis X. Sutton, deputy vice president of the International Division, to pose questions that during the ITR days would have been heretical. "Is it not possible," he asked his foundation colleagues in 1967, shortly after assuming his position as receiver of ITR,

that in some geographic areas, countries, and disciplines, "sufficient" area specialists have been trained to man the necessary positions, provide the basic research and reproduce themselves in adequate numbers without special pump-priming?[10]

With this rhetorical query, its negative-interrogative form notwithstanding, an era in philanthropic enterprise could be said to have ended.

§   II

It was one thing for Bundy and Sutton to declare the "revolution" in American international studies "permanent" and the enterprise sustainable without "special pump-priming," another that either be so. Spokesmen for academic international studies reacted to the termination of ITR—and the failure of Congress to fund the International Education Act—by declaring their enterprise to be in "a state of crisis." Since then, virtually all assessments emanating from within the enterprise, and some from supposedly more disinterested groups without, have adhered to this crisis theme. Indeed, nowhere is it more insistently presented than in the 1979 report of the President's Commission on Foreign Languages and International Studies. Convened by President Carter in 1978 and chaired by James A. Perkins, former president of Cornell University, the commission summarized the state of American international studies as "unlikely to survive, let alone maintain its quality."[11]

Among the sixty-five recommendations made by the commission, one called for the establishment of a National Council on Foreign Languages and International Studies to lobby for the other sixty-four. Such a council was established in 1980; a year later it began issuing a series of reports produced by panels of regional specialists in which "national targets" for additional specialists on a given region were established. Even more insistently than did the commission, the council has stressed both the magnitude of the "crisis" in academic international studies and its national security implications. For example, in calling for a fivefold increase in the number of Middle East academic specialists, the council presented its "expert assessments of need" with the surety that the need to understand "the area that has produced the 'oil shock,' Qaddafi's Libya and Khomeini's Iran will not decrease, whatever resources the nation musters to the task." Upon publishing these reports in 1982, the overall director of the council's Task Force on National Manpower Targets for Advanced Research on Foreign Areas, Allen H. Kassof, provided a prefatory summary: "To put it bluntly: The United States is losing the struggle with the Soviet Union for mastery of expert knowledge of foreign areas. . . . our stocks of specialized manpower, already inadequate to national needs, are dwindling."[12]

However urgently presented, the argument of the commission and the council that academic international studies in the late 1970s and early 1980s was so beset by crisis as to put the nation's security in jeopardy is not compelling. Three kinds of "evidence" accompany the argument but do not validate it. The first relates to Americans generally, specifically to what the commission called their "scandalous incompetence in foreign languages" and "dangerously inadequate understanding of world affairs." The commission went on to posit "a widening gap" between American needs and "American competence to understand and deal successfully with other people in a world in flux."[13] It is not simply a sense of *déjà vu*—although there is that!—that prompts resistance to such findings; it is also the dubious and historically disputable implication that more adequate funding of academic international studies would close this "gap." Had it narrowed in the ITR era?

A second kind of "evidence" accompanied the argument that the present fortunes of academic international studies put the United States at a growing strategic disadvantage vis-à-vis our international adversaries. In contrast to the "dwindling stocks of specialized manpower" in the United States, the council described the USSR as having "launched an amibitious, heavily financed, and successful campaign to arm itself with the information and know-how that are requisite to superpower status in the contemporary world." To substantiate the existence of this campaign the council report cited six institutes working on international affairs operating within the Soviet Academy of Sciences, along with the size of their respective staffs in 1980. The 2,750 specialists so identified, the council report went on, represents "only the tip of an iceberg." No figures on the size of these staffs at an earlier period are provided, so no conclusions about the growth of the Soviet effort can be drawn from those that are. Nor are American figures suitable for comparative purposes provided. The statement that the Soviet Academy had since 1956 "assembled almost 8000 specialists working on international affairs research and training," however, does lend itself to such comparative purposes, insofar as during that same period American universities produced easily twice that number of international studies PhDs.[14]

A third kind of "evidence" accompanied the case that the academic international studies enterprise was "deeply imperiled." As the commission characterized the situation in 1979, there had already occurred "a serious deterioration in this country's language and research capacity" and just ahead was "the threatened imminent loss of some of the world's leading centers for advanced training and research in foreign areas." Support for these findings consisted almost entirely of the unmediated opinions of international studies academics and university administrators during on-campus interviews. That they agreed that the enterprise needed "more money for program operating costs, more library support, more fellowships, more study abroad, and more sensible bureaucrats in Washington" might have been anticipated.[15]

Neither the 154-page report of the commission nor the 312 pages of accompanying background papers cited a specific instance of an important international studies program actually going under in the 1970s, much less analyzed such an instance for its representativeness. PhD-production figures and faculty-position counts were also omitted, as were curricular analyses or enrollment figures that might permit some conclusions as to trends both within the international studies enterprise and within the American academic enterprise generally. Only one of the twenty-five studies conducted for the commission, that by the Rand Corporation on the occupational demand for international studies specialists, did generate the kinds of data that might have served as a check against the possibility that the views expressed from within the enterprise did not fully describe the situation. Unfortunately, the Rand report, which concluded there were twice as many international studies PhDs being produced by American universities in the late 1970s as there were jobs for them, was the one report not included among those published by the commission.[16]

Neither the absolute nor the relative thinness of the commission's case deterred its membership, with one exception, from calling for the immediate expenditure of $180 million in new federal funds, two-thirds of which was to be earmarked for international studies academics. Among the specific requests: the establishment of sixty-five to eighty-five national centers for advanced international training and research to be funded by the Department of Education at an average of $250,000 annually for five-year periods; a program of 405 to 465 postdoctoral fellowships at $20,000 per year each; 240 to 280 fellowships for graduate students at $8,000 annually each for up to two years, tenable at home or abroad. To be sure, the commission recommended other expenditures as well, relating to language study in the schools, citizen education, and the needs of business, labor, and the media, but these were smaller and presented in considerably less detail than those emanating from—and for the direct benefit of—the academic international studies enterprise.[17]

To suggest that the case for the critical condition of academic international studies in the 1970s was not compelling as presented by the President's Commission or the National Council on Foreign Languages and International Studies does not require disproving it. Still less does it require acceptance of the contrary case that the enterprise flourished even more mightily in the 1970s than it had in the 1960s. Yet my own analysis of the state of academic international studies since 1966 does suggest that, at least through most of the 1970s, the enterprise held its own.

In point of fact, between 1966 and 1973, as measured by PhD productivity, academic international studies at the sixteen universities that constituted the sample used in chapter 8 doubled its size, increasing its share of the total output of PhDs in the social sciences and humanities from 22 percent to 25 percent (table 9.1). From 1973, the peak year in PhD production both nationally and among the sample universities, through the late 1970s the annual production of international studies PhDs did decline, but no more than did that of the social sciences and humanities generally. In 1980 international studies PhDs increased slightly and accounted for 30 percent of those produced in all the social sciences and humanities disciplines;

that was more a quarter larger than the enterprise's share in 1966, and twice what it had been back in 1940.

Why, then, in the face of these overall statistics, was the imminent demise of the enterprise so regularly predicted? Disaggregating them by institutional type, area, and discipline provides some clues. The institutional dispersion of the enterprise that became marked during the later years of the ITR era

TABLE 9.1. International Studies PhDs Awarded by Sample Universities As a Proportion of All Social Science and Humanities PhDs, 1966–1980

	Number of PhDs Awarded in:		
	All Social Sciences and Humanities	International Studies	Percentage
1966	1,717	379	22
1973	3,088	781	25
1976	2,728	745	27
1977	2,309	626	27
1980	2,121	569	30

Source: Association of Research Libraries, *Doctoral Dissertations Accepted by American Universities* (New York: H. W. Wilson, 1967, 1974, 1977, 1978, 1981).
Note: The universities included in this and the other tables in this chapter are those listed in tables 5.1 and 8.5.

persisted into the later 1970s, even if slowed somewhat (see table 9.2). This may have led some international studies academics at some of the "ancients" to mistake the declining standing of their own institutions within the enterprise for the decline of the enterprise itself. For example, whereas Harvard and Columbia in 1966 together accounted for one of every four international studies PhDs produced at all American universities, in 1980 they accounted for only one of every eight.

Continued dispersion of the enterprise's productive capacity in the 1970s led to a further leveling of institutional reputations. Unlike the 1940s, when Chicago could lay claim to being the center for Middle Eastern studies and Berkeley to being the center for Latin American studies, and Columbia and Harvard enjoyed joint suzerainty over Russian studies, in the 1970s

TABLE 9.2. International Studies PhDs at Sample Universities, 1966–1980, by Generational Clusters

	International Studies PhDs Awarded by:							
	Ancients		In-Betweens		Moderns		Total Sample	
	N	%	N	%	N	%	N	%
1966	203	54	122	32	54	14	379	100
1973	312	40	282	36	187	24	781	100
1976	319	43	266	36	160	21	745	100
1979	189	34	214	39	150	27	553	100
1980	226	38	244	41	124	21	594	100

Source: see table 9.1.
Note: For definitions of generations and for composition of clusters, see table 5.1.

all such claims came under multiple challenge. That some of the challengers—UCLA in Middle Eastern studies, Texas in Latin American studies, and Indiana in Russian studies—had begun to produce PhDs in any of the international studies disciplines in substantial numbers only in the 1950s simply conveyed the point of lost hegemony more urgently. So, too, did the fact that the sample universities' share of the estimated annual national production of international studies PhDs dropped throughout the 1970s (table 9.3). Not surprisingly, then, assessments from the perspective of the ancients recall the valedictory William Bradford pronounced upon the First Church of Plymouth in 1642:

TABLE 9.3. International Studies PhDs at Sample Universities, 1966–1980, as a Proportion of Estimated National Total of International Studies PhDs

	Estimated National Total	Sample Universities	Percentage
1966	550	379	69
1973	1,200	781	65
1976	1,200	745	62
1979	950	553	58
1980	950	594	62

Sources: see table 9.1.

And thus was this poor church left, like an ancient mother grown old and forsaken of her children . . . like a widower left only to trust in God. Thus, she that hath made many rich became herself poor.[18]

Another factor contributing to the perception of an entire enterprise beset by crisis in the 1970s was that some parts did experience sharp contraction, both relative and absolute. Russian and East European studies is the principal case in point. By the end of the 1970s, it accounted for a smaller share of the

TABLE 9.4. Russian and East European PhDs at Sample Universities, 1940–1980, as a Proportion of All International Studies PhDs

	Number of PhDs in Russian and East European Studies	As a Percentage of all PhDs in International Studies
1940	9	13
1951	31	17
1960	50	21
1966	71	19
1973	114	15
1976	102	14
1979	54	10
1980	66	11

Source: see tables 5.5, 8.2, and 9.1.

academic international studies enterprise than at any time since the 1930s (table 9.4). Its production of PhDs in 1980 had fallen to half what it had been a decade earlier. In some disciplines, perhaps most conspicuously economics, dissertations in Russian studies were rarer than they had been in the 1950s. Of the sixty-six Russian studies PhDs produced by the sample universities in 1980, one was in economics. Twenty-nine were in the humanities.[19]

Yet even if the relative decline of Russian studies within academic international studies dates from the early 1960s, it cannot be wholly attributable to funding difficulties following on the termination of ITR. Factors particular to the field, already operative in the ITR era, must also be considered. In any event, the troubles besetting Russian studies in the 1970s, however real and deserving of attention, ought not be viewed as characteristic of the entire enterprise. Quite the contrary: all the other regional constituents of academic international studies appear to have weathered the 1970s in reasonably stable condition (table 9.5). Only South Asian studies failed to be a beneficiary of the decline in Russian studies, while Latin American, Middle Eastern, and African studies all registered relative

TABLE 9.5. International Studies PhDs at Sample Universities, 1966–1980, by Area Focus

	1966		1976		1979		1980	
	N	%	N	%	N	%	N	%
Latin America	65	17	158	21	115	21	131	22
East Asia	60	16	116	16	103	19	97	16
Middle East	40	11	91	12	86	16	80	13
South Asia	58	15	115	15	81	15	80	13
International or other	36	9	64	9	39	7	69	12
Russia and East Europe	71	19	102	14	54	10	66	11
Africa	31	8	82	11	65	12	63	11
Canada	18	5	17	2	10	2	8	1
Total	379	100	745	100	553	102	594	99

Sources: see table 9.1.
Note: Percentages do not add up to 100 because of rounding.

gains. One suspects that the return of Latin American studies to the leading position among regional specialties by the end of the 1970s was even more decisive than production figures from the sample universities indicate, the bulk of its recent growth taking place in other institutions.[20]

The standing of the various disciplines within academic international studies during the fifteen years after ITR changed remarkably little (table 9.6). Except for a sharp drop in economics in the mid1970s and a comparable one in political science late in the decade, disciplines typically held their places. The relative growth of the humanities as a component in the enterprise, first discernible in the late 1950s, slowed somewhat in the late 1970s as the absolute production of humanities PhDs slumped sharply.

On balance, an analysis of the PhD-production pattern of academic international studies between 1966 and 1980 allows the conclusion that the enterprise survived the financial and organizational "crises" of the 1970s. Two other recent surveys of the enterprise, one undertaken in 1979 by the Ford Foundation and the National Endowment for the Humanities and

TABLE 9.6. International Studies PhDs at Sample Universities, 1966–1980, by Field and Discipline

| | International Studies PhDs in Each Field and Discipline Awarded in: | | | | | | | |
| | 1966 | | 1976 | | 1979 | | 1980 | |
	N	%	N	%	N	%	N	%
Social sciences	284	75	537	72	407	74	426	72
History	77	20	150	20	107	19	117	20
Political science	73	19	136	18	75	14	71	12
Economics	75	20	99	13	93	17	90	15
Anthropology	47	12	107	14	90	16	90	15
Sociology	12	4	45	6	42	8	58	10
Humanities	95	25	208	28	145	26	168	28
Language and literature	71	19	141	19	104	19	122	21
Other humanities	24	6	67	9	41	7	46	8
Total	379	100	745	100	553	100	594	100

Sources: see table 9.1.

the other in 1981 by the Rockefeller Foundation, support this view. "The broad picture," the report on the Rockefeller survey concluded, "is one of a robust, dynamic community which changed significantly during the 1970's but managed to stay reasonably healthy." Thus, to the extent that fifteen years constitutes a reasonable purchase on the ever thereafter, the assurances offered in 1966 by Ford Foundation officials that the "revolution" ITR had wrought was "permanent" and that academic international studies "are here to stay" have been borne out.[21]

ॐ III

Why then, in view of these cautiously positive and optimistic outside assessments, do the lamentations from within the international studies enterprises persist? Habit may provide part of the explanation. Since the enterprise achieved takeoff in the late 1940s, self-generated promotionalism has been one of its defining characteristics. Even during the "bonanza years" of the ITR era, a substantial proportion of the enterprise's collective energies went into arguing its own case. Those who continued to make the case for academic international studies in the 1970s were simply carrying on in the tradition of their predecessors.

A second explanation turns on the tendency of some of the spokesmen for academic international studies to interpret the difficulties encountered by academic enterprises generally since the late 1960s as peculiarly besetting their own. Clearly, international studies did not flourish as mightily in the 1970s as earlier; less clear is it that the enterprise fared worse than others within the university. Nor is it at all clear that its prospects for survival in the 1980s are more doubtful than any number of other academic enterprises. Like virtually all such enterprises, international studies stopped expanding in the early 1970s. Thereafter it contracted somewhat, as did the American graduate school enterprise generally. Like most parts of the social sciences and all parts of the humanities, international studies met with increased difficulties in securing tenure for its junior faculty. It also became harder to find academic jobs for its new PhDs, perhaps as many as half of whom in the late 1970s were obliged to obtain employment outside the university. Thus, international studies has been obliged to confront the same difficult choice confronting others in the universities in the postexpansionary 1970s: to cut back PhD production, thereby contracting further its university activities, or to maintain earlier levels, thereby increasing further its ranks of academically unemployable PhDs.[22]

In point of fact, academic international studies in the 1970s did a little of both. Between 1976 and 1980 the production of international studies PhDs dropped 19 percent, which was consistent with the overall cutback in the social sciences and humanities, though substantially less than in some specific disciplines, such as history, where the drop exceeded 29 percent nationally. At the same time, some enterprise advocates have argued that it ought not be bound by "a narrow market approach" in the determination of demand but ought to push for a doubling, trebling, or even, in the case of African and Middle Eastern specialists, a quadrupling of the number of area specialists available in 1980.[23]

It was one thing to argue that "the national interest" required nothing less than the exponential growth of academic international studies in an era of overall university growth, but quite another in the face of university retrenchment and what in the early 1980s was perceived to be a substantial and growing oversupply of PhDs generally and, according to the Rand Corporation's findings, of international studies PhDs particularly. Like the contention made in 1973 on behalf of the enterprise that "the necessities of the age are such that we must nurture and sustain in this country an ever increasing competence to deal with and understand the peoples and cultures of the rest of the world," such arguments invite the charge of special pleading. Moreover, to argue that with regard to such competence, "there can be no surplus, no oversupply," virtually obliges representatives of other equally pressed academic enterprises to respond, as per Talcott Parsons: "competence in any one field can only be acquired at the cost of expending scarce resources and hence at the sacrifice of competence in other fields."[24]

Yet to conclude with the recent difficulties encountered by academic international studies, even while trying to put them in a wider context than have its advocates, risks missing the still larger implications of what has happened to international studies in the four decades since 1940. It also risks missing the principal burden of this book's argument. The present predicament of American international studies has less to do with immediate problems than with, in its own terms, its long-term success. Having consciously set about in the 1940s to create an estimable and perdurable academic enterprise, those who directed the fortunes of American international studies succeeded only too well. International studies not only became an estimable academic enterprise, it became primarily and almost exclusively that.

Thus, the first of two tasks confronting those who seek to provide American international studies with a viable future is the same one confronting the historian who seeks a clearer understanding of its past: to accept the reality of the enterprise's academic enclosure. The second, which the historian may shun, is to reckon with the policy implications of enclosure. Surely one of the more obvious ones is that the enterprise cannot expect that, even in a revived university economy, growth of the magnitude that occurred in the late 1940s or from the late 1950s to the early 1970s will reoccur. At least within the university, international studies has become, and is likely to remain for some time, what Derek J. de Solla Price has characterized as "a saturated activity." If so, advocates of international studies might well consider ways of reconnecting their enterprise with its earlier nonacademic constituencies and nonprofessional audiences, which will require the enterprise's greater attention to their needs and somewhat less to its own.

At bottom, then, the predicament facing international studies academics in the 1980s is the same facing all Americans engaged in all kinds of intellectual pursuits that require underwriting by other Americans. Nor is the predicament new; it existed at least as far back as Tocqueville's visit to America. "In Boston," he recorded in his journal in 1831, "there are a certain number of persons, who, having no occupation, seek out the pleasures of the spirit." He then proceeded to note the prevailing "prejudice against those who do nothing (a very useful prejudice on the whole)."[25] Whether or not the history of American international studies confirms the utility of this prejudice, it attests to its enduring force. In America, at least, although the pursuit of learning may well be its own reward, it cannot for long among the otherwise occupied citizens be its own justification.

NOTES

࿇ PREFACE

1. Benjamin Keen, *The Aztec Image in Western Thought* (New Brunswick: Rutgers University Press, 1967); James A. Field, Jr., *America and the Mediterranean World, 1776–1882* (Princeton: Princeton University Press, 1969); James C. Thomson, Peter W. Stanley, and John Curtis Perry, *Sentimental Imperialists: The American Experience in East Asia* (New York: Harper and Row, 1981). Similar studies include Akira Iriye, *Across the Pacific: An Inner History of American–East Asian Relations* (New York: Harcourt, Brace, 1967); Harold R. Isaacs, *Scratches on Our Minds: American Images of China and India* (New York: Capricorn, 1958); Milton Singer, "Passage to More than India: A Sketch of Changing European and American Images," in Milton Singer, ed., *When a Great Tradition Modernizes* (New York: Praeger, 1972); and, though only marginally concerned with American perceptions and more insistently critical than the above, Edward Said, *Orientalism* (New York: Pantheon, 1978).

2. For an instructive discussion of this distinction, see Joseph Ben-David and Randall Collins, "Social Factors in the Origins of a New Science: The Case of Psychology," *American Sociological Review* (August 1966), 31:451–465; John Gross, *The Rise and Fall of the Man of Letters* (London: Macmillan, 1969).

3. Among these attempts, I would include Laurence R. Veysey, *The Emergence of the American University* (Chicago: University of Chicago Press, 1965), and Bruce Kuklick, *The Rise of American Philosophy: Cambridge, Massachusetts, 1860–1930* (New Haven: Yale University Press, 1977), two of the most important books in American intellectual history to have appeared in the last twenty years. For discussions of the relationship between the social history of intellectuals and the history of ideas, see John Higham and Paul K. Conkin, eds., *New Directions in American Intellectual History* (Baltimore: Johns Hopkins University Press, 1979), particularly the contributions of Veysey, David A. Hollinger, and Thomas L. Haskell.

4. *The Oxford English Dictionary* (Oxford: Clarendon Press, 1932), 3:147; "academicization" in William Barrett, *The Truants: Adventures Among the In-*

tellectuals (New York: Doubleday, 1981), p. 7; Max Weber, "Bureaucracy," in H. H. Gerth and C. Wright Mills, eds., *From Max Weber: Essays in Sociology* (New York: Oxford University Press, 1958), pp. 196–244; Edward Shils, "Tradition, Ecology, and Institution in the History of Sociology," in Edward Shils, ed., *The Calling of Sociology and Other Essays on the Pursuit of Learning* (Chicago: University of Chicago Press, 1980), pp. 165–256, 168.

5. Shils, "Tradition, Ecology, and Institution," p. 169.

ও্য 1. GENTLEMEN AND SCHOLARS

1. Mary Orne Pickering, *Life of John Pickering* (Boston: Wilson, 1887), p. 296.

2. Bernard Bailyn, *Education in the Forming of American Society* (New York: Vintage, 1960), pp. 3–4.

3. For an exhaustive coverage of the literature pertaining to American international studies prior to World War Two, see Stephen M. Arum, "A History of Foreign Language and Area Studies in the U.S., 1915–1941" (PhD dissertation, Columbia University, 1976).

4. Two issues of the *Annals of the American Academy of Political and Social Science* devoted to American international studies separated by sixteen years provide an interesting perspective on the changes and continuity in the enterprise's perception of itself: Donald K. Bigelow and Lyman H. Legters, eds., *The Non-Western World in Higher Education* (November 1964), vol. 356, and Richard D. Lambert, ed., *New Directions in International Education* (May 1980), vol. 449.

5. Irwin T. Sanders and Jennifer C. Ward, *Bridges to Understanding: International Programs of American Colleges and Universities* (New York: McGraw-Hill, 1970), p. 41; Stephen Blank, *Western European Studies in the United States* (Pittsburgh: Council for European Studies, University of Pittsburgh Press, 1974).

6. An exception to this tendency to stress academic international studies at the expense of nonacademic is Clarence A. Manning, *History of Slavic Studies in the United States* (Milwaukee: Marquette University Press, 1957).

7. J. P. Mayer, ed., *Alexis de Tocqueville: Journey to America* (New Haven: Yale University Press, 1960), p. 19; Alexis de Tocqueville, *Democracy in America,* J. P. Mayer, ed. (Garden City: Anchor Books, 1969), p. 454.

8. James Jackson, Sr., *Memoir of James Jackson, Jr., M.D.* (Boston: Hilliard, Gray, 1836), p. 80, quoted in Donald Fleming, "American Science and the World Scientific Community," *Journal of World History* (1965), 8:669; Richard Shryock, "American Indifference to Basic Science," *Archives internationales d'histoire des sciences* (1948), 28:50–65; Nathan Reingold, "American Indifference to Basic Research: A Reappraisal," in George Daniels, ed., *Nineteenth-Century American Science* (Evanston, Ill.: Northwestern University

Press, 1972), pp. 38–62; Richard Hofstadter, *Anti-Intellectualism in American Life* (New York: Vintage, 1963), ch. 6; William Stanton, *The Great United States Exploring Expedition* (Berkeley and Los Angeles: University of California Press, 1975), p. 11.

9. Tocqueville, *Democracy in America*, p. 228; Ralph Waldo Emerson, "The American Scholar," in Mark Van Doren, ed., *The Portable Emerson* (New York: Viking, 1946), p. 45.

10. George W. Pierson, *Tocqueville and Beaumont in America* (New York: Oxford University Press, 1940), p. 365.

11. Pickering, *Pickering*, p. 446.

12. *Ibid.*, pp. 140–143, 147.

13. *Ibid.*, pp. 524–525, 296; on Sir William Jones and English Sanskrit studies, see George D. Bearce, *British Attitudes Toward India, 1734–1858* (London: Oxford University Press, 1961), pp. 18–22.

14. Pickering, *Pickering*, pp. 231, 460.

15. *Ibid.*, p. 251; "Peter S. DuPonceau," *Dictionary of American Biography* (New York: Charles Scribners, 1930), 5:525–526 (hereafter cited as *DAB*).

16. Raymond Walters, Jr., *Albert Gallatin* (Pittsburgh: University of Pittsburgh Press, 1957), ch. 27; Pickering, *Pickering*, pp. 490, 491, 511.

17. Pickering, *Pickering*, p. 439; Stanton, *Exploring Expedition*, pp. 65–66, 373–377; on Hale, see Jacob W. Gruber, "Horatio Hale and the Development of American Anthropology," *Proceedings of the American Philosophical Society* (February 1967), 3:5–37.

18. Pickering, *Pickering*, pp. 323–324, 462–463.

19. William Jenks, "The Founding of the American Oriental Society," *American Oriental Society Journal* (1875), 10:lix–lxiv (hereafter cited as *AOS Journal*); see also Rosanne Rocher, "The Founding of the AOS: Boston Gentlemen and Foreign Missions" (Philadelphia: University of Pennsylvania, Department of South Asian Studies, 1976).

20. "Moses Stuart," *DAB*, 18:174–175; "Edward Robinson," *DAB*, 16:34–40.

21. "Barnas Sears," *DAB*, 16:537–538; "Bela B. Edwards," *DAB*, 6:27.

22. Rocher, "Founding of the AOS," p. 15; membership list in *AOS Journal* (1848), 1:xli–xliii.

23. Pickering, *Pickering*, p. 291.

24. Clifton Phillips, *Protestant America and the Pagan World: The First Half Century of the American Board of Commissioners of Foreign Missions, 1810–1860* (Cambridge: Harvard University Press, 1964), p. 239; see also Valentin H. Rabe, "Evangelical Logistics: Mission Support and Resources," in John K. Fairbank, ed., *The Missionary Enterprise in China and America* (Cambridge: Harvard University Press, 1974), pp. 56–90.

25. Phillips, *Protestant America*, p. 307; John K. Fairbank, "Introduction," in Fairbank, ed., *Missionary Enterprise*, pp. 1–19.

26. Phillips, *Protestant America*, p. 300.

27. "Justin Perkins," *DAB*, 14:475–476; "David O. Allen," *DAB*, 1:186–187; "Elias Riggs," *DAB*, 15:602–603.

28. Phillips, *Protestant America*, pp. 300, 307.

29. On "missionary literati," in addition to Phillips, *Protestant America*, pp. 300–305, see review of same by Maurice Freedman, "Eastward, Christian Soldiers," *Times Literary Supplement*, June 13, 1975, p. 671.

30. Francis A. Wayland, *A Memoir of the Life and Labors of the Reverend Adoniram Judson, D.D.*, 2 vols. (Boston: Phillips, Sampson, 1853); see also Courtney Anderson, *To the Golden Shore: The Life of Adoniram Judson* (Boston: Little, Brown, 1956).

31. Wayland, *Judson*, 1:159, 162.

32. Frederick Wells Williams, *The Life and Letters of Samuel Wells Williams: Missionary, Diplomatist, Sinologue* (New York: Putnam, 1889), p. 123; Pickering, *Pickering*, p. 284.

33. "George Bowen," *DAB*, 2:504.

34. John Pickering, "Inaugural Address to the American Oriental Society," *AOS Journal* (1843), 1:49, 59.

35. Pickering, *Pickering*, p. 455.

36. *Ibid.*, pp. 439, 462–463.

37. On American views of blacks in the nineteenth century, see William Stanton, *The Leopard's Spots: Scientific Attitudes Toward Race in America, 1815–1859* (Chicago: University of Chicago Press, 1960), and George M. Fredrickson, *The Black Image in the White Mind* (New York: Harper & Row, 1971), especially ch. 3. On "scientific racism" in nineteenth-century America, see Stephen Jay Gould, *The Mismeasure of Man* (New York: Norton, 1981).

38. Stanton, *Leopard's Spots*, p. 22.

39. *Ibid.*, pp. 50–51.

40. *Ibid.*, pp. 115–118.

41. *Ibid.*, p. 144.

42. *Ibid.*, pp. 175–180.

43. Charles Summer, *The Scholar, the Jurist, the Artist, the Philanthropist* (Boston: Ticknor, 1846), p. 9.

44. "John Lloyd Stephens," *DAB*, 17:579–580; Benjamin Keen, *The Aztec Image in Western Thought*, pp. 349, 402; James Baird, *Ishmael* (Baltimore: Johns Hopkins University Press, 1956), ch. 3; Paul Theroux, *The Great Railway Bazaar* (Boston: Houghton Mifflin, 1975), p. 3.

45. Arthur Christy, *The Orient in American Transcendentalism: A Study of Emerson, Thoreau, and Alcott* (New York: Columbia University Press, 1932), pp. 7, 191; Milton Singer, "Passage to More than India: A Sketch of Changing European and American Images," in Milton Singer, ed., *When a Great Tradition Modernizes* (New York: Praeger, 1972), pp. 11–38.

46. Henry David Thoreau, *Walden* (New York: Signet, 1960), p. 198; Christy, *Orient,* p. 191.

⟨∾ 2. ENCLOSURE DEFERRED

1. "Proceedings of the American Oriental Society," in *AOS Journal* (1891–1894), 16:lvii–lviii.

2. On academic revolutions, see Richard Hofstadter, "The Revolution in Higher Education," in Arthur M. Schlesinger, Jr., and Morton White, eds., *Paths of American Thought* (Boston: Houghton Mifflin, 1963), pp. 269–290; Laurence R. Veysey, *The Emergence of the American University* (Chicago: University of Chicago Press, 1965), pp. 1–2; Christopher Jencks and David Riesman, *The Academic Revolution* (New York: Doubleday, 1968), p. xiii; Robert A. McCaughey, "The Transformation of American Academic Life: Harvard University, 1821–1892," *Perspectives in American History* (1974), 8:241–242.

3. Samuel Eliot Morison, *Three Centuries of Harvard* (Cambridge: Harvard University Press, 1936), pp. 30–31, 57–58; Brooks Mather Kelley, *Yale: A History* (New Haven: Yale University Press, 1974), pp. 41, 109, 249; David C. Humphrey, *From King's College to Columbia, 1746–1800* (New York: Columbia University Press, 1976), pp. 122, 163.

4. Henry Adams, *The Education of Henry Adams* (New York: Random House, 1931), p. 54. See also McCaughey, "Transformation," pp. 246–275.

5. Francis J. Grund, *Aristocracy in America,* 2 vols. (London: Capen and Lyon, 1839), 2:34–35.

6. "Sidney Willard," *DAB,* 20:239–240; Sidney Willard, *Memories of Youth and Manhood* (Boston: J. Bartlett, 1855), 1:326.

7. George S. Hillard, "Memoir of Cornelius Conway Felton, LL.D.," *Proceedings of the Massachusetts Historical Society* (1868), 10:352–368; "Cornelius C. Felton," *DAB,* 11:442–443.

8. Cornelius C. Felton, ed., *A Memorial of the Rev. John Snelling Popkin, D.D.* (Cambridge: Harvard University Press, 1852); James Freeman Clarke, *Autobiography* (Boston: Houghton Mifflin, 1891), pp. 36–37; George S. Hillard, *North American Review* (1852) 75:479.

9. On Everett's and Ticknor's tenure at Harvard, see McCaughey, "Transformation," pp. 247–248; David B. Tyack, *George Ticknor and the Boston Brahmins* (Cambridge: Harvard University Press, 1967), pp. 86–128.

10. Mary Orne Pickering, *Life of John Pickering* (Boston: Wilson, 1887), pp. 231, 250.

11. Sidney Willard, "State of Learning in the United States," *North American Review* (1819), 10:240–269.

12. Eliot's inaugural address, reprinted in Nathan Pusey, ed., *A Turning Point in Higher Education* (Cambridge: Harvard University Press, 1969), p.

21; George N. Brush, New Haven, to C. W. Eliot, June 29, 1869 (Box 66, Eliot Papers, Harvard University Archives).

13. McCaughey, "Transformation," pp. 275–277.

14. "William Dandridge Peck," *DAB*, 14:383–384; Sven Peterson, "Benjamin Peirce: Mathematician and Philosopher," *Journal of the History of Ideas* (1955), 16:89, 110; A. Hunter Dupree, *Asa Gray* (Cambridge: Harvard University Press, 1959); Edward Lurie, *Louis Agassiz: A Life in Science* (Chicago: University of Chicago Press, 1960); Sally G. Kohlstedt, *The Formation of the American Scientific Community* (Urbana: University of Illinois Press, 1976).

15. Kohlstedt, *Formation*, ch. 5.

16. Edward Shils, "The Order of Learning in the United States: The Ascendancy of the University," in Alexandra Oleson and John Voss, eds., *The Organization of Knowledge in Modern America, 1860–1920* (Baltimore: Johns Hopkins University Press, 1976), p. 19.

17. Richard Hofstadter and Walter P. Metzger, *The Development of Academic Freedom in the United States* (New York: Columbia University Press, 1955); Frederick Rudolph, *The American College and University* (New York: Random House, 1962); Hugh Hawkins, *Pioneer: A History of The Johns Hopkins University, 1874–1889* (Ithaca, N.Y.: Cornell University Press, 1960); Veysey, *American University;* McCaughey, "Transformation," pp. 239–332.

18. Carl Diehl, *Americans and German Scholarship, 1770–1870* (New Haven: Yale University Press, 1973), p. 155; Kelley, *Yale*, pp. 185–187.

19. Yale University, *Doctors of Philosophy, 1861–1960* (New Haven: Yale University Press, 1961); Cornell University, Alumni Records Office, Cornell University, Ithaca, New York; Harvard University, *Doctors of Philosophy and Doctors of Science, 1873–1909* (Cambridge: Harvard University Press, 1910).

20. Hawkins, *Pioneer*, part 2; McCaughey, "Transformation," pp. 287–290.

21. *Graduates and Fellows of The Johns Hopkins University, 1876–1913* (Baltimore: Johns Hopkins University Press, 1914).

22. McCaughey, "Transformation," p. 331; Richard Storrs, *Harper's University: The Beginnings* (Chicago: University of Chicago Press, 1966), pp. 86–105, 154–163.

23. McCaughey, "Transformation," pp. 314, 310; John Barnard, *From Evangelism to Progressivism at Oberlin College, 1866–1917* (Columbus: Ohio State University Press, 1969), pp. 79–81; William James, "The Ph.D. Octopus," in William James, *Memories and Studies* (New York: Longman's, 1917), pp. 329–347.

24. McCaughey, "Transformation," p. 314; George Santayana, *Character and Opinion in the United States* (1920; reprint ed., New York: Norton, 1967), pp. 142, 143.

25. John Voss, "The Learned Society in American Intellectual Life," in Alexandra Oleson and Sanborn C. Brown, eds., *The Pursuit of Knowledge in*

the Early American Republic (Baltimore: Johns Hopkins University Press, 1976), pp. vii–xxv.

26. Allen Walker Read, "The Membership in Proposed American Academies," *American Literature* (October 1933), 7:145–165; Thomas L. Haskell, *The Emergence of Professional Social Science* (Urbana: University of Illinois Press, 1976), p. 110.

27. Haskell, *Professional Social Science,* chs. 8 and 9; on the founding of the AHA, see J. Franklin Jameson, "The American Historical Association, 1883–1909," *American Historical Review* (October 1909), 15:1–20; on the AEA, see A. W. Coats, "The First Two Decades of the American Economic Association," *American Economic Review* (September 1960), 50:556–573. See also Mary O. Furner, *Advocacy and Objectivity: A Crisis in the Professionalization of American Social Science, 1865–1905* (Lexington: University of Kentucky Press, 1975).

28. The academic economist's quote is in Robert L. Church, "Economists as Experts: The Rise of an Academic Profession in America, 1870–1917," in Lawrence Stone, ed., *The University in Society,* 2 vols. (Princeton: Princeton University Press, 1974), 2:571–609; Jameson's remarks are in Elizabeth Donnan and Leo F. Stock, eds., *An Historian's World: Selections from the Correspondence of John Franklin Jameson,* Memoirs of the American Philosophical Society (Philadelphia: The Society, 1956), p. 42.

29. Haskell, *Professional Social Science;* Bruce Kuklick, *The Rise of American Philosophy: Cambridge, Massachusetts, 1860–1930* (New Haven: Yale University Press, 1977).

30. McCaughey, "Transformation," pp. 312–314.

31. Diehl, *Americans and German Scholarship,* pp. 118–143.

32. "John Norton Johnson," Harvard College Alumni Files, Class of 1881 (Harvard University Archives).

33. William I. Chamberlain, obituary, *New York Times,* September 29, 1933; Harvey DeWitt Griswold, obituary, *New York Times,* May 19, 1945.

34. On DuBois, Herbert Aptheker, ed., *The Correspondence of W. E. B. DuBois, 1877–1934* (Amherst: University of Massachusetts Press, 1973).

35. "Isaac A. Hourwich," *DAB,* 9:257; see also Oscar Handlin, "Old Immigrants and New," in Oscar Handlin, *Race and Nationality in American Life* (New York: Doubleday, 1957), pp. 74–110.

36. W. Norman Brown, "South Asia Studies: A History," *Annals of the American Academy of Political and Social Science* (November 1964), 356:54–62.

37. McCaughey, "Transformation," pp. 290–291; Hawkins, *Pioneer,* pp. 156–157; "Edward Washburn Hopkins," *DAB,* Supplement 1, pp. 433–434.

38. "A. V. William Jackson," *DAB,* Supplement 2, pp. 338–339; Brown, "South Asian Studies," p. 55.

39. On Eliot's efforts to secure a Sanskritist, see McCaughey, "Transformation," pp. 289–290; on Columbia and Hebrew, Arthur Jeffrey, "The Department of Semitic Languages," in John Herman Randall, ed., *A History of*

the Faculty of Philosophy, Columbia University (New York: Columbia University Press, 1957), pp. 183–189.

40. David G. Lyon, "Semitics Department," in Samuel E. Morison, ed., *The Development of Harvard University since the Inauguration of President Eliot, 1869–1929* (Cambridge: Harvard University Press, 1929), pp. 231–240.

41. Charles R. Lanman, ed., *The Whitney Memorial Meeting* (Boston: Ginn, 1897), pp. 7, 93; "William Dwight Whitney," *DAB*, 20:166–168; Diehl, *Americans and German Scholarship*, pp. 120–130, 141–143.

42. Timothy Dwight, *Memories of Yale Life and Men* (New York: Mead, 1903), pp. 401–403.

43. George Wilson Pierson, *Yale: College and University, 1871–1937*, 2 vols. (New Haven: Yale University Press, 1952), 1:51, 70, 100; William Lyon Phelps, *Autobiography* (New York: Oxford University Press, 1938), p. 104; Henry Seidel Canby, *Alma Mater: The Gothic Age of the American College* (New York: Farrar and Rinehart, 1936), p. 89; Edgar Furniss, *The Graduate School of Yale: A Brief History* (New Haven: Yale University Press, 1965), pp. 31–34.

44. Hanns Oertel, Yale Ph.D., 1890, and Herbert Cushing Tolman, same class, did become academics after studying with Whitney, but Oertel went into administration at Yale and Tolman taught Latin at Vanderbilt.

45. Thomas W. Goodspeed, *William Rainey Harper* (Chicago: University of Chicago Press, 1928), pp. 26, 52, 79; Diehl, *Americans and German Scholarship*, p. 120.

46. On Whitney as popularizer, see *Nation* (June 23, 1894), 50:443–444.

47. Rosane Rocher, "The Founding of the AOS: Boston Gentlemen and Foreign Missions" (Philadelphia: University of Pennsylvania, Department of South Asian Studies, 1976).

48. See sources cited in notes 27 and 28 above.

49. Rocher, "Founding of the AOS," ch. 3; Cyrus Adler, *I Have Considered the Days* (Philadelphia: Jewish Publication Society of America, 1941), pp. 62–66; "Morris Jastrow," *DAB*, 10:3.

50. "Proceedings of the AOS at Its Meeting, Princeton, New Jersey, October 22nd and 23rd, 1890," in *AOS Journal* (1891), 15:xxxvi–xxxviii; restatement in *AOS Journal* (1894), 16:lvii–lviii.

ৡ 3. CYCLES OF CATHAY

1. George F. Kennan, *Memoirs, 1925–1950* (Boston: Little, Brown, 1967), p. 17.

2. Edward Shils, "Tradition, Ecology, and Institution in the History of Sociology," in Edward Shils, ed., *The Calling of Sociology and Other Essays on the Pursuit of Learning* (Chicago: University of Chicago Press, 1980), pp. 168–169; Bruce Kuklick, *The Rise of American Philosophy: Cambridge, Massachusetts, 1860–1930* (New Haven: Yale University Press, 1977), p. xxii.

3. Harlan Beach, ed., *World Atlas of Christian Missions* (New York: Stu-

dent Volunteer Movement, 1911); see also James A. Field, Jr., "Near East Notes and Far East Queries," in John K. Fairbank, ed., *The Missionary Enterprise in China and America* (Cambridge: Harvard University Press, 1974), pp. 23–55.

4. "William McCutchan Morrison," *DAB*, 13:231–232; "Robert Hamill Nassau," *DAB*, 13:390–391; "Adolphus Clemens Good," *DAB*, 7:375.

5. "Jacob Chamberlain," *DAB*, 3:597; "Samuel Henry Kellogg," *DAB*, 10:304–305; "George Edward Post," *DAB*, 15:116–117; "Cyrus Hamlin," *DAB*, 8:195; "Edwin Munsell Bliss," *DAB*, 2:371.

6. Field, "Near East Notes," pp. 37, 44; "W.A.P. Martin," *DAB*, 12:347–348; "Arthur H. Smith," *DAB*, 17:238–239; Akira Iriye, *Across the Pacific: An Inner History of American–East Asian Relationships* (New York: Harcourt, Brace, 1977), p. 17.

7. Frederick Wells Williams, *The Life and Letters of Samuel Wells Williams: Missionary, Diplomatist, Sinologue* (New York: Putnam, 1889), pp. 80, 174, 197, 234–235.

8. Earl Herbert Cressy, "Converting the Missionary," *Asia* (June 1919), 19:553.

9. Clifton J. Phillips, "The Student Volunteer Movement and Its Role in China Missions, 1886–1920," in Fairbank, *Missionary Enterprise,* pp. 91–109.

10. [William Ernest Hocking], *Re-Thinking Missions: A Laymen's Inquiry After One Hundred Years* (New York: Harper, 1932), p. 4.

11. *Ibid.,* p. iii; Harlan P. Beach, ed., *World Missionary Atlas* (New York: Institute of Social and Religious Research, 1925).

12. "Arthur W. Hummel, 1884–1975," *Journal of Asian Studies* (February 1976), 35:265–276; "Edwin Bliss," *DAB*, 2:371; Pearl Buck, *Essay on Myself* (New York: J. Day, 1966); Harold R. Isaacs, *Scratches on Our Minds: American Images of China and India* (New York: Capricorn, 1958); W. A. Swanberg, *Luce and His Empire* (New York: Charles Scribner's, 1972), pp. 15–24.

13. John Gunther, *A Fragment of Autobiography: The Fun of Writing the Inside Books* (New York: Harper & Row, 1962), p. 5; Cyrus L. Sulzberger, *A Long Row of Candles: Memoirs and Diaries, 1934–1954* (New York: Macmillan, 1969), pp. xiii, 33.

14. On American foreign correspondents generally, see John Hohenberg, *Foreign Correspondence: The Great Reporters and Their Times* (New York: Columbia University Press, 1969).

15. *Ibid.,* pp. 274–321.

16. William Henry Chamberlin, *The Confessions of an Individualist* (New York: Macmillan, 1940), p. 61; Edmund Taylor, *Awakening from History* (Boston: Gambit, 1969), p. xvi.

17. Gunther, *Fragment of Autobiography,* pp. 6, 32, 37.

18. *Ibid.,* p. 39.

19. Anna Louise Strong, *I Change Worlds* (Garden City, N.Y.: Doubleday, 1937); Vincent Sheean, *Personal History* (New York: Literary Guild, 1935); Warren I. Cohen, *The Chinese Connection: Roger S. Greene, Thomas*

W. Lamont, *George E. Sokolsky and American East Asian Relations* (New York: Columbia University Press, 1978), ch. 3; "Edgar Snow," in John K. Fairbank, *China Perceived* (New York: Knopf, 1974), pp. 179–186; Marion K. Sanders, *Dorothy Thompson: A Legend in Her Time* (Boston: Houghton Mifflin, 1973).

20. Sulzberger, *Long Row of Candles*, p. 37; Theodore H. White, *In Search of History: A Personal Adventure* (New York: Harper & Row, 1978), ch. 1.

21. Chamberlin, *Confessions*, pp. 4, 12.

22. Sulzberger, *Long Row of Candles*, p. xiii; Sue Berryman, Paul F. Langer, John Pincus, and Richard H. Solomon, *Foreign Language and International Studies Specialists: The Marketplace and National Policy* (Santa Monica: Rand Corporation, 1979), pp. 141–143.

23. James A. Reichley, "Our Critical Shortage of Leadership," *Fortune* (September 1971), 84:89.

24. Kennan, *Memoirs*, p. 23.

25. Warren Ilchman, *Professional Diplomacy in the United States, 1779–1939* (Chicago: University of Chicago Press, 1961), ch. 1.

26. Eugene Schuyler, *Selected Essays, with a Memoir by Evelyn Schuyler Schaeffer* (New York: Scribner's, 1901), pp. 17, 50–51.

27. *Ibid.*, p. 170.

28. *Ibid.*, p. 204.

29. *Ibid.*, p. 15.

30. The principal sources on Rockhill are Paul A. Varg, *Open Door Diplomat: The Life of W. W. Rockhill* (Urbana: University of Illinois Press, 1952), and Peter W. Stanley, "The Making of an American Sinologist: William W. Rockhill and the Open Door," *Perspectives in American History* (1977–1978), 11:419–460.

31. Varg, *Open Door Diplomat*, p. 126.

32. *Ibid.*, pp. 114, 125.

33. *Ibid.*, p. 4.

34. Ilchman, *Professional Diplomacy*, chs. 3 and 4. See also Robert D. Schulzinger, *The Making of the Diplomatic Mind* (Middletown, Conn.: Wesleyan University Press, 1975), and Martin Weil, *A Pretty Good Club* (New York: Norton, 1977).

35. Kennan, *Memoirs*, pp. 33–34; Daniel Yergin, *Shattered Peace: The Origins of the Cold War and the National Security State* (Boston: Houghton Mifflin, 1977), pp. 20–21.

36. Russell D. Buhite, "Stanley K. Hornbeck and American Far Eastern Policy," in Frank J. Merli and Theodore A. Wilson, eds., *Makers of American Diplomacy* (New York: Scribner's, 1974), pp. 431–457. See also John K. Fairbank, *Chinabound: A Fifty-Year Memoir* (New York: Harper & Row, 1982), pp. 176–177.

37. O. Edmund Clubb, *The Witness and I* (New York: Columbia University Press, 1974), p. 34; E. J. Kahn, Jr., *The China Hands: America's Foreign Service Officers and What Befell Them* (New York: Viking, 1975).

38. On Hoover's Commerce Department, see Joseph C. Brandes, *Herbert Hoover and Economic Diplomacy* (Pittsburgh: University of Pittsburgh Press, 1965); on the Department of Agriculture in the 1930s, Allen Weinstein, *Perjury: The Hiss-Chambers Case* (New York: Vintage, 1979), pp. 132–134; on the Army, Barbara Tuchman, *Stilwell and the American Experience in China, 1911–1945* (New York: Macmillan, 1970); John K. Fairbank, "David D. Barrett," in Fairbank, *China Perceived*, pp. 199–204; and David D. Barrett, *Dixie Mission: The US Army Observer Group in Yenan, 1944* (Berkeley, Cal.: Center for Chinese Studies, 1970).

39. Kennan, *Memoirs*, pp. 294–295.

40. Kahn, *China Hands*, ch. 9.

41. Clubb, *Witness and I*, pp. 123, 142; Fairbank, "Barrett," p. 204.

42. Kennan, *Memoirs*, pp. 17, 76–77; Bohlen, *Witness to History*, p. 4; Clubb, *Witness and I*, pp. 143–144; Tuchman, *Stilwell*, p. 76.

43. Lewis Coser, *Men of Ideas: A Sociologist's View* (New York: Free Press, 1965), p. 263.

44. *Webster's New Collegiate Dictionary*, 2d ed. (Springfield, Mass.: G. & C. Merriam, 1953), p. 330.

45. R. A. Humphreys, "William Hickling Prescott: The Man and the Historian," in Howard F. Cline, ed., *William Hickling Prescott: A Memorial* (Durham, N.C.: Duke University Press, 1959); John W. Caughey, *Hubert Howe Bancroft: Historian of the West* (Berkeley and Los Angeles: University of California Press, 1946), p. 86.

46. Milton Singer, "Passage to More than India: A Sketch of Changing European and American Images," in Milton Singer, ed., *When a Great Tradition Modernizes* (New York: Praeger, 1972), p. 20; Isaacs, *Scratches on Our Minds*, p. 155; Alice Payne Hackett, *70 Years of Best Sellers* (New York: Bowker, 1967), pp. 71–81; "Isabel Florence Hapgood," in Edward T. James, ed., *Notable American Women*, 3 vols. (Cambridge: Harvard University Press, 1971), 2:129–130; Isabel Florence Hapgood, obituary, *New York Times*, June 27, 1928.

47. Granville Hicks, *John Reed: The Making of a Revolutionary* (New York: Arno, 1936); Max Eastman, *Love and Revolution: My Journey Through an Epoch* (New York: Random House, 1964); Bertram Wolfe, *A Life in Two Centuries* (New York: Stein and Day, 1978). On Edmund Wilson, see Sherman Paul, *Edmund Wilson: A Study of Literary Vocation in Our Time* (Urbana: University of Illinois Press, 1965); also Simon Karlinsky, ed., *The Nabokov-Wilson Letters* (New York: Harper & Row, 1979); Edmund Wilson, *A Window on Russia* (New York: Farrar, Straus, and Giroux, 1972); for Wilson on journalism Elena Wilson, ed., *Letters on Literature and Politics* (New York: Farrar, Straus, and Giroux, 1972), p. 354; Dorothy L. Guth, ed., *Letters of E. B. White* (New York: Harper & Row, 1976), p. 146.

48. Lawrence W. Chisholm, *Fenollosa: The Far East and American Culture* (New Haven: Yale University Press, 1963); E. A. Robinson, ed., *Selections From the Letters of Thomas Sergeant Perry* (New York: Macmillan, 1929), p. 4.

49. Letter of Ralph Waldo Emerson to William R. Alger, Concord, Massachusetts, October 19, 1856, Beinecke Library, Yale University. This citation and other material relating to Emerson's interest in the Orient was provided to me by Professor Eleanor M. Tilton, Barnard College.

50. George N. Kates, *The Years That Were Fat* (New York: Harper & Row, 1952), pp. 2, 24.

51. *Ibid.*, p. 267.

₷ 4. ACADEMIC AMBASSADORS

1. Harold Jefferson Coolidge and Robert H. Lord, *Archibald Cary Coolidge: Life and Letters* (Boston: Houghton Mifflin, 1932), p. 18.

2. Thomas L. Haskell, *The Emergence of Professional Social Science* (Urbana: University of Illinois Press, 1977), p. 19; Mary O. Furner, *Advocacy and Objectivity: A Crisis in the Professionalization of American Social Science, 1865–1905* (Lexington: University of Kentucky Press, 1975); Robert A. McCaughey, "The Transformation of American Academic Life: Harvard University, 1821–1892," *Perspectives in American History* (1974), 8:239–332; Joseph Ben-David and Randall Collins, "Social Factors in the Origins of a New Science: The Case of Psychology," *American Sociological Review* (August 1966), 31:451–474; Arnold Thackray and Robert K. Merton, "On Discipline-Building: The Paradoxes of George Sarton," *Isis* (December 1972), 63:473–494.

3. Coolidge and Lord, *Coolidge*, pp. 17, 26.

4. *Ibid.*, pp. 31, 40.

5. *Ibid.*, pp. 40–59; Ephraim Emerton and Samuel Eliot Morison, "History, 1838–1929," in Samuel Eliot Morison, ed., *The Development of Harvard University, 1869–1929* (Cambridge: Harvard University Press, 1930), pp. 166–167. See also Robert F. Byrnes, "Archibald Cary Coolidge: A Founder of Russian Studies in the United States," *Slavic Review* (December 1978), 37:651–666.

6. Coolidge and Lord, *Coolidge*, p. 47; William Bentinck-Smith, *Building a Great Library: The Coolidge Years at Harvard* (Cambridge: Harvard University Press, 1976).

7. Clarence A. Manning, *A History of Slavic Studies in the United States* (Milwaukee: Marquette University Press, 1957), ch. 1; Philip E. Mosely, "The Growth of Russian Studies," in Harold H. Fisher, ed., *American Research on Russia* (Bloomington: Indiana University Press, 1959), pp. 1–22.

8. Coolidge and Lord, *Coolidge*, p. 166; Emerton and Morison, "History," p. 166; Manning, *Slavic Studies*, pp. 27–28; Bentinck-Smith, *Great Library*, p. 191.

9. Bentinck-Smith, *Great Library*, p. 12; Coolidge and Lord, *Coolidge*, pp. 51–52, 72–73, 85–86; George Parker Winship, "A.C.C.," *Harvard Library Notes* (1928), 20:157–162.

10. Coolidge and Lord, *Coolidge*, pp. 58–59.

11. *Ibid.,* p. 18.

12. William Phillips, *Ventures in Diplomacy* (Boston: Beacon, 1952), pp. 5–6.

13. Waldo H. Heinrichs, Jr., *American Ambassador: Joseph C. Grew and the Development of the United States Diplomatic Tradition* (Boston: Little, Brown, 1966); Coolidge and Lord, *Coolidge,* p. 71.

14. Roger B. Merriman, "Introduction" to Archibald Cary Coolidge, *Suleiman the Magnificent* (Cambridge: Harvard University Press, 1944); Coolidge and Lord, *Coolidge,* pp. 93–94; George Santayana, *Persons and Places,* 3 vols. (New York: Scribner, 1963), 2:162.

15. On Reinsch, see Merle Curti and Vernon Carstensen, *The University of Wisconsin: A History, 1848–1925,* 2 vols. (Madison: University of Wisconsin Press, 1949), 1:637, 2:338–339; on T. J. Coolidge, see Ernest R. May, "American Imperialism: A Reinterpretation," *Perspectives in American History* (1967), 1:155.

16. Coolidge and Lord, *Coolidge,* p. 140; Bentinck-Smith, *Great Library,* p. 192.

17. Lawrence E. Gelfand, *The Inquiry: American Preparations for Peace, 1917–1919* (New Haven: Yale University Press, 1963), pp. 53–67; Coolidge and Lord, *Coolidge,* pp. 192–233.

18. Coolidge and Lord, *Coolidge,* pp. 306–330; see also Hamilton Fish Armstrong, *Peace and Counterpeace: From Wilson to Hitler* (New York: Harper & Row, 1971), pp. 144–145, 220–221.

19. Coolidge and Lord, *Coolidge,* p. 315.

20. *Ibid.,* pp. 340–345. Haskins' remarks are recorded in Archibald Cary Coolidge Obituary Notebook, Harvard University Archives.

21. Kenneth Scott Latourette, "Chinese Historical Studies During the Past Seven Years," *American Historical Review* (July 1921), 26:703–716; *idem.,* "Chinese Historical Studies During the Past Nine Years," *AHR* (1930), 35:778–797; *idem.,* "Far Eastern Studies in the United States: Retrospect and Prospect," *Far Eastern Quarterly* (November 1955), 15:3–11.

22. "Far Eastern Studies," p. 5.

23. Brooks Mather Kelley, *Yale: A History* (New Haven: Yale University Press, 1974), p. 252; K. S. Latourette, "Harlan P. Beach," *DAB,* Supplement 1, pp. 62–63.

24. George Pierson, *Yale: College and University, 1871–1937,* 2 vols. (New Haven: Yale University Press, 1952–1955), 1:292; Frederick Wells Williams, *The Life and Letters of Samuel Wells Williams: Missionary, Diplomatist, Sinologue* (New York: Putnam, 1889).

25. Kenneth Scott Latourette, *Beyond the Ranges: An Autobiography* (Grand Rapids, Mich.: William B. Eerdmans, 1957), pp. 31–32; E. Theodore Bachman, "Kenneth Scott Latourette, Historian and Friend," in Wilbur C. Harr, ed., *Frontiers of the Christian World Mission since 1938* (New York: Harper & Row, 1962), p. 238.

26. Latourette, *Beyond the Ranges,* p. 30; Clifton J. Phillips, "The Student

Volunteer Movement and Its Role in China Missions, 1886–1920," in John K. Fairbank, ed., *The Missionary Enterprise in China and America* (Cambridge: Harvard University Press, 1974), pp. 91–109.

27. Latourette, *Beyond the Ranges*, pp. 31–40.

28. Bachman, "Latourette," pp. 240–243.

29. Latourette, *Beyond the Ranges*, pp. 57, 61.

30. *Ibid.*, p. 78.

31. John K. Fairbank, *Chinabound: A Fifty-Year Memoir* (New York: Harper & Row, 1982), pp. 134–135; Bachman, "Latourette," p. 246.

32. Latourette, *Beyond the Ranges*, p. 63; Kenneth Scott Latourette, *Missions Tomorrow* (New York: Harper, 1933), p. iv.

33. Latourette, *Beyond the Ranges*, pp. 74–75; Edward C. Carter, ed., *China and Japan in Our University Curricula* (New York: Institute of Pacific Relations, 1929); Kenneth S. Latourette, ed., *Progress of Chinese Studies in the United States of America* (Washington, D.C.: American Council of Learned Societies, 1931).

34. Latourette, *Beyond the Ranges*, p. 86; on Lindbeck, see the preface to John M. H. Lindbeck, *Understanding China: An Assessment of American Scholarly Resources* (New York: Praeger, 1971).

35. Carter, *China and Japan*, p. 78; Latourette, "Chinese Historical Studies (1931)," p. 747.

36. Pierson, *Yale*, 2:296.

37. Latourette's frustration with his colleagues is conveyed in *Beyond the Ranges*, pp. 94–95, 63; his lasting satisfactions, in Kenneth Scott Latourette, *Christian Adventure at Yale: 75 Years of the Yale YMCA* (New Haven: Yale University Press, 1956).

38. Phillips, "Student Volunteer Movement," p. 106. On the Greenes, see Warren I. Cohen, *The Chinese Connection: Roger S. Greene, Thomas W. Lamont, George E. Sokolsky and American East Asian Relations* (New York: Columbia University Press, 1978), ch. 1. See also Maurice Freedman, review of Fairbank, *Missionary Enterprise*, in *Times Literary Supplement*, June 13, 1975.

39. Biographical materials on Bolton have been drawn from the following sources: John W. Caughey, "Herbert Eugene Bolton," in Howard F. Cline, ed., *Latin American History: Essays on Its Study and Teaching, 1898–1965* (Austin: University of Texas Press, 1965), pp. 179–184; Frederick E. Bolton, "The Early Life of Herbert Eugene Bolton," *Arizona and the West* (Spring 1962), 4:65–73; John Francis Bannon, "Herbert Eugene Bolton," *DAB*, Supplement 5, pp. 76–78; author's interview with Professor Jeffrey Johnson, Palo Alto, California, May 13, 1976.

40. Lewis Hanke, "The First Lecturer on Hispanic American Diplomatic History in the United States," in Cline, *Latin American History*, pp. 6–18; Howard F. Cline, "Latin American History since 1898," in *ibid.*, pp. 30–32; Benjamin Keen, "Introduction" to Edward Gaylord Bourne, *Spain in America, 1450–1580* (New York: Harper & Row, 1962).

41. On Bancroft and his library, see John W. Caughey, *Hubert Howe Bancroft: Historian of the West* (Berkeley and Los Angeles: University of California Press, 1946); on Moses and Stephens, see Lincoln Constance, *Berkeley and the Latin American Connection* (Berkeley and Los Angeles: University of California Press, 1978), pp. 1–7.

42. Bolton, "Early Life," p. 73; Bannon, "Bolton," p. 77.

43. Caughey, "Bolton," p. 180.

44. *Ibid.*, p. 181.

45. Lewis Hanke, "Development of Bolton's Theory," in Cline, *Latin American History*, pp. 184–194; John Francis Bannon, ed., *Bolton and the Spanish Borderlands* (Norman: University of Oklahoma Press, 1964).

46. Caughey, "Bolton," p. 180.

47. Johnson interview; Caughey, "Bolton," pp. 179–181.

48. Adele Ogden, ed., *Greater America: Essays in Honor of Herbert Eugene Bolton* (Berkeley and Los Angeles: University of California Press, 1945).

49. Johnson interview.

50. Bolton's PhDs (through 1945) listed in Ogden, *Greater America*, pp. 549–672.

51. Irving Leonard, "A Survey of Latin American Studies at Twenty Universities," *Notes on Latin American Studies* (1943), 1:7–43; Constance, *Latin American Connection*, p. 34.

52. David Riesman, "Ten Years On," *New Republic* (July 1, 1978), pp. 15–17.

53. Charles Breasted, *Pioneer to the Past* (New York: Scribner's, 1945), p. 216. This work is the principal source for Breasted's career and a splendid book in its own right.

54. *Ibid.*, pp. 21, 30, 65.

55. John A. Wilson, "James Henry Breasted, 1865–1935," in National Academy of Sciences, *Biographical Memoirs* (1938), 18:98; Breasted, *Pioneer*, p. 28.

56. Breasted, *Pioneer*, p. 108.

57. *Ibid.*, p. 109.

58. *Ibid.*, pp. 212–213.

59. *Ibid.*, pp. 216, 221.

60. *Ibid.*, pp. 230, 239; Wilson, "Breasted," p. 102.

61. Breasted, *Pioneer*, p. 226.

62. On Harper, see Richard Storrs, *Harper's University: The Beginnings* (Chicago: University of Chicago Press, 1966); on Merriam, see Barry D. Karl, *Charles E. Merriam and the Study of Politics* (Chicago: University of Chicago Press, 1974); on Samuel Harper, see his autobiographical work, *The Russia I Believe In* (Chicago: University of Chicago Press, 1945); and on Hale, see Daniel J. Kevles, "George Ellery Hale, the First World War, and the Advancement of Science," *Isis* (Winter, 1968), 59:427–440.

63. Breasted, *Pioneer*, pp. 224–225, 391–392.

64. *Ibid.,* pp. 354, 374–377.

65. *Ibid.,* pp. 385, 392.

66. *Ibid.,* pp. 372–377, 398.

67. James Henry Breasted, "Introduction," in James Henry Breasted, ed., *The Oriental Institute* (Chicago: University of Chicago Press, 1935); George M. Beckmann, "The Role of the Foundations [in the Non-Western World in Higher Education]," in Donald N. Bigelow and Lyman H. Legters, eds., *Annals of the American Academy of Political and Social Science* (1964), 356:12–22.

68. James T. Shotwell, *The Autobiography of James T. Shotwell* (Indianapolis: Bobbs-Merrill, 1961); Harold Josephson, *James T. Shotwell and the Rise of Internationalism in America* (New Brunswick, N.J.: Rutgers University Press, 1975).

69. Ernest Bender, ed., *Indological Studies in Honor of W. Norman Brown* (New Haven: Yale University Press, 1962); George E. Simpson, *Melville Herskovits* (New York: Columbia University Press, 1973); *Webster's New Collegiate Dictionary,* 2nd ed. (Springfield, Mass.: G. & C. Merriam, 1953), p. 356; figures for years prior to 1934 from annual reports of sample universities, thereafter from Association of Research Libraries, *Doctoral Dissertations Accepted by American Universities* (New York: H. W. Wilson, 1934–41).

70. Faculty figures calculated from listings in the university bulletins of the six sample universities; affiliations with international studies determined by course offerings.

71. Curti and Carstensen, *University of Wisconsin,* 2:338.

72. Fairbank, *Chinabound,* pp. 133–135.

73. John N. Thomas, *The Institute of Pacific Relations: Asian Scholars and American Politics* (Seattle: University of Washington Press, 1974).

74. Committee for the Promotion of Chinese Studies, "Report," *Bulletin of the American Council of Learned Societies* (June 1937), 26:62.

75. "William L. Langer," in Harvard College, *Class of 1915: 25th Anniversary Report* (Cambridge: Harvard University Press, 1940), p. 420.

ࣾ 5. WAR, BLESSED WAR

1. Alfred Kazin, *New York Jew* (New York: Knopf, 1977), p. 4.

2. Edward Shils, "Intellectuals and the Center of Society in the United States," in Edward Shils, *Intellectuals and the Powers* (Chicago: University of Chicago Press, 1972), p. 168; Carleton Coon, *A North Africa Story: An Anthropologist as OSS Agent* (Boston: Gambit, 1980), pp. 3, 7.

3. William L. Langer, *In and Out of the Ivory Tower* (New York: Academic Publications, 1977), ch. 9; Stewart Alsop and Thomas Braden, *Sub Rosa: The OSS and American Espionage* (New York: Reynal and Hitchcock, 1946), p. 10. See also R. Harris Smith, *OSS: The Secret History of America's First*

Central Intelligence Agency (Berkeley and Los Angeles: University of California Press, 1972), and Anthony Cave Brown, *The Last Hero: Wild Bill Donovan* (New York: Time, 1982).

4. Alsop and Braden, *Sub Rosa,* pp. 18–19; Smith, *OSS,* pp. 1–35.

5. Alsop and Braden, p. 23; on OWI, see John K. Fairbank, *Chinabound: A Fifty-Year Memoir* (New York: Harper & Row, 1982), pp. 289–301.

6. Wendell C. Bennett, "The Ethnogeographic Board," *Smithsonian Institution Miscellaneous Collections* (1947), 107:1–135.

7. "James H. Gaul," in Harvard College, *Class of 1932: 15th Anniversary Report* (Cambridge: Harvard University Press, 1947), p. 132; "John C. Campbell," in Harvard College, *Class of 1933: 25th Anniversary Report* (Cambridge: Harvard University Press, 1958), p. 165; Smith, *OSS,* pp. 13–14, ch. 11.

8. Hugh Borton, "Reminiscences," in Oral History Collection, Columbia University, pp. 31–32; "Jacob C. Hurewitz," in *American Men and Women of Science,* 13th ed. (New York: R. R. Bowker, 1978), 7:586.

9. Langer, *Ivory Tower,* ch. 10; "Philip E. Mosely," folder in Columbiana Room, Columbia University Archives, Columbia University, New York City; Philip E. Mosely to Cleon O. Swayzee, New York City, October 5, 1954, in International Training and Research Program Files, Ford Foundation Archives, New York City.

10. Theodore H. White, *The Making of the President 1960* (New York: Atheneum, 1961), p. 188.

11. John K. Fairbank, *Chinabound: A Fifty-Year Memoir* (New York: Harper & Row, 1982), p. 173.

12. On antiwar campus sentiment into 1941, see Seymour Martin Lipset, "Political Controversies at Harvard, 1636–1974," in Seymour Martin Lipset and David Riesman, *Education and Politics at Harvard* (New York: McGraw-Hill, 1975), pp. 173–176; on its decline, Robert A. Divine, *Second Chance: The Triumph of Internationalism in America During World War II* (New York: Atheneum, 1971), ch. 3.

13. On Columbia's wartime efforts, see Nicholas Murray Butler, "Report of the President," in *Annual Reports to the Trustees of Columbia University* (New York: Columbia University Press, 1944, 1945); L. Gray Cowan, *A History of the School of International Affairs* (New York: Columbia University Press, 1954), chs. 1 and 2; William G. Boardman, *Columbia in Peace and War* (New York: Columbia University Press, 1944).

14. Cowan, *School of International Affairs,* chs. 1 and 2.

15. I. L. Kandel, *The Impact of the War upon American Education* (Chapel Hill: University of North Carolina Press, 1948), pp. 145–165; J. S. Gibson, "Area Language Training: An Army Experiment," *Education* (January 1945), 65:291–297.

16. Columbia University, *Annual Report* (1946), p. 27.

17. Boardman, *Columbia in Peace and War,* p. 95.

18. Butler, "Report of the President" (1944), p. 3; Ernest R. May, *"Les-*

sons" of the Past: The Use and Misuse of History in American Foreign Policy (New York: Oxford University Press, 1973), p. 7.

19. May, "Lessons", pp. 19–51; Divine, Second Chance, chs. 11 and 12.

20. Walter Johnson, The Battle Against Isolation (Chicago: University of Chicago Press, 1944), p. 239.

21. On interwar revisionism, Warren I. Cohen, The American Revisionists: The Lessons of Intervention in World War I (Chicago: University of Chicago Press, 1967); Samuel F. Bemis, "First Gun of a Revisionist Historiography for the Second World War," Journal of Modern History (March 1947), 19:55–59.

22. William L. Langer and S. Everett Gleason, The Challenge to Isolation: The World Crisis of 1937–1940 and American Foreign Policy (New York: Harper, 1952); William L. Langer and S. Everett Gleason, The Undeclared War, 1940–1941 (New York: Harper, 1953); Langer, Ivory Tower, pp. 200–201, 209.

23. Langer and Gleason, Challenge to Isolation, p. 11; Thomas A. Bailey, The Man in the Street: The Impact of American Public Opinion on Foreign Policy (New York: Macmillan, 1948), pp. 126, 150.

24. Ibid., pp. 133, 160.

25. Ibid., pp. 2, 319.

26. Ibid., p. 319.

27. Ibid., pp. 151, 202; for self-serving imputation, Christian Science Monitor, May 11, 1948, p. 14.

28. Martin Kriesberg, "Dark Areas of Ignorance," in Lester Markel, ed., Public Opinion and Foreign Policy (New York: Harper, 1949), pp. 49–64.

29. John W. Gardner, "Are We Doing Our Homework in Foreign Affairs?," Yale Review (March 1948), 37:400–408, 405.

30. Frederick S. Dunn, "Education and Foreign Affairs: A Challenge to the Universities," in Joseph E. McLean, ed., The Public Service and University Education (Princeton: Princeton University Press, 1949), p. 139 (entire article, pp. 121–143).

31. Ibid., p. 141; Grayson L. Kirk, The Study of International Relations in American Colleges and Universities (New York: Council on Foreign Relations, 1947). See also William T. R. Fox, "Interwar International Relations Research: The American Experience," World Politics (October 1949), 2:67–83.

32. Robert B. Hall, Area Studies: With Special Reference to their Implications for Research in the Social Sciences (New York: Social Science Research Council, 1947), pp. ii–iii.

33. Ibid., pp. 2, 22, 23.

34. Wendell C. Bennett, Area Studies in American Universities (New York: Social Science Research Council, 1951), pp. v–vi.

35. Hall, Area Studies, p. 32; Bennett, Area Studies, pp. 10–20.

36. Bennett, Area Studies, pp. 21–26.

37. Ibid., part 2.

38. John K. Fairbank, "Assignment for the '70's," *American Historical Review* (February 1969), 74:871; Denis Sinor, "Uralic and Altaic: The Neglected Area," *The Annals of the American Academy of Political and Social Science* (1964), 356:86–92; Robert E. Ward, "A Case for Asian Studies," *Journal of Asian Studies* (May 1973), 32:391–403.

39. Bennett, *Area Studies,* p. 41; President's Commission on Higher Education [George F. Zook, chairman], *Higher Education for American Democracy* (New York: Harper and Brothers, 1948), pp. 8, 17–20; see generally Alice M. Rivlin, *The Role of the Federal Government in Financing Higher Education* (Washington: Brookings Institution, 1961).

40. On the Fulbright-Hays Act, see *A Quarter Century: The American Adventure in Academic Exchange* (Washington: Board of Foreign Scholarships, 1971), and Walter Johnson and Francis J. Colligan, *The Fulbright Program: A History* (Chicago: University of Chicago Press, 1965); on Point Four and its impact on universities, Edward W. Weidner, *The World Role of Universities* (New York: McGraw-Hill, 1962), ch. 9.

41. On the Carpentier bequests, see L. Carrington Goodrich, "The Department of Chinese and Japanese," in John Herman Randall, ed., *A History of the Faculty of Philosophy, Columbia University* (New York: Columbia University Press, 1957), p. 246; on Crane, see Samuel Harper, *The Russia I Believe In* (Chicago: University of Chicago Press, 1945), ch. 2; on Hall, *DAB,* 8:122–123.

42. On Graves and Stevens, see Kenneth Scott Latourette, "Far Eastern Studies in the United States: Retrospect and Prospect," *Far Eastern Quarterly* (November 1955), 15:3–11; on Fairbank, *Chinabound,* pp. 98–99, 135–136. On Rockefeller and Carnegie efforts in the 1930s for international studies generally, see Stephen M. Arum, "A History of Foreign Language and Area Studies in the United States, 1915–1941," PhD dissertation, Columbia University, 1976.

43. George M. Beckmann, "The Role of the Foundations," *Annals of the American Academy of Political and Social Science* (November 1964), 356:12–22; *Annual Reports of the Rockefeller Foundation* (New York: The Foundation, 1945–1951).

44. *Annual Report of the Carnegie Corporation of New York* (New York: The Corporation, 1946), pp. 20–24.

45. The grant to Harvard's Russian Research Center is discussed in Carnegie Corporation 1948 report; Beckmann, "Foundations," p. 14.

46. *Annual Report of the Rockefeller Foundation* (1949), pp. 6–14.

47. The concept of "takeoff" is borrowed from Walt W. Rostow, *The Stages of Economic Growth: A Non-Communist Manifesto* (Cambridge: Cambridge University Press, 1960).

48. For quality rankings, see Hayward Keniston, *Graduate Study and Research in the Arts and Sciences at the University of Pennsylvania* (Philadelphia: University of Pennsylvania Press, 1959); Allan M. Cartter, *An Assessment of*

Quality in Graduate Education (Washington: American Council on Education, 1966); Kenneth D. Roos and Charles J. Andersen, *A Rating of Graduate Programs* (Washington: American Council on Education, 1970).

ᔰ 6. TO ADVANCE HUMAN WELFARE

1. Allan Nevins and Frank E. Hill, *Ford: The Times, the Man, the Company* (New York: Scribner, 1954), p. 621.

2. On Ford, Sr., see Nevins and Hill, *Ford;* William Greenleaf, *From These Beginnings: The Early Philanthropies of Henry and Edsel Ford* (Detroit: Wayne State University Press, 1964); "Henry Ford," *DAB,* Supplement 4, pp. 291–304.

3. Merle Curti and Roderick Nash, *Philanthropy in the Shaping of American Higher Education* (New Brunswick, N.J.: Rutgers University Press, 1965); Howard J. Savage, *Fruit of an Impulse: Forty-Five Years of the Carnegie Corporation, 1905–1950* (New York: Harcourt, Brace, 1953); Merle Curti, *American Philanthropy Abroad: A History* (New Brunswick, N.J.: Rutgers University Press, 1963).

4. *DAB,* Supplement 4, p. 298.

5. Greenleaf, *From These Beginnings,* pp. 133–170.

6. Waldemar A. Nielsen, *The Big Foundations* (New York: Columbia University Press, 1972), pp. 78–79.

7. *Ibid.,* pp. 79–81.

8. C. Rowan Gaither, *Report of the Study for the Ford Foundation on Policy and Program* (Detroit: Ford Foundation, 1949); description of Gaither Report in Waldemar A. Nielsen, Oral History Interview, p. 41, transcript in Ford Foundation Archives, Ford Foundation, New York City, p. 7; Nielsen, *Big Foundations,* p. 80. Hereafter oral history interviews will be identified by interviewee and O/H; all interview transcripts are available at the Ford Foundation Archives.

9. Gaither Report, pp. 21, 27, 47.

10. For Henry Ford II quote, see *The Ford Foundation Annual Report for 1950* (Pasadena, Cal.: Ford Foundation, 1951), pp. 3–4; Nielsen, *Big Foundations,* pp. 81–83. Hereafter annual reports of the Ford Foundation will be identified by *A/R* and year.

11. On Hoffman, as on much else about the inner workings of the Ford Foundation from the early 1950s to the mid-1960s, see John Howard, O/H (February 1973), pp. 4–23.

12. Nielsen, *Big Foundations,* pp. 81–82; Dwight Macdonald, *The Ford Foundation: The Men and the Millions* (New York: Reynal and Hitchcock, 1956), pp. 15–20.

13. George F. Kennan, O/H (March 1972), pp. 6–7.

14. Howard, O/H, p. 6.

15. Ibid.; *A/R,* 1951, p. 13.

16. Kennan, O/H, pp. 6–7.

17. Ibid.; George F. Kennan, *American Diplomacy, 1900–1950* (New York: New American Library, 1952), p. 5.

18. For a critical rendering of Hutchins' views on nonacademic education, see Macdonald, *Ford Foundation,* pp. 55–60. See also *A/R,* 1953, pp. 16–17.

19. Howard, O/H, p. 54.

20. *Ibid.,* p. 11.

21. As an example of what Spaeth had in mind, see the proposal submitted to the Ford Foundation [Stanford University], *A Survey of Asian Studies* (Palo Alto: mimeographed pamphlet, 1951), copy in Ford Foundation Archives, Ford Foundation, New York City.

22. *A/R,* 1951, pp. 12–13.

23. On the Redfield project, see Milton Singer, "Robert Redfield's Development of a Social Anthropology of Civilizations," in John Murra, ed., *American Anthropology: The Early Years* (Minneapolis: American Ethnological Society, 1976); on the labor movements study, James L. Cochrane, *Industrialism and Industrial Man in Retrospect* (New York: Ford Foundation, 1979).

24. *A/R,* 1952, pp. 18–21.

25. *A/R,* 1952, pp. 21–24; *A/R,* 1953, pp. 31–34; Howard, O/H, p. 14. On the Foreign Area Fellowship Program, see Dorothy Soderlund, ed., *Directory, Foreign Area Fellows, 1952–1972* (New York: Social Science Research Council, 1973), pp. x–xii; on the Board of Overseas Travel and Research, Cleon Swayzee, "International Training and Research in the Ford Foundation, 1951–1966," draft report, June 1967, Ford Foundation Archives, Ford Foundation, New York City.

26. *A/R,* 1953, pp. 16–17.

27. John Howard, O/H, p. 53; Melvin J. Fox, O/H (October 1972), p. 15.

28. On the foundation and the CIA, see Howard, O/H, p. 109; Fox, O/H, p. 113.

29. Nielsen, *Big Foundations,* pp. 83–85; Chester C. Davis, O/H (April 1972), p. 8.

30. Nielsen, *Big Foundations,* p. 85; Macdonald, *Ford Foundation,* p. 75.

31. Howard, O/H, p. 42; author interview with Don K. Price, May 21, 1982, Cambridge, Massachusetts.

32. Nielsen, O/H, p. 38.

33. *Ibid.,* p. 28; Fox, O/H, pp. 31, 48–49; Don K. Price, Cambridge, Massachusetts, to author, May 26, 1982.

34. Howard, O/H, p. 67.

35. On this general subject, see John Lankford, *Congress and the Foundations in the Twentieth Century* (Madison: University of Wisconsin Press, 1964).

36. *Ibid.,* ch. 2; Macdonald, *Ford Foundation,* pp. 25–35.

37. John N. Thomas, *The Institute of Pacific Relations: Asian Scholars and American Politics* (Seattle: University of Washington Press, 1974), pp. 77–99, 110.

38. Norman Dodd, "Research Report of Special Congressional Committee Investigation of Tax Exempt Foundations, B. Carroll Reece, Chairman,"

submitted to 83rd Congress, April 29, 1954. See also René A. Wormser, *Foundations: Their Power and Influence* (New York: Devin-Adair, 1958).

39. Nielsen, O/H, pp. 10–16.

40. H. Rowan Gaither, "Statement to Special Committee to Investigate Tax Exempt Foundations," House of Representatives, 83d Congress, July 16, 1954, pp. 2, 3; see also "Supplement" to Gaither Statement; Lankford, *Congress and the Foundations*, ch. 3.

41. *A/R*, 1956, p. 24; Office of Reports, "Summary of news coverage of Reece hearings," to John B. Howard, January 27, 1955, Ford Foundation Archives, Ford Foundation, New York City; *New York Times*, July 24, 1954; *New York Herald Tribune*, July 27, 1954.

42. Robert M. Hutchins, "The Fund, Foundations, and the Reece Committee," in Robert M. Hutchins, *Freedom, Education, and the Fund: Essays and Addresses, 1946–1956* (New York: Meridian, 1956), pp. 22–23; Nielsen, O/H, p. 4.

43. Macdonald, *Ford Foundation*, pp. 58–64.

44. Thomas, *Institute of Pacific Relations*, pp. 87–88; John K. Fairbank, *Chinabound: A Fifty-Year Memoir* (New York: Harper & Row, 1982), ch. 25. See also Theodore H. White, *In Search of History: A Personal Adventure* (New York: Harper & Row, 1978), ch. 9.

45. Howard, O/H, pp. 87–88.

46. William L. Langer, "The Russian Research Center at Harvard University," *Proceedings of the American Philosophical Society* (January 1955), 99:34–35.

47. Gaither, "Statement to Reece Committee," p. 34.

7. THE BONANZA YEARS

1. Howard, O/H, p. 67.

2. Author interview with Niel Smelser, University of California, Berkeley, March 26, 1976.

3. Waldemar A. Nielsen, *The Big Foundations* (New York: Columbia University Press, 1972), pp. 86–87; *A/R*, 1955, pp. 5–6.

4. McCloy quoted in Lally Weymouth, "Foundation Woes: The Saga of Henry Ford II: Part Two," *New York Times Magazine*, March 12, 1978, p. 66; Howard, O/H, p. 128.

5. *A/R*, 1955, pp. 11–13.

6. Nielsen, *Big Foundations*, p. 88.

7. Dwight Macdonald, *The Ford Foundation: The Men and the Millions* (New York: Reynal and Hitchcock, 1956), p. 167.

8. Don K. Price to author, Cambridge, Massachusetts, May 28, 1982.

9. "New England's First Fruits," in Perry Miller and Thomas Johnson, eds., *The Puritans*, 2 vols. (New York: Harper & Row, 1963), 2:701.

10. *A/R*, 1954, p. 1.

11. [Devereux C. Josephs], *President's Committee on Education Beyond the High School: Second Report to the President* (Washington: Government Printing Office, 1957), ch. 1.

12. *Historical Statistics of the United States: Colonial Times to 1970*, 2 vols. (Washington: Government Printing Office, 1975), 1:385–386.

13. For a full discussion of the faculty labor-market controversy, see Allan M. Cartter, *Ph.D.'s and the Academic Labor Market* (New York: McGraw-Hill, 1976), ch. 2.

14. Bernard Berelson, *Graduate Education in the United States* (New York: McGraw-Hill, 1960), pp. 69–80; Harold Orlans, *The Effects of Federal Programs on Higher Education* (Washington: Brookings Institution, 1962), pp. 14–15; Don Cameron Allen, *The Ph.D. in English and American Literature* (New York: Rinehart and Winston, 1968), p. 18.

15. Cartter, *Academic Labor Market*, pp. 14–16.

16. *A/R*, 1954, pp. 1–4; *A/R*, 1955, pp. 2–3, 11–12.

17. "Report of Committee Z on the Economic Status of the Profession," *AAUP Bulletin* (Spring 1956), 42:5–18.

18. *President's Committee* (1957), p. 6.

19. Something of the flavor of these boom times is conveyed in Clark Kerr, *The Uses of the University* (Cambridge: Harvard University Press, 1964); also, David G. Brown, *The Mobile Professors* (Washington: American Council of Education, 1967).

20. Academic salaries were generally reported in the summer issues of the *AAUP Bulletin* throughout this period. For ten-year review, see *AAUP Bulletin* (Summer 1965), 51:248–253.

21. Robert W. Hodge, Paul M. Siegel, and Peter H. Rossi, "Occupational Prestige in the United States: 1925–1963," *American Journal of Sociology* (November 1964), 70:286–302; Claude Bowman, *The College Professor in America: An Analysis of Articles Published in the General Magazines* (Philadelphia: University of Pennsylvania Press, 1938), p. 12.

22. Hodge et al., "Occupational Prestige," p. 290.

23. Arthur M. Schlesinger, Jr., *A Thousand Days: John F. Kennedy in the White House* (Boston: Houghton Mifflin, 1965), p. 209. On the rise of academics in federal government in 1960s, see Kenneth Prewitt and William McAllister, "Changes in the American Executive Elite, 1930–1970," in Heinz Elau and Moshe M. Czudnowski, eds., *Elite Recruitment in Democratic Politics* (New York: Wiley, 1976), pp. 105–132.

24. James A. Davis, *Great Aspirations: The Graduate School Plans of America's College Seniors* (Chicago: University of Chicago Press, 1964).

25. Daniel Bell, *The Reforming of General Education* (New York: Anchor, 1968), p. 87.

26. Macdonald, *Ford Foundation*, pp. 98, 103; Nielsen, O/H, p. 40.

27. Francis X. Sutton, "The Foundation's Strategy Towards University-

Level International Studies Programs . . . ," Ford Foundation Internal Memorandum, Social Science Research Council Files, Ford Foundation Archives, New York City, October 19, 1967; Melvin J. Fox, O/H, p. 124.

28. Weymouth, "Foundation Woes," p. 66; Ford's resignation letter is excerpted in *New York Times* (January 12, 1978), II, 6:5; Macdonald, *Ford Foundation,* p. 24.

29. Nielsen, *Big Foundations,* pp. 89–92.

30. Fox, O/H, p. 86; Nielsen, O/H, p. 22.

31. *A/R,* 1967, p. 7.

32. Howard, O/H, pp. 44, 59; Don K. Price to John W. Gardner, March 24, 1954, ITR Files, Ford Foundation Archives, Ford Foundation, New York City.

33. Fox, O/H, p. 86; Nielsen, O/H, p. 22.

34. *A/R,* 1958, pp. 129–135; Macdonald, *Ford Foundation,* p. 165; on the labor movements study, see James L. Cochrane, *Industrialism and Industrial Man in Retrospect* (New York: Ford Foundation, 1979).

35. Howard, O/H, pp. 52–53; Fox, O/H, pp. 80–82.

36. *A/R,* 1953, p. 90; *A/R,* 1954, pp. 28, 79. On such grants not working out, see Fox, O/H, pp. 100–103.

37. On Ford's favoring private universities, see George Grassmuck to Elinor Barber, Madison, Wisconsin, January 15, 1969, International Division Files, Ford Foundation.

38. Howard, O/H, p. 69; for institution-by-institution funding by ITR, see "Report on the $9,000,000 Special Transitional Program in Support of International Studies in American Universities," Ford Foundation Information Paper, November 1972, p. 11.

39. Howard, O/H, pp. 77–82.

40. *A/R,* 1964, p. 28; Cleon O. Swayzee, "International Training and Research in the Ford Foundation, 1951–1966—A Draft Report" (June 1967), ITR Files, Ford Foundation, pp. 5–6.

41. On the "neglect" of Uralic and Altaic, see Donald N. Bigelow and Lyman H. Legters, eds., "The Non-Western World in Higher Education," *Annals of the American Academy of Political and Social Science* (November 1964), 356:86–92.

42. Howard, O/H, p. 44; John Howard to author, Scarsdale, New York, June 10, 1982.

43. Fox, O/H, p. 86; Fox to author, New York City, July 28, 1978.

44. Fox, O/H, p. 27; Howard, O/H, p. 66.

45. Howard to author, June 10, 1982.

46. Committee on the University and World Affairs (J. L. Morrill, chairman), *The University and World Affairs* (New York: The Committee, 1961), pp. 2, 3; hereafter cited as Morrill Report.

47. Morrill Report, pp. 77–78.

48. Ibid., pp. 62–63.

49. *A/R*, 1960, pp. 67–69.

50. *A/R*, 1961, pp. 20–21, 32; *A/R*, 1962, pp. 12, 21–22; Howland Sargeant, "Status Report on ITR Program," December 15, 1961, ITR Files, Ford Foundation.

51. Doak Barnett to John Howard, August 3, 1961, ITR Files, Ford Foundation.

52. Howard, O/H, pp. 87–88; *A/R*, 1963, p. 29–30.

53. On "resource base" grants, see Swayzee, "ITR," pp. 40–44; *A/R*, 1963, p. 125.

54. *A/R*, 1965, p. 34; *A/R*, 1966, pp. 19–20.

55. On NDEA, Donald N. Bigelow and Lyman H. Legters, *NDEA Language and Area Centers: A Report on the First 5 Years* (Washington: Government Printing Office, 1964); on IEA, U. S. Congress, House Document No. 527, Committee on Education and Labor, *International Education: Past, Present, Problems and Prospects: Selected Readings to Supplement H.R. 14643*, 89th Cong., 2d sess., 1966.

56. *International Education*, p. 97.

57. *Ibid.*, p. 100.

ᏅᏴ 8. THE FRUITS OF PHILANTHROPY

1. Adam Smith, *An Inquiry into the Nature and Causes of the Wealth of Nations* ([1776] Chicago: Encyclopedia Brittanica, 1952), p. 65.

2. John K. Fairbank, *Chinabound: A Fifty-Year Memoir* (New York: Harper & Row, 1982), p. 360; Philip E. Mosely, "International Affairs," in Warren Weaver, ed., *U.S. Philanthropic Foundations: Their History, Structure, Management, and Record* (New York: Harper & Row, 1967), p. 395.

3. William H. Whyte, Jr., "What Are the Foundations Up To?," *Fortune* (October 1955), 52:140–141.

4. On Chicago and Berkeley, see Ellen McDonald Gumperz, *Internationalizing American Higher Education: Innovation and Structural Change* (Berkeley and Los Angeles: University of California Press, 1970); on Harvard, Robert E. Klitgaard, *Harvard International: A Report on Some International Activities at the University* (Cambridge: John F. Kennedy School of Government, 1979), ch. 4.

5. University totals for ITR funding are provided in Ford Foundation Information Paper, "Report on Special Transitional Program in Support of International Studies in American Universities" (November 1972), p. 11.

6. On expansion of American higher education at the margins, see David G. Brown, *The Mobile Professors* (Washington: American Council on Education, 1967), ch. 2.

7. On UCLA, see Neil J. Smelser, "Growth, Structural Change, and Conflict in California Public Higher Education, 1950–1970," in Neil J. Smelser and Gabriel Almond, eds., *Public Higher Education in California* (Berkeley

and Los Angeles: University of California Press, 1974), pp. 9–41; on Michigan State, Warren Hinckle, "MSU: The University on the Make," *Ramparts* (April 1966), 4:11–23; author interview with Ralph Nicholas, Chicago, March 25, 1976; author interview with Rose M. Hayden, Washington, D.C., July 6, 1976.

8. Gumperz, *Internationalizing American Higher Education*, p. 209; Robert Nisbet, *The Degradation of the Academic Dogma: The University in America, 1945–1970* (New York: Basic Books, 1971), ch. 6.

9. Fred H. Harrington to Francis X. Sutton, Madison, Wisconsin, June 27, 1979, International Division File, Ford Foundation.

10. On placement of Chicago PhDs, see Southern Asian Studies Committee, *Programs and Dissertations in Southern Asian Studies* (Chicago: The Committee, 1977).

11. [Abram Bergson], *Annual Report of the Russian Research Center, Harvard University, 1965–1966* (Cambridge, 1966), p. 22. On the general topic, see Derek J. de Solla Price, "Citation Measures of Hard Science, Soft Science, Technology, and Non-Science," in Carnot E. Nelson and D. K. Pollock, eds., *Communication Among Scientists and Engineers* (Lexington, Mass.: Heath, 1970); Brown, *Mobile Professors*, ch. 2.

12. On MA students shifting to PhD programs, see D. W. Lockard, *A Brief History of the Harvard Center for Middle Eastern Studies* (Cambridge: Harvard University Press, 1969), p. 22.

13. Author's calculations, drawing on fellowship lists in *A/R*, 1953, pp. 96–108, and occupational data in Dorothy Soderlund, ed., *Directory, Foreign Area Fellows, 1952–1972* (New York: Social Science Research Council, 1973).

14. *A/R*, 1956, p. 90; Max Weber, "Politics as a Vocation," in H. H. Gerth and C. Wright Mills, eds., *From Max Weber: Essays in Sociology* (New York: Oxford University press, 1946), pp. 77–128; *A/R*, 1962, pp. 21–22; Soderlund, *Directory*.

15. Howland Sargeant, "Status Report on ITR Program," December 15, 1961, ITR Files, Ford Foundation; Dorothy Soderlund, "History of the Foreign Area Fellowship Program," in Soderlund, *Directory*, pp. i, ii.

16. Richard D. Lambert, *Language and Area Studies Review* (Philadelphia: American Academy of Political and Social Science, 1973), ch. 3.

17. Lambert, *Review*, p. 43, table 3.6; Patricia A. Graham, "Expansion and Exclusion: A History of Women in American Higher Education," *Journal of Women in Culture and Society* (Winter 1978), 3:759–773. See also David Chaplin, "The Careers of Women Latin Americanists, Interim Report to Latin American Studies Association," (Atlanta, Ga.: Mimeographed draft, 1976).

18. Leonard Binder, "Area Studies: A Critical Reassessment," in Leonard Binder, ed., *The Study of the Middle East: Research and Scholarship in the Humanities and the Social Sciences* (New York: Wiley, 1976), p. 7; author interview with Ralph Nicholas, Chicago, March 25, 1976.

19. Nicholas interview; Wm. Theodore de Bary, "East Asian Studies: A Comprehensive Program," *Annals of the American Academy of Political and Social Science*, 356:63–69, 64; Robert F. Byrnes, "The Future of Area Studies," *ACLS Newsletter* (November 1968), 19:12–18.

20. Howard, O/H, p. 147; Doak Barnett to John Howard, November 19, 1959, ITR Files, Ford Foundation; John K. Fairbank, *Ten-Year Report of the Director* [of the Harvard East Asia Research Center] (Cambridge: East Asia Research Center, 1965), pp. 36–38.

21. On released-time arrangements, David E. Bell to Howard Swearer, October 13, 1966, Harvard materials, International Division File, Ford Foundation; John K. Fairbank to John Howard, Cambridge, Mass., September 25, 1963, Harvard materials, ITR File, Ford Foundation.

22. John K. Fairbank, "Assignment for the '70's," *American Historical Review* (February 1969), 74:871; Richard M. Morse, "The Challenge for Foreign Area Studies," *Bulletin* [of the National Association of Secondary School Principals] (January 1967), 50:18.

23. Fairbank, *Chinabound*, p. 329.

24. Hinckle, "MSU," p. 20.

25. Alvin W. Gouldner, "Cosmopolitans and Locals: Toward an Analysis of Latent Social Roles," *Administrative Science Quarterly* (December 1957, March 1958), 2:281–306, 444–479; Fairbank, "Assignment for the '70's," p. 867.

26. On the AAASS, see Jacob Ornstein, "The Development and Status of Slavic and East European Studies in America Since World War II," *Slavic Review* (October 1957), 16:369–388; on the AAS, Charles O. Hucker, *The Association of Asian Studies: An Interpretative History* (Seattle: Association of Asian Studies, 1973); on the ASA, Philip D. Curtin, "African Studies: A Personal Assessment," *African Studies Review* (December 1971), 14:357–368; on the LASA and its predecessors, Howard F. Cline, ed., *Latin American History: Essays on Its Study and Teaching, 1898–1965*, 2 vols. (Austin: University of Texas Press, 1967), chs. 17–19, 99. On Ford support for these associations, see Cleon O. Swayzee, "International Training and Research in the Ford Foundation, 1951–1966," draft report, June 1967, Ford Foundation Archives, Ford Foundation, New York City, pp. 46–52.

27. Membership figures from *Encyclopedia of Associations* (Detroit: Gale Research, 1968). On lack of connection between the area associations and the APSA, see Robert E. Ward, "Culture and the Comparative Study of Politics, or the Constipated Dialectic," *American Political Science Review* (March 1974), 68:190–201; between them and the AHA, Fairbank, "Assignment for the '70s," p. 867.

28. On the AAS, see Hucker, *Association of Asian Studies;* also Fairbank, *Chinabound*, pp. 399–402; on the ASA, Africa Research Group, *Africa Report* (Cambridge, Mass.: Africa Research Group, 1970).

29. Hucker, *Association of Asian Studies*, p. 59.

30. On ITR's program in international legal studies, see Howard, O/H, pp. 66–69; Swayzee, "ITR," pp. 61–62.

31. Robert D. Schulzinger, "Whatever Happened to the Council on Foreign Relations?," Diplomatic History (Fall 1981), 5:277–289.

32. On popularization and its academic critics, see Edward Shils, "The Calling of Sociology," in Edward Shils, ed., The Calling of Sociology and Other Essays in the Pursuit of Learning (Chicago: University of Chicago Press, 1980), pp. 85–86; James N. Rosenau, International Studies and the Social Sciences (Beverly Hills, Calif.: Sage, 1973), tables 32 and 33.

33. Edward Shils, "The High Culture of the Age," in Edward Shils, Intellectuals and the Powers (Chicago: University of Chicago Press, 1972), p. 117.

34. Robert M. Rosenzweig to author, Palo Alto, California, December 30, 1975.

35. Allen S. Whiting, "The Scholar and the Policy-Maker," in Raymond Tanter and Richard Ullman, eds., Theory and Practice in International Relations (Princeton: Princeton University Press, 1972), pp. 229–247; Louis J. Halle, "On Teaching International Relations," Virginia Quarterly Review (Winter 1964), 40:11–25; Fairbank, Chinabound, p. 397.

36. Irving Louis Horowitz, ed., The Rise and Fall of Project Camelot (Cambridge: MIT Press, 1967); Hinckle, "MSU"; Ithiel de Sola Pool testimony quoted in Horowitz, Camelot, pp. 267–280.

37. Richard E. Neustadt, "White House and Whitehall," Public Interest (Winter 1966), 1:55–69; Merton dictum quoted in Eytan Gilboa, "The Scholar and the Foreign Policy Maker in the United States" (Ph.D. dissertation, Harvard University, 1974), ch. 1; Horowitz, Camelot, pp. 339–376.

38. Derek J. de Solla Price's distinction between science as "papyrocentric" and technology as "papyrophobic" might be adapted to distinguish between scholars, who are given to regarding publication as the determinant of intellectual stature, and advisers, who are leery of publication because it reduces their value as consultants. See Price, "Citation Measures."

39. Galbraith quote in Everett Carl Ladd, Jr., and Seymour Martin Lipset, The Divided Academy (New York: McGraw-Hill, 1975), p. 25.

40. Irving Kristol, "Teaching In, Speaking Out: The Controversy over Vietnam," Encounter (August 1965), 25:68; Meg Greenfield, "After the Washington Teach-In," Reporter (June 3, 1965), 32:17–18; William F. Buckley, "Hope in Academe," Washington Star, September 1, 1965.

41. Noam Chomsky, American Power and the New Mandarins (New York: Vintage, 1967), p. 3; Marshall Windmiller, "International Relations: The New Mandarins," in Theodore Roszak, ed., The Dissenting Academy (New York: Random House, 1967), pp. 110–134; Everett Carl Ladd, Jr., "American University Teachers and Opposition to the Vietnam War," Minerva (October 1970), 8:542–556; Eric F. Goldman, The Tragedy of Lyndon Johnson (New York: Knopf, 1974), pp. 433–434; Charles Kadushin, The American Intellec-

tual Elite (Boston: Little, Brown, 1974), p. 320; Ladd and Lipset, *Divided Academy*, pp. 66–67, 109–111.

42. For a discussion of the statistical basis of my disagreement with Ladd, see Robert A. McCaughey, "American University Teachers and Opposition to the Vietnam War: A Reconsideration," *Minerva* (Autumn 1976), 14:307–329. For Lerner's comments, see *New York Post*, April 30, 1965.

43. Columbia University, *Bulletin, Graduate School of Arts and Sciences, 1966–67*, and *Bulletin, School of International Affairs, 1966–67*; University of Chicago, *Graduate Programs in the Divisions, 1966–67*; University of Michigan, *Horace H. Rackham School of Graduate Studies, 1966–67*; Stanford University, *Bulletin, Courses, and Degrees, 1966–67*; Harvard University, *Center for International Affairs, 1966–67*.

44. Rosenau, *International Studies*, appendix A.

45. Wesley Fishel et al., "Experts Reply to Critics of United States," *New York Journal American* (October 20, 1965), reprinted in L. Monashe and R. Radosh, eds., *Teach-Ins USA* (New York: Praeger, 1967), pp. 110–111. See also United States Senate, *The Anti-Vietnam Agitation and Teach-In Movement* (Washington: Government Printing Office, 1966).

46. Letter from Robert Scalapino to Berkeley Vietnam Day Committee, Spring 1965, reprinted in Monashe and Radosh, *Teach-Ins*, pp. 29–30.

࿔ 9. THE AFTERNOON OF ENTERPRISE

1. Derek J. de Solla Price, *Science since Babylon* (New Haven: Yale University Press, 1961), p. 117.

2. Howard, O/H, p. 76.

3. *Ibid.*, p. 78.

4. On IE Act hearings, U. S. Congress, House Document No. 527, Committee on Education and Labor, *International Education: Past, Present, Problems and Prospects: Selected Readings to Supplement H.R. 14643*, 89th Cong., 2d sess., 1966; *A/R*, 1967, p. 7, 9.

5. *A/R*, 1967, p. 7.

6. McGeorge Bundy, "Were Those the Days?" *Daedalus* (Summer 1970), 49:531–567.

7. *A/R*, 1967, pp. 6–7.

8. Ford Foundation Information Paper, "Report on the $9,000,000 Special Transitional Program in Support of International Studies in American Universities" (November 1972, Ford Foundation Archives, Ford Foundation, New York City).

9. On foundation support in the 1970s, see [Francis X. Sutton], "Docket Statement on U.S. and International Affairs Programs," International Division, Ford Foundation, FY 1982, supplied to author by Francis X. Sutton.

10. Francis X. Sutton, "The Foundation's Strategy Toward University-Level International Studies Programs, the Joint Committees of the

SSRC/ACLS, the FAFP, Professional Area Studies Associations and All That" (October 19, 1967), International Division Files, Ford Foundation, pp. 10–11.

11. Irwin T. Sanders and Jennifer G. Ward, *Bridges to Understanding: International Programs of American Colleges and Universities* (New York: McGraw-Hill, 1970), p. ix; James A. Perkins, *Strength through Wisdom: A Critique of U.S. Capability,* Report to the President from the President's Commission on Foreign Language and International Studies (Washington: Government Printing Office, 1979), p. 8.

12. Perkins, *Strength through Wisdom,* pp. 139–141; Allen H. Kassof, ed., "Report of the Task Force on National Manpower Targets for Advanced Research on Foreign Areas," draft form (New York: National Council on Foreign Language and International Studies, 1981), pp. 35, 13.

13. Perkins, *Strength through Wisdom,* p. 7, which contains the statement, "Americans' scandalous incompetence in foreign languages also explains [!] our dangerously inadequate understanding of world affairs."

14. Kassof, "Task Force on Manpower Targets," pp. 20–21. Similarly, comparisons between American capacities and those available in western Europe would seem to weaken the argument for America's "scandalous" condition. See David Heaps, ed., *International Studies in Six European Countries* (New York: Ford Foundation, 1976).

15. Perkins, *Strength through Wisdom,* pp. 1, 134–138.

16. Sue E. Berryman, Paul F. Langer, John Pincus, and Richard H. Solomon, *Foreign Language and International Studies Specialists: The Marketplace and National Policy* (Santa Monica, Calif.: Rand Corporation, 1979); on Rand and the commission, see John Pincus, "Rand Meets the President's Commission: The Life-Cycle of a Non-Event," *Annals of the American Academy of Political and Social Science* (May 1980), 449:80–90.

17. Perkins, *Strength through Wisdom,* pp. 12–27.

18. William Bradford, *Of Plymouth Plantation,* Samuel E. Morison, ed. (New York: Modern Library, 1952), p. 334; for an appreciation of the institutional impact of dispersion, [Steven Marcus], *Presidential Commission on Academic Priorities in the Arts and Sciences—Columbia University* (New York: Columbia University, 1979), pp. 1–4.

19. For a mid-1970s rendering of the state of American Slavic studies, see Gregory Grossman, "Report to the Ford Foundation" (Berkeley, Calif.: April 1975), International Division Files, Ford Foundation. See also Jesse J. Dossick, *Doctoral Research in Russia and the Soviet Union, 1960–1975* (New York: Garland, 1976); Jesse J. Dossick, "Doctoral Dissertations on Russia, the Soviet Union, and Eastern Europe, 1980–1981," *Slavic Review* (Winter 1981), 40:700–711.

20. For example, sample universities accounted for only 54 percent of the PhDs in Latin American history and 34 percent of those in Latin American literature, according to *American Doctoral Dissertations, 1979–1980.*

21. Edwin A. Deagle, Jr., *A Survey of United States Institutions Engaged in International Relations Research and Related Activities: A Preliminary Report* (New York: Rockefeller Foundation, 1981); for equally "non-crisis" renderings of the enterprise as it entered the 1980s, see Robert E. Klitgaard, "On Reviewing International Studies," Discussion Paper Series, No. 81D (Cambridge, Mass.: John F. Kennedy School of Government, 1980); Robert E. Klitgaard, *Harvard International: A Report on Some International Activities at the University* (Cambridge: John F. Kennedy School of Government, 1979); Elinor G. Barber and Warren Ilchman, *International Studies Review* (New York: Ford Foundation, 1979); Robert A. McCaughey, "The Current State of International Studies in American Universities: Special Consideration Reconsidered," *Journal of Higher Education* (July–August 1980), 51:381–399.

22. On the general state of American graduate education, cast in its most pessimistic terms, see Nathan Keyfitz, "The Impending Crisis in American Graduate Schools," *Public Interest* (Summer 1978), 52:85–97, and Roy Radner and Charlotte Kuh, *Preserving a Lost Generation: Policies To Assure a Steady Flow of Young Scholars until the Year 2000* (New York: Carnegie Council on Policy Studies in Higher Education, 1979). For a more sanguine rendering, see Robert E. Klitgaard, "The Decline of the Best?," Discussion Paper Series, No. 65D (Cambridge, Mass.: John F. Kennedy School of Government, 1979).

23. Perkins, *Strength through Wisdom,* p. 2; Kasoff, "Task Force on Manpower Targets," p. 13.

24. Pendleton Herring, "Preface" to Richard D. Lambert, *Language and Area Studies Review* (Philadelphia: American Academy of Political and Social Science, 1973), p. xvii; Talcott Parsons and Gerald M. Platt, *The American University* (Cambridge: Harvard University Press, 1973), p. 77.

25. George W. Pierson, *Tocqueville and Beaumont in America* (New York: Oxford University Press, 1940), p. 365.

INDEX